Making a Difference in Academic Life:
A Handbook for Park, Recreation, and Tourism Educators and Graduate Students

Making a Difference in Academic Life:
A Handbook for Park, Recreation, and Tourism Educators and Graduate Students

Dan Dustin and Tom Goodale
Editors

Venture Publishing, Inc.
State College, PA

Venture Publishing, Inc.
1999 Cato Avenue
State College, PA 16801
Phone: 814-234-4561; Fax: 814-234-1651
E-mail: vpublish@venturepublish.com
Web site: http://www.venturepublish.com

Production Manager: Richard Yocum
Manuscript Editing: Christina Manbeck, Valerie Fowler

Library of Congress Catalogue Card Number: 2007940628

ISBN-10: 1-892132-73-7

ISBN-13: 978-1-892132-73-4

Dedication

to our mentors and students

Table of Contents

Acknowledgments xi

Preface xiii

Part I

On Being a Professor 1

Chapter 1 The Gift 3
    Dan Dustin

Chapter 2 Does This Path Have a Heart? 9
    Mary Faeth Chenery

Chapter 3 On Privilege and Obligation 21
    Larry Beck

Chapter 4 Sometimes It Feels Like Moonlighting 31
    Ruth Russell

Chapter 5 The Joys of Doing Research 43
    Roger Mannell

Chapter 6 On Reading and Professing: Recounting a World
of Privilege 57
    Geof Godbey

Chapter 7 On Professing, Publishing, and Sometimes
Writing 71
    Tom Goodale

Part II

For the Good of the Order 83

Chapter 8 Caring for the Alma Mater 85
    Andy Young

Chapter 9 On Being an Administrator 93
Doug Sessoms

Chapter 10 The Academic Animateur 101
Bert Brantley

Chapter 11 Building a Program at MSU............................107
Lou Twardzik

Chapter 12 Thoughts from a Green Twig..........................119
Phyllis Ford

Chapter 13 Advancing a Social Agenda............................129
Jim Murphy

Chapter 14 A Day at the Office..135
Nick DiGrino

Chapter 15 First Among Peers 147
Mark Searle

Chapter 16 Managing in Times of Retrenchment............155
Bob Rossman

Chapter 17 The Changing Proportions of My Life............161
Peter Witt

Chapter 18 A Once and Future Chair................................167
Steve Smith

Part III

Making a Difference..179

Chapter 19 A Very Privileged Form of Service................181
Geof Godbey

Chapter 20 "Faith-Based" Teaching 189
Dan Dustin

Chapter 21 Things That We Believe In 195
Karla Henderson

Chapter 22 A Gleam in the Eye 203
Leo McAvoy

Chapter 23 My Parents Led the Way 211
Deb Kerstetter

Chapter 24 Deb's Feel Good Folder 217
Deb Bialeschki

Chapter 25 On Undergraduate "Benevolent Coercion"
and Graduate Collegiality 225
John Crompton

Chapter 26 Beyond the Social Science Citation Index 237
Dennis Howard

Chapter 27 A Fair Share for All 245
Jim Murphy

Chapter 28 The Accidental Administrator 253
Bob Wolff

Chapter 29 When You Come to a Fork in the Road 259
Frank Guadagnolo

Chapter 30 Connecting with Others 263
Gene Lamke

Chapter 31 Accentuate the Positive 267
Marilyn Jensen

Chapter 32 Doing What Needs to Be Done 273
Patricia Delaney

Chapter 33 Embracing Serendipity 281
Linda Caldwell & Ed Smith

Chapter 34 Pardon My Reservations 287
   Tom Goodale

About the Authors.. 295

NOTES... 311

Acknowledgments

We are indebted to several individuals and organizations for helping us complete this work. Gene Lamke, Director of San Diego State University's Institute for Leisure Behavior (ILB), graciously gave permission to incorporate two earlier books published by the ILB into this expanded work: *Beyond Promotion and Tenure: On Being a Professor* (1990) and *For the Good of the Order: Administering Academic Programs in Higher Education* (1993). Florida International University's College of Education, under the leadership of Dean Linda Blanton, Associate Dean Robert Wolff, and Assistant Dean Carmen Mendez, provided significant funds to host a writing workshop in Key West, Florida for the contributors to the newest section of the book. For that learning experience, and for those tropical memories, we are most grateful. Finally, Venture Publishing, Inc., under the direction of Drs. Frank Guadagnolo and Geof Godbey, took the ultimate "leap of faith" by agreeing to publish the final product.

We would also like to thank the 31 contributors, who took time out from their busy academic lives to reflect on, and then write about, the meaning of their work. This truly has been a collaborative effort, and the rewards of participation far exceeded our modest expectations. This book was motivated by a desire to be of service to others. The friendships cultivated along the way now constitute the proverbial frosting on the cake.

Preface

This book is the culmination of a 20-year inquiry into the nature and meaning of academic life. When the inquiry began, however, there was no thought given to this particular end. The impetus for publishing *Beyond Promotion and Tenure: On Being a Professor* was rooted in a concern for better understanding a professor's life. *For the Good of the Order: Administering Academic Programs in Higher Education* was prompted by an interest in trying to better understand just what it is about administration that draws some professors to it. The idea for this book was motivated by a desire to "put things in order" as our generation of professors makes way for the next. Combining the first two books with what was to be the content of a third book was fortuitous: a matter of good timing and good luck. This larger book will give the first two a longer life, and it will round out their meaning.

Making a Difference in Academic Life parallels the careers of many of its contributors. Larry Beck, for example, was an untenured assistant professor at San Diego State University (SDSU) when he penned "On Privilege and Obligation." Larry is now a tenured full professor at SDSU with an international reputation in natural and cultural resource interpretation. When Roger Mannell wrote "The Joys of Doing Research," he was an associate professor of leisure studies at the University of Waterloo in Ontario, Canada. Roger is now a full professor and Dean of Waterloo's College of Applied Health Sciences. And when Mark Searle recorded his thoughts on being a Programme Head at the University of Manitoba in "First Among Peers," little did he know that today he would be Vice President of academic personnel at Arizona State University.

One thing is clear from reading these essays. An enduring passion for academic life has sustained all the authors. While some have migrated into administration, others have remained teaching professors and scholars. They have each, in their own way, followed their bliss and led a productive and meaningful life. We should all be so lucky.

Part I

On Being a Professor

Part I is for students considering a life in the university, new and seasoned faculty members, and anyone else interested in the question of what it means to be a professor. Issues explored include the place of teaching, research, service, reading, and writing in a professor's life, as well as the privileges and obligations that accompany that life. The rewards and frustrations of being a professor are also discussed, as are the demands placed on a professor's time.

Although the authors are all professors of recreation, park, and leisure studies, the issues raised and questions pondered will be familiar to all residents of the university. The authors include a professor on leave from university life, a newly appointed professor, a professor renowned for her love of teaching, a professor renowned for his love of research, and two professors renowned for their love of the life in toto. Collectively, they paint a good picture of what being a professor is all about.

A professor's life, like life in general, can always use improvement. At the same time, a professor's life is seldom as bad as it seems to some people. If this section helps you distinguish more clearly the good points from the bad, if it assists you in making a more informed career choice, then it will have served its modest purpose.

The Gift
Dan Dustin

The essays that follow are testimonials to university life written by people who care deeply about the question of what it means to be a professor, even as they differ in their responses. The essays are personal statements: labors of love.

In the first few pages, I share my perspective on the question, not because I necessarily know what it means to be a professor, but because I want to whet your appetite for the kinds of issues that are explored later on in a more personal way. I see my responsibility as getting you ready for the main fare.

I will focus on four issues central to the question of what it means to be a professor: 1) the role of freedom in the life of a professor, 2) the demonstration of scholarship, 3) the connection between scholarship and teaching, and 4) the professor as student. Some of the contributors to this section see these issues differently than I do. That's okay. In fact, that's precisely what makes life in the university interesting. I think we would all agree, however, that you must ultimately judge these issues for yourself.

For one who likes to think, I can imagine no better life than that of a professor. I still find it hard to believe that society is willing to pay us to think, and then to share our thoughts with others through our teaching, scholarship, and service. What an incredible act of faith in our ability, indeed our integrity, to put that opportunity to good use.

By design, colleges and universities give us increasing degrees of freedom to carry on our work. First we go through a probationary period when we are expected to try on our thinking caps. Then, to the extent we please our colleagues with our efforts, we are given more and more freedom through promotion and tenure. Finally, as tenured professors, we are awarded academic freedom in its ultimate sense. We are entrusted to ourselves. The use to which we put that trust is the final measure of our professional worth.

Colleges and universities take a calculated risk when they award promotion, tenure, and academic freedom to professors. The risk is that some of us might abuse the privilege. Rather than understanding academic freedom for what it is—the right to pursue truth wherever it may lead—some of us see it only as an opportunity to take off our thinking caps, to escape the responsibilities attendant to being a professor. To some among us, tenure signifies nothing more than a paid-up insurance policy whose dividends are counted in more free time to pursue other interests or outside employment.

Fortunately, more saints than scamps populate colleges and universities. For every professor who sees promotion only as a chance to earn more while doing less, there might be five others who see it as a vote of confidence that more is expected of them. For every professor who sees tenure as a license to be irresponsible, there might be five others who see it as a mandate to be more responsible. For every professor who thinks academic freedom means being less accountable, there might be five others who understand it as the necessity to be more so. In sum, the life of a professor is a gift enjoyed by relatively few people. Society intends the gift to be used for its betterment, but like all true gifts there are few, if any, strings attached. We professors are free to make of the gift what we will. As hard as it is to accept, that includes the freedom for some of us to squander it.

How do we know if we are doing justice to our gift? What is the mark of a good professor? The first test is in our scholarship. "Scholarship in essence means continuing to develop [our] own abilities and at some point placing [our] work, [our] preparation, [our] results in public view for others to see and evaluate."[1]

Typically, evidence of good scholarship is in our publication record. While heavy reliance on this criterion has contributed to the "publish or perish" syndrome, I do believe the public display of our written thoughts is a good indicator of intellectual involvement within our field of study. As Steven Cahn puts it, "Few who oppose the 'publish or perish' principle would object to the demand that faculty members 'think or perish'; yet to publish is to make available to all the results of one's best thinking."[2]

Notice here that my concern is going public with our thinking. It is the external display of our work that is essential to its evaluation. But what can be said of those of us who do not seek a public forum? Paraphrasing Cahn, are our ideas of worth? We do not know, for we have not been willing to test them against professional standards. Would our work be a significant contribution to the field? We can only guess, for our peers have not been given the opportunity to read what we have to say. We have thus done a disservice to ourselves and to the subject we value. We have, in short, failed to fulfill our obligation as scholars.[3]

While I agree with Cahn, I also think it is possible to demonstrate scholarship in many ways. Presentations at professional meetings, consulting work, organizational leadership, grants and contracts, public lectures, community service, and our teaching evaluations all can be evidence of our intellectual currency and our scholarship. All of these activities deserve attention in promotion and tenure decisions.

But if I were asked to pick the most important measure, I would still choose the publication record. I see writing as the principal medium through which we professors conduct our individual and collective quests. Unlike other forms of communication, writing is a slow, painstaking process through which we work and rework our thoughts until we are satisfied they represent our best thinking. Then we offer them up for public scrutiny. Writing is our means of going on record.

The second test of our professional worth is in our teaching. And what is the relationship between our scholarship and our teaching? Good scholarship is inseparable from good teaching. Borrowing from the Indian teacher and poet Rabindranath Tagore, teachers can never truly teach unless they are still learning themselves. A lamp can never light another lamp unless it continues to burn its own flame. Teachers who have come to the end of their subject, who have no living traffic with knowledge but merely repeat their lessons to students, can only load their minds; they cannot quicken them. Truth not only must inform but also inspire. If the inspiration dies out, and the information only accumulates, then truth loses its infinity.[4]

A good teacher must be actively engaged in scholarship, in the pursuit of his or her own learning. Of course such involvement does not guarantee good teaching, but it is integral to it. That is why one of the most important measures of teaching effectiveness is demonstrated scholarship. It provides evidence that the conditions are ripe for a productive learning environment. In its presence, students are more likely to be inspired by the professor's living traffic with knowledge.

I realize it doesn't always turn out this way. We all know scholars who care little for teaching, who do not invest the same energy and enthusiasm into their classroom that they do into their research and writing. This does not mean, however, that good teaching can happen in the absence of good scholarship, only that there are good scholars who are not good teachers.

Is the opposite also true? Are there good teachers who are not good scholars? I think not. Most professors I know who proclaim teaching effectiveness in the absence of demonstrated scholarship base the claim on student evaluations of their teaching. While I value student assessments of a professor's enthusiasm and energy toward them and their subject matter, I am skeptical of students' ability to judge a professor's currency of thought, the degree to which his or her traffic with knowledge is living or dead. In the same way that I would not expect passengers on an airplane to know whether their pilot is really using up-to-date knowledge in flying the aircraft, I would not expect students to be able to judge the relevance of what they're being taught. Just like airline passengers, students may be the best judges of how exciting or enjoyable the ride is, but that is a fundamentally different issue. Judgments of intellectual currency are best left to other professors in the same way that judgments of skillful piloting are best left to other pilots.

Were we to employ a more robust measure of teaching effectiveness, one that included in-depth peer review of the content of a professor's teaching, what would actually be revealed would be evidence, or lack thereof, of a professor's scholarship: the degree to which the professor is employing up-to-date knowledge in class. Such peer review would simply be another way of having the professor go public with his or her thinking. In its absence, however, the professor is limited to students as the critical public audience, and their assessment of a professor's teaching effectiveness is incomplete for reasons already discussed.

What I'm suggesting here is that good teaching is more difficult to affect than good scholarship because it asks more of the professor. Good teaching demands coupling one's own scholarship with an ability to instill a love of scholarship in others. The existence of either condition by itself, however, is not enough to ensure good teaching. Both conditions are necessary.

"Ideally," as William Nelson concludes, "the college professor [should] be a widely respected scholar excited about learning and capable of communicating this excitement to others, a teacher deeply concerned with the welfare of students and eager to have them learn and grow, one who teaches imaginatively both by books and by personal example, a demanding yet compassionate person who respects the moral worth of students and their potential for growth."[5] From this perspective, Ernest Boyer continues, "Scholarship is not an esoteric appendage; it is at the heart of what the profession is all about. All faculty, throughout their careers, should, themselves, remain students. As scholars, they must continue to learn and be seriously and continuously engaged in the expanding intellectual world."[6]

Living up to this ideal is a tall order. Nonetheless, I take it as axiomatic that we are obliged to try. A good professor is, in the final analysis, a good student, and a good student recognizes there is always more to learn. Such recognition brings with it a fundamental sense of humility toward the learning process as well as that which is thought to be known. Seldom are questions put to rest permanently. The debate is ongoing. The enduring challenge is to remain open to the possibilities.

In closing, I am reminded of the late A. Bartlett Giamatti's characterization of university life:

> You are here to be thrown upon the resources of your own mind. And that means defining and refining those resources by drawing upon the resources of the place and of the other people in the place. To what end? So that the individual mind and spirit, made civil and capacious and curious, can foster the good and the knowledge it wishes for itself on behalf of others. The ultimate goal is to make the one, through fulfillment of the self, part of the many.[7]

Professor Giamatti's remarks, directed to students, apply equally to those of us who serve them.

Does This Path Have a Heart?

Mary Faeth Chenery

When I was 16, I wrote to my grandfather and asked him about careers—what should I do? How does one choose? How do you know what is right for you? A week later, one of his single page wonders arrived—40 lines of support, understanding, love and advice, this letter contained the recommendation: "Find out what you want to do, and find someone to pay you to do it." With this beacon, I moved forward into college and graduate school, with teaching in a university never on the list of, "what I want to do."

But what you do changes you, and I found myself teaching: first teaching sailing at a camp, then teaching swimming to children who were blind, then teaching interpersonal skills and creativity in management school, then psychology, and finally recreation when I reached my doctoral program. Teaching was fascinating and challenging, and the university setting seemed to be a good one. When I finished my doctoral program in psychology, I looked for two kinds of jobs: directing a camp, or teaching in a university. Camping had been the theme that united all my education and was really my work aim in life. The day after I asked my recreation advisor to find me a job, he called to say that there was a position at Indiana University combining teaching in a university with working at the university-owned camp. Surely they designed that job for me, and so I went. I taught in the Department of Recreation and Park Administration at Indiana University for six years. The first three were split between teaching responsibilities in the department and work at Bradford Woods, the department's camp and conference facility about half an hour away from the university. I was on the tenure track as far as the university was concerned, and, despite my unusual job arrangement, I needed to meet the expectations for teaching, research, and service the same as any faculty member. I wanted to succeed on the terms that the university established, and I wanted to succeed on my own terms: to do it my way.

As it turned out, I did succeed; I received tenure and promotion. And then I decided to leave.

I went to the west coast, wanting to live nearer to the ocean, nearer to friends, and wanting to find a new challenge. The University of Oregon had a temporary position to fill in my areas of outdoor recreation and philosophy of leisure, and I was fortunate to be hired. I received the "permanent" tenure-track position the next year, being given the rank of Associate Professor but not tenure, despite having received tenure elsewhere. However, I had not had any *years* of tenure, but had only just received it when I left Indiana University, and I understand that universities have different systems and different expectations for granting tenure; they often wish to apply their own standards to the incoming person. No problem. I was interested in the job, and tenure and rank have never had much hold on me.

I taught three years in the Department of Leisure Studies and Services at the University of Oregon, and again I left. This time I moved to Seattle, again to be nearer to water, nearer to friends, and nearer to what I wanted to do. In addition I wanted to be able to have the time to do things well (which results from having the time to think things through, the time to read and keep current on the developments in one's area, and the time to get feedback before the final draft). I also wanted to do my work without having to give up the rest of life. Here in Seattle I left professorship and academe and started my own business with two other colleagues, wanting to see if that business could provide enough income for me to live well. Synergies Research and Resources Group, Inc., was designed to provide research, consulting, education, and publication in the fields of organized camping and leisure services. We also created Human Development Research Associates to provide a not-for-profit structure within which to do research in camping. Fortunately, I don't need much money to live well.

That's quite a brief synopsis of 14 years of university teaching, four while in graduate school at two universities, and ten spent in tenure-track positions at two universities. Will I go back to teaching in the university? Well, I didn't know I was going into it to begin with, so it feels a bit unwise and unimportant to hazard a prediction. In many ways, everything I do feels like teaching (whether I'm educating myself or others), and I feel strongly about teaching in the university, about being a professor, and about the professors' responsibilities to students. My commitment to the goals of university education remains strong; thus, I would like to offer some of my philosophy about this matter through the remainder of this essay. I hope we will both learn through the process.

The Basic Themes

To understand how I approach teaching, it seems useful to know about some of the central themes in my life. I grew up going to camp in the summer, usually for four or five weeks, then for the whole summer when I became a staff member at 17. At home I was told I was capable and was expected to do well in school (and in everything else); I experienced unconditional love, and a valuing of both the artistic and the scientific rationale. I can remember one moment of complete flow as a child: complete engagement in a creative, shared, timeless afternoon of play. At camp I was believed in and supported; I made deep and lasting friendships; I learned self-confidence in sailing; I saw and was inspired by beauty and talent; I was challenged by a progressive program of opportunities to learn; I experienced community; and I found moments of oneness with the universe through times spent alone in the outdoors. As I grew up, I began to ask a few questions which have remained with me through the years: Why are we here? What is the purpose of life? What are we supposed to be doing? What is worth doing? What makes meaningful work? How should I spend my time?

It seems to me that I had a glimpse of how life could be led, and led well, through my child's-eye view of camp. People supported one another, celebrated the successes of others, and they cared for one another and said so. Beauty, talent, and music inspired them, and they took time to wonder about the spirit. People worked and played and lived together. Learning was fun, and the teachers (counselors) were your friends. Work was meaningful, and everyone made a contribution to the community.

I never have understood why life and work can't be peaceful, challenging, fun, loving, active, and meaningful; why we can't experience community more often; why there isn't enough time for the things that are important, like relationships and caring, beauty, craftsmanship, deep thought, service to others and to the earth, and spiritual growth. Thus, I have not understood why the university can't be like camp in its best sense.

I guess I was also brought up having most of the things that I wanted (possibly in part through being guided not to want things I couldn't have), fixing things that broke, solving problems, smoothing conflict, and believing that I could change things that didn't seem right to me. Then I went to management school, where the content and the process of our education branded us with a permanent action orientation: if you don't like it, take action to make change (and here's how). This leadership orientation, combined with a valuing of individuals and a participative management philosophy, created a strong student rights focus that I brought to my teaching positions. If I am honest, I must also add that I believe I have always identified more with the student role than the teacher role, thus I probably have a bias in the direction of student concerns.

On Being a Professor

The job of professor, as it was explained to me in my first tenure-track position, has three major aspects: teaching, research, and service. That explanation was brief and to the point. However, what it means is a little more complex. Perhaps if I describe explicitly what the job entailed, you will see the framework within which I spent my ten years of professorship. The structure of being a professor—expectations and demands—had quite a life of its own. As much as I might have liked to have been independent of its pull and "do it my way" attitude, this was the river of work to be done. I could choose my style of getting down the river; but unless one opted out of the tenure track, whether tacitly or vocally, this was the only river to run. Here's the interpretation that unfolded for me:

In order to do your job, you are expected to teach well. The teaching stream involves curriculum development, course design (and updating), class preparation (thinking, reading, writing, materials preparation), in-class leadership, evaluation of and giving feedback on assignments, grading, and student conferences. From that teaching, it is expected that the students will learn needed content and process and that they will give the teacher good student evaluations at the end of each term. The teaching assignment may be in small or large classes, with undergraduates, master's students, or doctoral students; you are expected to have experience with all these. Ideally, your teaching will be seen as dynamic and innovative.

Further, you are expected to do research in your chosen area of study. The research stream involves the creative act of problem formulation, research design, data collection, analysis, report writing, and seeking outlets for publication (which may require several revisions of your paper). In your research you may or may not have co-workers, some of whom may be students in need of supervision, some of whom may be colleagues in other, perhaps distant, universities. Your research publications are expected to be numerous, and will likely be viewed as important contributions to the field—preferably ones that break new ground. The work should follow a theme that you pursue over time (as distinct from being a series of separate, unrelated studies). At least some of your publications should be under your sole authorship. The expected number of publications per year may or may not be explicitly stated; the number, and the comparative status of journals in which you publish, often remain a mystery. (The expectation for "productivity" expanded over the ten years, and by the time I left, I felt that two to three publications each year were expected, at least one in a high status, refereed journal.)

Finally, you are expected to do service—to your department, the college or school where your department resides, the university, to the profession (local, state, and/or national, and in some cases international), and to the community. Advising students who are majors or graduate students in the department may fit in this category, or this may be considered part of the teaching stream. Committee membership or leadership, offices in professional organizations, publications in journals of the professional organizations, advising of student groups—all these are signs of service. The amount of service you are expected to do is a tricky calculation (and, of course, a paradox). If untenured, do as little as possible because it will take time away from research; however, if untenured, do a good deal of service, beginning with the department and moving into the university, with a dose of national professional service as well, because it will make you known. When I took my first tenure-track position, the department head told me, "I'll give you five years to be President of the American Camping Association." I was on the national board of directors in three years, and Vice President in four. It has been a wonderful way to get involved and to serve, but I can't say I'd recommend it to an untenured professor, unless you are truly "beyond promotion and tenure" in your mental state.

An area of service that is sometimes hidden is the realm of administration. If your job description involves an explicit administrative role (like department chairperson), you may get "forgiven" the time that this takes away from research and teaching; the expectations for your productivity may be reduced a bit in acknowledgment of the energies you are putting into administration. However, if you have a role (like head of the undergraduate or graduate curriculum) which is not a specific and recognized title in your job description—and may often be a job rotated around to different faculty—the energy you put into getting these tasks done doesn't appear to count as much. Each department has a number of jobs that must be done, and usually it is regular faculty members who must do them. They are important and worth doing, but they are time-consuming.

Research and service ideally will contribute to your teaching, and they do, if you have time to make that integration. The priorities of teaching, research, and service vary among universities and vary within units of the university, although it is a rare occasion when research is not the foremost task.

The final aspect of your job, or at least your life in the university, is governance or participation in the running of the university. Most faculty want to have some say in the decisions that affect them, and most universities have some form of faculty governance. It's amazing how much time democracy can take—again, it's worth doing, but time-consuming.

All these aspects of being a professor—teaching, research, service, administration, participation—have the potential to create a wonderful, meaningful, challenging job which contributes to worthy purposes and the development of the individual carrying out this good work. If integrated well, teaching, research, and service make quite a productive whole. The design of the job is quite good, at least until the dimension of time is added, the dimension of time that says, for example, that you must produce three refereed publications per year, teach four courses per year, advise the student recreation group, chair the committee revising the curriculum or preparing for the accreditation visit, and serve as a national officer for the professional organization. Who determines how much is enough? When did the time frame begin to shrink? Has anyone truly examined the amount of research, teaching, service, administration, and governance that can be done well in one academic year? Are the expectations based on that analysis?

I must admit that the time frame, the expectation for what feels like a tremendous amount of work in a short amount of time, seems quite arbitrary to me. I found that I was being encouraged by the expectations, and the reward system (of tenure, promotion, and merit increases), to be away from the office as much as possible, and out of the classroom. In order to do all of the things that "being a professor" means, I could not do them well, up to my own standards.

For a time, in my first years as a professor, I was learning so much personally about how to be a professor and what the content was in my new field that it really didn't matter that I worked all the time. I knew that I was working up to meeting my own standards, but I didn't need to be there yet, because it was still very new. After a while, though, as I became more comfortable with teaching, more knowledgeable about the field, and more effective in my role, it began to disturb me that I wasn't meeting my own standards (which, of course, had probably changed with my own growth). I had only written one paper (out of probably 15 papers) that I thought was truly ready for publication, was truly a good piece of work.[1] I had come to realize the importance of human relationships, of truly listening to students, of showing them my caring by making my time and my self available to them. I had come to want a community that included students and faculty and professionals. I had come to want a life that included more than work. After teaching the philosophy of leisure for ten years, I had come to realize that not living one's philosophy is unhealthy; how can you teach about leisure and have none? I had learned that while I like the holistic concept that one's work and recreation and other dimensions of life can run together in healthy ways, there are more aspects of a human life which, for me, should be allowed to unfold. While I loved my work as a university teacher, I needed to turn other facets of myself to the light. Ideally, the university would acknowledge this for all of its members. I did not find a way within the system to make this happen. I thought that I would take on the university and change it in my best "take initiative way," but I found that it was not time for me to do this now.

The need for community, even for intellectual community, the community of sharing ideas, did not seem to be as great for others as for me. Or, perhaps it is closer to the truth to say that others wanted such a community but could not find where it would fit in with the demands on their time from the named and recognized job functions of research, teaching, and service. The reward structure does not encourage such sharing of ideas, the taking of time to nurture dialogue, and ultimately to promote individual and community growth. When I found that the intellectual community I sought did not seem to be present in my department or college, I created a number of structures for community to happen, such as "Breakfast and Ideas," brown bag lunches, and finally, having given up on getting other faculty to attend, an evening doctoral student seminar. Nothing lasted, because no one had the time to give to it.

John Dewey pointed out that we must create the conditions for teachers that we wish them to create for students. If we want growth in students, we must enable growth for faculty; we must create the conditions for faculty members to experience personal and intellectual growth. I understand that by the correct performance of the professor's job of teaching, research, and service, personal and intellectual growth is supposed to happen. I think the "correct performance" of the professor's job, as it is currently designed, is a bit like the correct performance of being a working mother: Just as being Super Mom has its costs, being Super Professor perhaps does too. When you are unable to do the job well—to fully experience its challenges and grow from them, the very real danger of becoming bored emerges. As amazing as that may seem in the stimulating and relatively free climate of the university, it is possible to get so tied up in just doing the basic tasks (go from classroom, to meeting, to office hours, to research lab) that there is no time to do anything truly new and

creative. When nothing new is happening, you get bored—even if uncon-
sciously. For me, it was sacrilege to even contemplate being bored. I was
always of the mindset that one could only blame boredom on oneself.
What I didn't see was the power of routine tasks to fill all the time and
squeeze out new activity. Even though I was finding new ways to teach
and new research efforts, the size of the innovations didn't match my
need as I grew in the last few years.

What would happen if we removed the time frame, and only asked
that everything that the professor does be done with the highest quality
of which the individual is capable, with integrity in giving at least 40
hours of work to the university each week, and with the aim of personal
and intellectual growth for the individual, knowing that those conditions
are necessary for the growth of the students in the professor's care? What
happens when we are free...?

But perhaps I am listening to a different drummer than the larger
world, because I admit to being at odds with a good deal of how society
operates. It seems to me that much of the motivation of what happens in
the world stems from greed, and I cannot accept that for myself. I suspect
that the university administrators will tell me that while what I would like
to change may be a worthy idea, economic considerations will prevent
doing what I suggest. Yet, the time to scale back the economic desires of
people will come, I suspect. The New Age that we see unfolding is revealing the desire of many people to live lives of high quality. As Jennifer
James puts it, "success is the quality of the journey." Achieving quality
will require some sacrifice of what we are used to, for example, of material goods and disposable income. Many professors are looking at the
option of leaving the university in order to restore harmony and balance
in their lives, and to begin to grow, not only intellectually, but spiritually
and physically, as often their health needs to be restored. Several of us in
the leisure services field joke about starting a new university, one where
the job will not stifle life and growth. It is unfortunate that leaving seems
like the most viable option for change.

Who is to say that the way the professor's job is structured is correct? One of the reasons for living in communities, marriages, and
organizations, is to get the necessary tasks done. The path of life is
many-faceted. We must sustain the physical body, nurture relationships,
become educated and provide for the education of others, do meaningful work, rest, express ourselves creatively, and care for our souls: that
is, have a spiritual life. Learning is the life stream; it is the vitalizing
force in human development. Maybe it takes more than one person to do
the educator's job. Perhaps it requires assistance and/or assistants along

the way. If the time frame is to stay as it is, maybe the professor needs a team; perhaps the university should contract each position out to a small group, a job sharing collective. Perhaps being a professor does need to be redefined... but I will come back to that.

The most meaningful part of being a professor for me was the teaching part of the job. Let me explain some of my thinking there.

How I Taught/How I Want to Teach

I enjoy teaching, though I inevitably experience some anxious moments prior to each class. Sometimes during, and almost always after the classroom performance, I *really* enjoy teaching. If I have had enough time to prepare adequately (to my standards) for the class, then going into the classroom is easier. It was a rare occasion that I felt adequately prepared, though as the years progressed, so did my feeling that I could survive the classroom hours, and in fact, that they would go well.

I must confess that despite having spent a good deal of time teaching, I am still not sure that the classroom is needed. Relationships are needed, and community is helpful; but the classroom, as it is traditionally and regularly used in the universities I know most about, probably isn't needed. Feeling such doubt about the classroom made it hard to go into it, but I did. Students can read; therefore, the purpose of the classroom must be something other than the giving of information.

Sometimes I felt that I had only one course (though I have taught probably 15-20 different courses over time); that course was a process course. Irrespective of the course title, the framework was the same: teaching students to think and write well, nurturing creativity, and encouraging students to take initiative on their own behalf when they wanted something changed. It seems to me that students can always read, can always learn content on their own. What they may need help with is process—thinking, analysis, synthesis, the use of content, the consideration of values in relation to content, the drawing out of the implications of the information. Writing forces students (and professors) to confront what is inside them; it brings up issues of discipline, creativity, values, self-concept, and meaning. It is a difficult challenge—perhaps an Outward Bound experience for the mind. The act of writing, and rewriting, then is as important as the content of the paper produced.

I wondered from time to time whether my emphasis on process was a smokescreen for my lack of knowledge of content; after all, my primary background was not in leisure studies or outdoor recreation, and the way most university positions are set up, you really don't have time to do all the necessary reading to be adequately informed of the current content. However, my tentative conclusion here is that process is truly important, because once process is acquired, then a person has ultimate freedom to learn anything. Then the challenge becomes finding out what one really wants to learn.

Ideally, I also wanted students to feel part of a community in the classroom, and in the department. That meant taking some time to build relationships; it meant helping students overcome years of expectations to be silent and distant in the classroom and in relation to professors and administrators. Being a professor puts you in relationship to others, the key link being to students. The relationship of professor and student is a power relationship in that the professor can make decisions that govern a student's progress through the university. I believe we should not act out the power in the relationship. Rather, students and faculty should come together, recognizing that each has something to offer the other. For example, using titles like Doctor or Professor, and/or using last names, reinforce distance and power, which is why I prefer the use of first names for everyone in or out of the classroom. Mutual respect and the desire to learn from one another will establish a basis for a relationship of equality (a healthy model for other relationships beyond the university as well). Equality and closeness are more likely than power and distance to help students want to do their highest level of work.

I learned over time to tolerate silence, to be patient enough to allow students to speak at their own rate, and to create a receptive, safe climate within which to express their ideas. To create community, especially where other faculty may not share this objective, also means creating some demands on your time to be available outside the classroom — worthwhile, but risky to other expectations and responsibilities. Community building also requires vulnerability: a willingness to be wrong and to show your brokenness.[2]

When I look at the personal highlights of my professorship, I think of the following: a few, special students, lots of whom played their own role in my personal/professional growth; quotes in students' papers that stretched me; a lecture I gave about writing, using different colored felt pieces, sewing them together as I talked to demonstrate how a proposition or thesis should be carried through a paper; an intensive summer school class taught in residence in the woods; the Lilly Postdoctoral Teaching Fellowship that gave me the time and resources to learn how to design classes and develop teaching materials; learning by walking alongside mentors like Rey Carlson; being forced to articulate my beliefs through the philosophy class I taught; designing the entrepreneurship curriculum with its process emphasis; advising the graduate student groups; being present at the nearly unanimous acceptance of the revised American Camp Association (ACA) standards after long hours of service on the National Standards Board; and having the opportunity due to proximity to be of service to the national headquarters of ACA for six years. The patterns I see in these personal highlights are of growth unfolding, through teaching and being taught; of confidence gained and potential neared; of people admired; of giving service, and being acknowledged and valued for service given; and of moments of flow in the classroom and office. Clearly, I have had many gifts from being a professor.

How I want to teach is, I hope, fairly close to how I have been teaching, with the difference that how I want to teach takes a lot more time, which I like to think I now have and will continue to have. I want to teach the processes of centering, thinking, analysis, synthesis, creativity, initiative, and giving and receiving feedback. I want to work within a community that supports its members and values caring and learning and service. I want to learn from students and to create new knowledge with them. I want to use many different modes of teaching, and to do the teaching in many different settings. I want to be able to live my philosophy and model what is important to me. I want to be able to offer my values to others and to discuss what is important. I want students to take action to change what they feel needs changing, including how and what I teach. I want to take time to read, to discuss, to write, and to be able to give informed feedback on what others have written. Sometimes I want to play with the members of the community, and sometimes I want to have time to be by myself.

Redefining Professor

One of the students I have worked with, Jess Schload, brought this quote to me via a class paper: "We continue to accept the established as real; we assume that if we know more about teaching and learning, we can solve our educational problems. Faced by curricular needs we turn to technology and neglect ways of being together. Faced with non-responsive students, we turn to psychology to understand and control behavior instead of reflecting on the meaning of two persons in relationship. Confronted by difficulties in classroom discussion, cooperation, or morale, we consider the latest group dynamics technique instead of rethinking the nature of community."[3]

I think it is time to rethink the nature of community, and also the nature of university education and the meaning of being a professor. Although another term for the changed role would perhaps be more accurately descriptive (such as enabler or resource person), I don't need to play in semantics, as jargon is a distancer. How we live the role will speak louder than its title. Being a professor should mean being one who is chosen to walk alongside. In my case, I hope that students would choose me as their professor because I have been on this path a bit longer than them; because I am willing to do and want to do the tasks of teaching, inquiring, writing, and serving them; because I have some skills to offer and the ability to translate those skills to them; because I am eager to learn and willing to be in a relationship of equality with them; because I know how to create and nurture community; and because I model some of what the university thinks is important and wants its students to know.

The commitment of the Dominican Sisters, whom we think of as the Catholic teaching order, is not to teaching per se, but to lifelong learning—for themselves and for others; that seems a good model. Being a professor should mean creating and being a part of a caring community, being committed to the equality and growth of all its members, in all their dimensions. Finally, another gift from a student friend, Almut Beringer: "…be patient toward all that is unresolved in your heart and… try to love the questions themselves like locked rooms and like books that are written in a very foreign tongue. Do not seek the answers, which cannot be given to you because you would not be able to live them. And the point is, to live everything. Live the questions now. Perhaps you will then gradually, without noticing it, live along some distant day into the answers."[4] Together, as professors and students, we can ask questions, and "live along… into the answers."

Ultimately, the questions about being a professor are really, "Does this path have a heart, for me?" "Can I be who I want to be in this environment, under these conditions, within this value system?" "Am I growing and continuing to learn?" "If I can truly lay aside the benefits of the financial reward and the relative freedom of schedule, is this the path I should be on?" "Am I being led toward my highest potential?" "Am I able to unfold who I am with honesty and integrity, and with pleasure?" "Is who I am when I am in the classroom, or in the office, or in the field, good for the people I am around, especially for the students who come to me to learn from my highest self?" "Am I living my philosophy?" "Do I truly want to be here doing this?" "Does this path have a heart, for me?"

On Privilege and Obligation

Larry Beck

Off in the distance is Mt. Laguna, behind which the sun has just risen. It is a brisk autumn morning. My office window is slightly ajar and the crisp air is invigorating. I listen to the cavorting of various birds: woodpeckers and jays, flickers and sparrows, juncos and warblers, and the rustling leaves of poplar and birch. Earlier I sat by the fireplace in my living room, reading the paper and drinking coffee. The fire is still crackling, but now it is time for work. My profession demands that I take time to write; however, where I choose to accomplish this task is of no consequence.

It is Monday and I imagine most people in San Diego, some 50 miles to the west, are battling traffic on their way to work. Their days, for the most part, will be structured and routine. Later today, as I get stuck or as I require breaks, I will go out and work in the yard, split wood, take a walk in the forest. I'll put in eight hours today, maybe more. But I'll set my own pace and that makes all the difference. How did I get so lucky?

On August 30, 1982, with a Bachelor of Science degree and an abundance of enthusiasm, I began teaching at San Diego State University as a lecturer. I remember well that first fall semester. In addition to teaching a course at SDSU, I taught courses at Mesa College and San Diego City College. I carried 12 units in a master's program at Azusa Pacific University. I worked weekends at Cabrillo National Monument. And because all of this didn't add up to much in the way of a paycheck, I delivered pizzas.

Prior to my employment in higher education I worked for the National Park Service in some of the most scenic country on the continent—in Alaska, Arizona, California, and Utah. Most of my work was conducted outdoors. My job was enviable.

Hard work and sacrifice characterize the years since those carefree times as a national park ranger. But the effort has been well worth it. This fall, after completing a Ph.D. at the University of Minnesota, I was appointed to a tenure-track position. After serving as a lecturer for several years, what has changed can be measured in terms of job security, opportunity for advancement, and esteem. From my perspective, the chance to work toward tenure is a tremendous luxury. The actual job I do, however, remains the same. Whether "before promotion and tenure" or "beyond promotion and tenure," the significance of the job, and the obligation to do it well, remain the same. My lecturer position, to the credit of the faculty in my department, allowed time for university service and professional growth activities. Teaching, however, brought me into the profession.

The Joy of Teaching

My passion for teaching stems from the courses I conduct in the areas of wilderness and resource management, natural history interpretation, and environmental education. Especially in these courses I have a solid grounding of book knowledge and personal experience. The subjects are captivating; I want to learn more.

Through teaching, I continue to be a devoted student. I enjoy researching topics for inclusion into the courses I teach. My obligation is to seek out the most current and the most relevant material. I also find satisfaction in determining the best method of organizing the material and getting the information across. I teach based upon a "modular system" in which each topic is a self-contained unit with supporting classroom experiences and readings. I take pride in assembling a well-organized course. Carrying out a deliberate instructional plan is also rewarding. The degree of attention a professor devotes to course preparation is revealed in the overall success of the class. If care in course structure is evident, it gives students confidence they are in good hands. I strive for a balance between authority and humility in the classroom. I also attempt to create a balance between a sense of order and definiteness, and a stimulus for students to take control of their own learning.

For the most part I look forward to class. I begin with the assumption that students are sincerely interested in what I have prepared. I am aware that I must be excited about the subject to expect to arouse the interest of students. Enthusiasm is contagious. We sometimes forget that students need to be excited about what they learn. Mihaly Csikszentmihalyi once wrote: "Perhaps the most important accomplishment of influential teachers is that they are able to transform the usual drudgery of the classroom into an enjoyable experience." This approach, of course, demands innovation and creativity from the professor. An atmosphere that is conducive to learning is evident in the replacement of student impassiveness by their attentiveness, blank expressions by warm eyes, and scowls by occasional laughter.

The use of humor, periodically, has the tendency to contribute to the positive mood of the class and reduces the social distance between students and professor. Humor should be relevant and central to the theme of the lesson. Little is more pathetic, or inappropriate, than a professor wasting excessive time regaling students with irrelevant jokes and personal anecdotes. Humor should be incorporated in moderation. A respect for the subject must be evident on the part of the professor.

I teach from the conviction that my subjects are genuinely important. I launch each semester by explaining that the course is among the most pivotal offered at the university. The point is to provide the students a rationale for why the subject is worthy of study. Likewise, it is valuable to leave students with a direction for further pursuit of the course material. I conclude each course I teach with a lecture titled, "The End... Or The Beginning... Where To Go From Here." In this lecture I present specific steps for continued attention to the subject.

At a panel discussion I recently attended, Charles Sykes, the author of *Profscam*, declared that we are experiencing a revolution in attitudes toward teaching. The revolution stems from the obligation professors have to serve students. To me, it is an honor to have a forum for my subject, my thoughts, and my passion. It is remarkable, I think, that every semester there will be 100 or more students who will gather in the classrooms in which I teach at the appointed times. To have an audience is a tremendous responsibility. It is important to remember who is paying, and who is getting paid, for being in the classroom. There is a reciprocal relationship, I believe, in which the professor is responsible to students and students are responsible to the professor. It is in this balance that education can be most effective.

On Making a Difference

One of the outcomes of devoting much time to the teaching process is to see evidence from students that you have made a difference. I am always moved when students bring in articles of interest, small gifts, or cards. It is also rewarding when a past student returns to say that I have made a difference in his or her life. This is a powerful commentary on the high degree of influence professors have.

Professors also affect students outside of the classroom. Office hours are set aside for those who want clarification on a course topic or advice about pursuing graduate school or a particular avenue of employment. It is often this direct contact, this intimacy of conversation outside of class that has a strong effect on students. I enjoy this interaction.

I have found that students are most likely to seek counsel if they feel welcome. I encourage students several times during the course of a semester to stop by during office hours. Some, on occasion, will confront me with a serious personal problem. These students are always referred to our university counseling division.

There are professors who don't believe that they can make a difference in the lives of students, and they structure their priorities accordingly. These cynical individuals maintain that students who show interest in outside reading or bring in small gifts are trying to bribe the professor. Perhaps this is true. Still, I have more faith in the human capacity to be moved out of genuine absorption with a subject and personal integrity. I also know the difference a handful of professors have made in my life.

Wilbur Mayhew was one of my biology professors at the University of California. I took 15 units of vertebrate field biology from him. Professor Mayhew's courses were interesting. Along with traditional texts in vertebrate biology he also required what might be described as "popular" readings by Aldo Leopold and Barry Commoner, among others. I now employ this same strategy in my own teaching.

Professor Mayhew's passion for his subject and his depth of knowledge were most evident on our field trips. During these outings he also revealed something of his personal life and his sense of humor. I respected him all the more for this. Overall, he inspired in me a deep respect for natural environments and species other than our own. He set me in a direction that has contributed greatly to how I experience the world.

There was another influential professor. Alann Steen taught Journalism at Humboldt State University. The course I took was titled "Technical Writing." Contrary to the course title, Professor Steen contended that writing should be clear, concise, and non-technical. "It's easy to write," he said, "in incomprehensible, scientific gibberish. What is tough is to write crisply—in a style that is easily understood." He provided us with handouts of the most vital information. I still have his "Forty Rules for Vivid Writing."

Most students, I remember, were not inclined to move beyond their indifference to writing. I was sufficiently inspired, after the class, to write a lengthy essay for a popular magazine. I spent more time on that article than anything else I've ever written, save my dissertation. I asked Professor Steen to review the paper and he filled the pages with re-written passages and suggestions. I recall fondly his insightful teaching and his encouragement. I always left his class feeling good. Now, for my own students, I strive to develop with them a stronger sense of their own possibilities.

There was a third professor who impacted me. Doris Meek was my professor of higher education. Professor Meek worked hard for students. Her syllabus was the most comprehensive I'd ever seen. We knew exactly what was expected of us. Her class sessions were always well-executed, with a diversity of activities. I was never bored. I learned from Professor Meek to be innovative in my own teaching—to keep trying new things.

I remember being startled, early in the course, when she called me by name. In fact, she knew the name of every student in the class. To this day I strive to learn the names of the students in my classes, large or small. I know many professors who consider this an idle task. Maybe so. Still, in a small way, this mitigates some of the impersonal flavor of a university of 35,000.

A fourth professor, Richard Knopf, taught the research course at the University of Minnesota. Like the others, Professor Knopf gave only meaningful assignments. It was in his class that I conceptualized my thesis topic. He made learning about research an adventure. He wanted us to experience how a research orientation changes the way you look at the world.

Professor Knopf was always available for consultation. I think he liked our brainstorming sessions. He made me work through various perplexities by raising questions rather than telling me the answers, thereby allowing me to shape the direction of my dissertation He forced me to think on my own. I remember his words: "Arm yourself with knowledge." We also talked about a wide range of topics in addition to those related to class. It seemed that he was sincerely concerned that I leave with more than a broadened education, that I learn something about Minnesota. And at his insistence I did.

I have also had dozens of other professors. Some good, some fair, some poor. The inadequate professors taught me about aloofness, indifference, and arrogance. From their bad example I learned never to mock or berate students. I learned not to return exams and papers weeks after receiving them. I learned not to embarrass myself by not staying current. I learned, from their bad example, about integrity.

There was a "professor" I had in graduate school who used to come into class and read to us from a text. I remember once when a student asked a question. The "professor" paused, read ahead in the text until he found the answer, and then reported back without the least amount of embarrassment. He once told the class that we weren't fit to be in graduate school. Worthy graduate students, he insisted, sit quietly and take notes and don't ask questions.

What Professors Mayhew, Steen, Meek, and Knopf represent can be summed up in their selflessness. These exemplary educators had agendas that included time for students. Together, and in different ways, they prepared me for where I am now. Their courses, without exception, were tough. They demanded much of their students. They also demanded much of themselves. They projected a vision of excellence and, not surprisingly, represent some of the top scholars in their respective fields.

Professor Mayhew and Professor Knopf are still teaching. Professor Meek has retired, although she is still active in the university community. I don't know what events led to Professor Steen taking a teaching position at the University of Beirut. Tragically, he was one of the Americans held hostage in Lebanon.

The Rewards of Writing

The 25th rule for vivid writing from Professor Steen's handout is: "Pay attention to each word, each sentence, each paragraph, and each transition." Writing is hard work. It's tedious.

My role at this university, initially, was to teach. For the past three years I have also been expected to write articles for publication—from research findings to thought pieces to book reviews. At about the same time I began to feel confident with my teaching, I was faced with this new challenge. Writing can be a demanding chore—as difficult to do well as most anything I can think of. The challenge is high, and, therefore, so are the rewards. I don't resent having to write. On the contrary, I relish it. Good writing requires the same care and many of the same skills that are employed in good teaching. Like good teaching, the best writing is that which is so deliberate and smooth it appears to be effortless.

There are at least three reasons why professors are required to write. First, a discipline advances only if there are contributions to the body of knowledge. If those who are most highly trained to advance the field don't contribute to the literature, who will? This is what distinguishes a college professor, who is paid in part to generate knowledge, from a teacher, who is paid primarily to convey knowledge.

Another reason for writing is that it forces us to sharpen ideas, to extend our critical thinking skills. We demand critical thinking from our students. Can we demand anything less of ourselves? Putting ideas in written form is indispensable to precise thinking.

A third reason for writing is that professors may utilize this investment in focused thinking in their teaching. Among other activities, this is how professors stay current in the field. A professor's own thoughts-turned-to-print can be of tremendous value in the teaching of graduate courses and may sometimes be as useful in undergraduate teaching.

I used to think that a department could function like a team. The chair would serve as manager in his or her utilization of varying faculty talent. Many professors have a preference for either teaching or writing, and each could pursue his or her passion accordingly. The chair would orchestrate the faculty strengths to build an effective whole. The problem with this approach is that, at the university level, writing and teaching are complementary tasks. Writing articles relates directly to pedagogic responsibilities. To take a prolific thinker and writer out of the classroom would be a disservice to students. Similarly, to take great teachers away from time for writing would be undesirable, for they too have much to offer the profession in the advancement of knowledge. Teaching and writing are mutually reinforcing activities.

The most difficult barrier for me to overcome is setting aside time for writing. I require large blocks of uninterrupted time to be productive. Once I'm settled into the writing process, time passes quickly. I become absorbed in the task. Writing is a creative process and I prefer not to be hurried. It feels good to find that right word, to make an effective transition, to capture an elusive line of thought on paper. It feels good to generate a cadence, a rhythmic sequence of words. Introductions and conclusions are particularly tricky. But, there is a tremendous sense of satisfaction upon completing a writing assignment. The 33rd rule for vivid writing is: "Write, revise, edit—then revise and edit again." Again, writing is hard work. It demands time and focus.

A Way of Life

Being a professor is not so much a job or occupation to me as it is a way of life. The dichotomizing of work and leisure is transcended. There is little separation between the two. I don't make a conscious connection between the work I do and a monthly paycheck. Being a professor is an inextricable component of my life. I feel like I belong in this profession and realize my good fortune to be paid for what I like to do.

I appreciate the diversity of duties the profession demands. One day might include an early committee or faculty meeting, a couple of office hours when I meet with students, and several hours in the classroom. Another day might encompass preparing for classes, grading term papers, and reviewing a manuscript for journal publication. Another day might be devoted solely to writing.

It is not possible for me to touch on all the intricacies, the nuances, of what it means to be a professor. The job is enormously complex and the duties vary according to the institution where one teaches. For example, my entomology professor at the University of California taught one class a year. The bulk of his time was spent on research. I also know a friend from graduate school who teaches four courses a quarter. As a result, aside from teaching, little else is expected.

In a spectrum of research to teaching universities, I find myself somewhere in between. The expectations at SDSU lie on the balance of teaching and writing. I like it that way. Some aspects of the job, of course, are more rewarding than others. I would be remiss to suggest that my employment is without irritations. I'm not particularly fond of grading exams. It is sometimes difficult to conduct my work, especially writing, at my university office. There are almost constant interruptions by the phone, friendly colleagues, and students stopping by to chat outside of office hours. I often wish there were more time in a day, especially to read and write. Finally, I am sometimes bothered by the complacency of some students in the university. But these are, in the course of things, minor annoyances. In my other jobs I always dreaded Mondays and couldn't wait for the workday to end. Now I cherish Mondays, and days set aside for writing. I am also astonished at how quickly other workdays go by.

Many of the desirable qualities of my lifestyle are associated with involvement in higher education. There are few other professions, I suspect, where there is such a high degree of intellectual stimulation. An academic environment affords many opportunities. Over the years I have attended university-sponsored lectures by such luminaries as Carl Rogers and Stephen Jay Gould. Within this department we have hosted noted professors in our discipline. Beyond the exchange of ideas on campus, my wife and I have hosted several scholars at our home including Jim Murphy, Richard Schreyer, and Roderick Nash. As much as I respect what these professors have contributed to our field, I also admire their warm and gracious manner.

One of the highlights of last year was three days spent hosting Barry Lopez, the writer, during his contribution to our lecture series, "Promoting Environmental Messages through the Arts." He is among the most articulate and scholarly men I have ever met. I learned much from his passion for ideas, language, and landscape. He had an enormous impact on me.

The three greatest attributes of a life in higher education, a close colleague once told me, are: June, July, and August. I agree, because as much as I love my work, it is refreshing to get away now and then. The time of rejuvenation enables me to be a better professor. Also, for someone who likes to travel this is a great business to be in. Summer trips in the past few years have taken me to Martha's Vineyard, Yellowstone, and Banff National Park, Canada. Winter excursions have been to Yosemite, Kauai, and New Zealand. Various aspects of this travel are employed in my teaching and, on occasion, in my writing.

With so much time off in the winter and summer I often find myself completing work-related activities that I don't have time for during the academic year. This work generally encompasses designing or revising curriculum, keeping up with the literature, and writing articles. That I choose to work during vacation is a revealing commentary on the intrinsic rewards of my vocation.

On Privilege and Responsibility

What I worked for at the University of Minnesota was a ticket into this lifestyle. My diploma reads that I earned a Doctor of Philosophy degree "with all its privileges and obligations." That phrase sums up what it means to be a professor. I thrive on the high degree of freedom and appreciate the flexibility of my schedule. I may work over a weekend only to take some time off during the week. I might choose to work 14 hours one day and two the next. So long as I meet my classes, committee assignments, and office hours each week, the way I structure the balance of my work hours is basically up to me. That time is ultimately accounted for in the form of well-designed classes, publications, conference presentations, and other professional growth activities.

Promotion and tenure are designed to keep me honest. Ideally, there will be some form of accountability throughout my career. The problem with tenure is that it can be abused. "Professors" who take advantage of the privileges make a mockery of the enterprise. The freedom of the job carries with it responsibility. Academic freedom does not mean freedom not to do the job.

In the beginning of this section, Dan Dustin claims that the life of a professor is a gift, and like all true gifts there are no strings attached. I see it differently. My employment at this university isn't a present. I've worked hard for this. And there are strings attached. If I'm not doing my job, the university is obligated to fire me for the sake of my discipline, my students, my hardworking colleagues, and the tax-paying public. But in another respect I agree with Professor Dustin that a life in higher education is a gift. The gift is in the freedom and privilege afforded professors. It is being paid to pursue, create, and share knowledge. The gift is adding another dimension to the lives of others, helping them to realize their goals and potentials. It is enabling others to develop a passion for lifelong learning, to become more responsible, to deliberate over what it means to live well, with honesty and integrity. The gift is to be shared, not squandered. The gift, all told, has privileges and obligations.

Sometimes It Feels Like Moonlighting

Ruth Russell

Bracing myself for yet another challenge, I again catch a ride with George, one of the motor pool drivers. Careening around corners onto wide eight-lane boulevards, we travel mostly in silence. Occasionally he mumbles about the Armenians. We enter the teeming caverns of the airport. George and I maneuver toward new arrivals. For the fourth time in as many days I show my entry documents to the police and then search the left-luggage rooms, lost and found, and new arrivals conveyer belt areas. Again I pantomime my dilemma to the officials. Again no luggage.

I arrived in Moscow on July 4th. I came as part of my teaching responsibilities in Indiana University's Department of Recreation and Park Administration. Several years ago I began to work on the idea of a practicum course for my students with the American Embassy in Moscow. For two summers now we have sent a team of four students to provide day camp services for the children of American, British, French, West German, Mexican, Danish, Icelandic, and other diplomatic staff.

The camp is held within the Embassy compound and in its two country dachas (retreats). Students are provided housing and a stipend by the American Embassy; Pan American Airlines helps with the round-trip transportation; my department provides logistical assistance, training, Russian language tutoring, program supplies, and moral support; and the University's Russian and East European Institute offers orientations to Moscow culture and manners.

It's a big project—we probably use too many departmental and faculty resources for the number of students who benefit—but I persist and even seek ways to expand it. This made my trip to Moscow a necessity in order to explore improvements for the project, particularly better ways to prepare students for it. I felt insecure helping students get ready for a place and a responsibility I had never experienced. Of course I have helped hundreds of other students prepare for careers in other places I'd never experienced—like Forest Park, Illinois and Kokomo, Indiana. Somehow, sending four students to Moscow to run a summer day camp without having firsthand knowledge seemed more irresponsible. However, after wearing the same outfit for five days in a row, I'm beginning to feel less of a need to know Moscow for myself.

The student counselor team arrived earlier and the first camp session was already under way. Therefore, I expected my role here would be simply to inventory program supplies and facilities and establish face-to-face relationships with the Embassy staff whose telexed writing styles I had come to know well. I would critique the counselors' performances and write a progress report for the department. I was especially looking forward to the free time I would have to write up several research projects that had been idle in my office for months.

Instead, upon arrival at the apartment in the Embassy compound where the counselors were living, I realized my expectations would be challenged. My role as teacher for the next two weeks would be drastically different from any teaching role I had known previously.

Regularly I teach under frightening circumstances. In one of my courses I lecture before 200 undergraduates. Some of them are sitting so high in the back of the auditorium I am sure they can only see the top of my head. I've taught a doctoral level research design seminar with six students in which I was only a chapter ahead. I have taught workshops to recreation personnel on Air Force bases in ten countries in Europe and the Pacific. I've piled students in university vans and driven for miles and days, all in the name of teaching. Nonetheless, since my arrival here, I have been newly anxious.

Immediately I notice the kitchen situation. Across the countertops, like neatly ordered books, are boxes of macaroni and cheese instant dinners. Just add water. In the refrigerator is a six-pack of beer and a six-pack of soda. This is the extent of the kitchen inventory. Is this the foreign cultural experience I envisioned for the students? I realize that in expecting to use my time to catch up on my research writing, I had forgotten the purpose of my trip. Likewise, I realize the students had forgotten the purpose of their adventure.

Because of an Embassy staff shortage, no one had been available to show the students how to function within Moscow's day-to-day lifestyle. They had leapt right away into running the day camp, using only resources found inside the Embassy compound. They ate breakfast in the Embassy cafeteria, skipped lunch because the camp schedule didn't allow them to return to the cafeteria, and for dinner relied on the very expensive Embassy commissary, which imports all American products via Helsinki,

Finland. Each box of macaroni and cheese, for example, cost about $5.00. At that rate the students' stipend from the Embassy would be literally eaten up halfway through the summer. Far worse was their admission that they had only been outside the Embassy a couple of times and had only seen the area within a few blocks of the compound.

So my role as their teacher immediately changed. I had to spend my first days teaching myself about Moscow. Now my goal is to teach the students what I learned. So far I have learned how to use a long fork to test the freshness of the bread, where dollars and not rubles are required for purchases, how to finesse the "three-line" system to buy things, how to get a taxi by holding a pack of Marlboros in the palm of my hand, how to stand in line at a Pepsi kiosk to drink out of the same glass as everyone else in line, and how to negotiate the metro route to Chekhov's house.

Teachers by definition teach students from their own store of knowledge and experience. Here, however, I am teaching students with only minutes between my knowledge acquisition and the instruction. For example, I have seen no homeless people. A teacher in the Anglo-American school tells me that everyone has a place to live. Most are living in two to three room apartments (not two to three bedrooms) with their extended families. I explain to the students that the single-family dwelling is very rare in Moscow and that it is usually found only outside the city. When a couple gets married they usually live with the husband's family until they can find an apartment of their own. Throughout the city there are "trade boards" where people post notices in hopes of exchanging apartments.

On Saturday I took the students to Red Square where we spent a fascinating hour watching newlyweds place large bouquets of fresh gladiolas at the Grave of the Unknown Soldier. A man and woman who wore identical red ribbon sashes across their shoulders attended each couple. Solemnly the young foursomes posed for photographs taken by friends and family.

Last night I cajoled my charges away from the large selection of American videos in their Embassy apartment for a late evening stroll down Arbat Street, the only pedestrian mall in Moscow. We joined Muscovites listening to street musicians, laughing with impromptu comedians, and watching nuns silently display protest posters on the plight of hungry Armenian Catholics. "Where is Armenia?" the students asked. "Why are they hungry?" Although it was close to midnight, the Moscow summer sky was still light.

For tomorrow I have arranged for the wife of the Brazilian ambassador to take us to a "workers club." This is a recreation center for the workers in a shoe factory. Most Moscow factories have these facilities, and they are active providers of recreation services. Inside, we are told, we'll find a gymnasium, auditorium, meeting rooms, dining area, and a childcare playground. This will be appropriate subject matter for the students.

Perhaps other lessons can be learned from our guide for this outing. Having recently lived in five east European countries, she speaks six languages. She was born in London, the daughter of a Syrian mother and a Pakistani father. She met her husband, the Brazilian ambassador, while on vacation in Katmandu, Nepal. Her great passion is architecture. She spends her days with her Soviet driver roaming around Moscow discovering old buildings that escaped the Stalin era of annihilation-of-things tsarist. What conclusions should I help the students draw from this alternative lesson?

I have come here as "the teacher" for this student practicum course. But I am not teaching recreation program planning, or camp leadership, or the development of a budget. The day camp is going well; the students are adequately prepared. Instead I am teaching how to experience another culture, how to appreciate its differences, and how to be curious and adventuresome.

The American children in the camp are extremely patriotic. They name their sport teams "The Yanks" and "Uncle Sam"; they write I-heart-America on giant mosaics during a crafts session. The students and I sit down after a camp day to discuss this. What does it mean to be patriotic? Does living without Batman and Dairy Queen instill patriotism? Do the American children living in the Embassy compound understand their own culture? We have this discussion for over two hours. Sometimes I am teaching, sometimes I am learning. It is exciting.

I realize that I am teaching every minute of my waking hours and even these are extended by later and later bedtimes. I have taught college students at two universities for over 11 years, won two outstanding teaching awards, and written two textbooks. But never before had I felt as excellent at my craft. For the first time I am completely immersed in my teaching. I live with these students and share myself with them continually. My classroom is everywhere—on the boat that ferries us down the Moscow River, in the courtyard at the Australian Embassy cookout, on top of the giant Ferris wheel in Gorky Park. But the students are also teaching me. Even I am searching shops for the Paul McCartney album that was released only in the Soviet Union! Though I am only four days into this, it holds the intensity of a lifetime. At last I am a professor.

Over the stretch of years since I enrolled as a freshman in my first recreation course, I have found my motives for wanting to be a professor have changed. Originally I observed my own college teachers and thought it looked easy. After all, how difficult could it be to teach only two or three courses a semester that met only two or three times a week? Lectures that came from our assigned textbook and exams written and graded by graduate assistants gave me an impression that college professors taught mostly from habit—not preparation, talent, or skill.

After several years of working in a variety of recreation and park settings (in order to get real examples to use in class), I stood before my own college classroom. The price of getting there, however, was high. The pursuit of my first college teaching position cost in salary, friendships and relationships, self-esteem, and a great deal of time. Worse, it cost me my notion that it was an easy occupation.

Working with college students themselves is certainly not easy. Coming from a wide variety of backgrounds, they sit in my classrooms with wildly different expectations, as well as preparedness, for the course and subject. Demographically, they have ranged in age from 15 years to 82 years. Some of them carry a full load of coursework, work full-time, and are single parents to many children. Others find it difficult to attend class due to the demands of television cartoons and soap operas. (I've been told in student evaluations that the only problem with my 12:20 p.m. class is that it starts too early!)

I work with students from small Indiana towns and inner city Chicago. Some are the children of research scientists; others are children of welfare families whose members have never seen a college campus. More frequently these days I have students in my courses from Thailand, Malaysia, Taiwan, Korea, and Japan. For them, oral and written English expression is more challenging than any course subject. Adnan comes to me every week requesting additional readings to those required in the course. Chung-Ying bows as I enter the classroom and greets, "Good morning, Sir!"

Some of my students are not intrinsically motivated to attend classes. They're here to learn a trade—to get a good paying job. As a result they are less likely to tolerate a class discussion on human or environmental issues, and instead care more for entrepreneurship. In my freshman class I ask if they think leisure in a conserver society is possible. Some find it impossible to even imagine the concept and certainly deem it ludicrous to discuss. Instead, they say "I see college as a risk I am willing to take for the sake of a profit." They want to be told exactly what they should know and the easiest, fastest way to learn it.

Then there is Terry. Fortified with two degrees in business, Terry arrived this year ready to breeze through a doctorate in leisure behavior. Her goal is to be a college professor in tourism. After surviving the initial shock that her coursework would include things like creativity, human development, freedom, transitory experience, social existentialism and other "new" ideas, she settled into a spellbound curiosity about the subject. Now she's thirsty for more understanding about her new field. She makes connections and distinctions in her reading and writing without being asked. When I see her coming down the hall, I hope she'll stop to ask a question or share an insight. Where did this student come from?

Working with the curriculum is also not easy. As my profession has grown, matured and become more specialized, so has the subject matter supporting it. Our department offers five different emphases for students. They can choose among therapeutic recreation, outdoor recreation and resource management, sports management, tourism management, and park and recreation management. Each option is supported by courses that are necessary to prepare students for the specialized work professionals in the field seem to demand of our graduates. Thus I've taught 15 different courses in the past six years. Do I really know that much?

Also, the curriculum requires that professors have their intellectual feet in the mire of a wide assortment of disciplines: sociology, business, economics, psychology, geography, environmental science, and the medical sciences. Add to this, of course, the need for classes in the curriculum to attract masses of students who are non majors. This leisure education mission within our university is an important political tool because it generates high student enrollments that in turn harvest library holdings, new faculty lines, and offices with windows.

Besides the diversity in students and curriculum, there is the faculty. It is not easy for professors to work with one another. We come from a variety of training origins, have divergent notions of priorities, and envision "the good of the profession" very differently. No wonder collegial consensus takes years to accomplish. Our faculties are trapped in lengthy and unresolved discussions on not only what courses should be taught in the curriculum, but also on the more emotionally charged topic of what should be the name of the department. Worse, we suffer from disparate beliefs on the importance of the teaching role itself.

At my university the sanctity of teaching has endured. Outstanding teachers are honored each year with sizable cash awards, strategy workshops are frequently scheduled, there is money available for developing new teaching methods and courses, and the mission of teaching is always listed first in the trinity statement.

Nonetheless, everyone knows that teaching prowess is not truly supreme. I should teach well, but teaching with inspired excellence could be considered a waste of time. As I prepared for the tenure decision this year, I was warned over and over again by my colleagues not to spend too much of myself on teaching. Only when enrollments threaten to drop do we seem to worry about the quality of teaching.

College professors seem to teach in a vacuum. I do not feel a sense of academic collegiality through my role as teacher. It is difficult for me to think that teaching is my prime purpose; it feels like moonlighting. I have no teaching friends—only research and service buddies. Last semester my students told me about a teacher in anthropology whom they admired. They raved about her abilities and enthusiasm. One day I attended her class, introduced myself afterwards, and asked if we could be friends. She was caught off guard and barely able to respond. Who ever heard of two professors from different fields working cooperatively on teaching endeavors! She asked, instead, if I had some research project in mind.

I decided to wake the students from their macaroni and cheese stupor and take them out to dinner. "The Havana," a government restaurant, had been recommended, so I made reservations. I had read in a tourist book that reservations are required in Moscow restaurants, even if there are only a few diners there. This advance notice assures that there will be enough food.

At 6:00 p.m. we arrive. It takes me until 6:30 p.m. to negotiate the bribe payment ($3.00 worth of rubles) to the doorman for allowing us to enter the restaurant and be seated. At 6:45 p.m. the menu is presented. We make up our minds and call over the waiter. They have nothing that is listed on the menu. What do you have? Chicken. Good, we'll have five orders of chicken. And what do you have to drink? Pepsi and cognac. Fine, we'll have both. At 7:30 p.m. the Pepsi arrives. The chicken, with canned peas, is served at 8:00 p.m. The cognac never makes it. I am worried. I can't decipher the bill. So I put it on my American Express card. In September I'll finally learn what this all cost me. I am crushed. My first teaching lesson in Moscow has failed. The students are hungry and tired, and I am humiliated.

The next evening after the camp day we walk to Red Square. From the guidebook I read out loud to the students: "The austere-looking structure of red granite and black labradore near the Kremlin wall is the Lenin Mausoleum, built after the death of Lenin, the leader of the revolution. During the hours when the Mausoleum is open, there is always an endless stream of people wishing to pay homage to our hero."

We too get in line. The mood is solemn. We are required to stand two by two facing forward; no talking; no packages or cameras allowed; no stopping; a slow, regular march to the Mausoleum's entrance, guarded on all sides by Soviet military. Inside it is very dark and there are small steps everywhere. Where do I look? At the waxy reclined body of Lenin draped in red cloth and red lights, or at the floor to ensure that I don't embarrass my own government by falling down? Keep moving; never stop; no talking. One of the students is yanked from the line; they suspect she has a camera. Why do I try so hard? Why do I teach?

I enjoy the boldness of reaching for goals. Teaching combines the exhilaration of both succeeding and failing. Even though my classroom syllabi are mostly about the skills and facts that are necessary for performing as leaders and managers in recreation and park service agencies, or as researchers and instructors in leisure studies academic units, my joy in teaching lies in striving for larger goals. Right now I can think of four.

First, I want my students to learn intellectual independence. Beginning with freshmen who are in my large introductory course and extending to doctoral students in my statistics class, I find there are great amounts of work to be done in teaching students how to think critically. They balk at open-ended writing assignments, preferring true-false exam questions, and request that I place samples of term projects on reserve in the library. But I want them to be able to solve difficult problems, make considered decisions, and think discerningly.

I continually seek ways of managing my classes for intellectual independence. Rather than ending a lecture on the history of the U.S. recreation movement with questions, I often begin with a question from the writings of Jane Addams and ask the students to participate in a brief discussion. Or I ask students to bring to class an advertisement from a magazine or newspaper and, working in small groups, explain how that ad appeals to one or more of the levels of Maslow's need(s) hierarchy. Or before class begins I display on the screen a statement about the no rescue wilderness controversy. With a long rope I divide the lecture hall in half and ask the students to sit on the right side if they are in favor, or on the left side if they are against the position in the controversy. Throughout the lecture I ask students to comment on the presented material according to the position they've taken in the class seating. Sometimes there aren't enough seats on their preferred side and students who may be for the issue are forced to sit (and contribute to the lecture) from the opposite side of the room.

Some students thrive on it, and others flounder. I have formulated a hypothesis of sorts. I find that structured classes with large amounts of teacher-directed learning is better for insecure students with less prior achievement in the subject area. In contrast, for students high in internal locus of control and command of the subject matter, less structured and teacher-dictated learning environments seem best.

My attempts to create more secure, internally controlled students include other techniques such as requesting short, ungraded reaction papers following class lectures. Several days before each exam in the large freshman class I pass out essay questions, go over the generic structure of good answers, and ask them to work in teams to hammer out answers. The exam is a selection from these questions. In some of my classes students are asked to keep journals about what they learn. I regularly read these and provide written feedback. I also keep a journal of my thoughts about the class material and give excerpts to them to read and likewise respond to.

I'm not afraid to let students see and hear me think, to spy on my slippings from rational deliberation, to catch my excitement over a newly shaped thought. Sometimes I work through their questions aloud or on the board and ask them to join me for a "blackboard" dialogue.

A second goal for my teaching is to instill creativity as a habit of thought. Breaking old expectations of seeing things from only one perspective and becoming dissatisfied with consistently doing things in the same way requires patterns which vary from rational thinking. Creativity means going beyond the obvious, playing with ideas, being flexible, and embracing foolishness. Just looking at the typical classroom wardrobe demonstrates that my students have creativity in that domain, but even there it is carefully chosen creativity that conforms to some norm.

Bolstered by a strong belief in the vital role of innovation to success in professional and personal life, I try to translate the creativity ethic into each course. In my program-planning course we spend several days talking about creativity and doing exercises designed to release the kind of thinking required for creative results. In advising students about course schedules and degree progress I ask them to brainstorm some nontraditional solutions to their problems and consider them along with the more customary ones. Periodically I offer a one-credit workshop specifically focused on creativity to students from any major in the university. I invite field practitioners to the leadership and supervision class to describe ways in which they are creative in fulfilling their positions in recreation and park agencies. We discuss barriers to their creativity.

Last semester I became excited about the possibility of using fiction in my teaching. I read descriptions of bullfighting from Hemingway to introduce the concept of flow. I assigned readings from the works of Sarton, Oates, and Cheever to generate discussion on leisure's role in life satisfaction. It failed miserably. Students were unable to see the connections; they were even uninspired by the chance to simply read a good story. At best, they considered it "time off" from the serious tasks of the class. I've put the effort on hold. I need to develop better ways of using fiction in my teaching, better ways of preparing the students for learning from fiction.

My third goal is to enable students to develop a strong sense of professional pride and commitment. We all know the story they share with us: "I'm afraid to tell my parents that my major is recreation and that I want a career in Boy Scouting." I continually remind students that they are part of an eminent and vital cultural force. I explain over and over again leisure's central position in the health of society. I run the risk of unpopularity by assigning historical reading that illustrates leisure's importance to people for thousands of years. I use adjectives such as lofty, illustrious, noble, and magnificent.

Sometimes this means I'm faking it. Sometimes I must be honest and tell them of the failings of our profession—for example, of our own shortsightedness in destroying irreplaceable natural resources with recreation developments. But I label these things "challenges" and describe them as "acute," hastening to add that acute means keen or quick of mind, which I explain is our professional mandate. I've committed other crimes. I've driven students in my own car to meetings of professional associations. I've even passed out membership applications in class.

As my fourth goal I like to stir up dissatisfaction. I want students to one day contribute to their chosen career by always seeking ways to improve themselves and the work they do. I want them to question the status quo. I want them to wonder about better ways of doing and being, to have critical minds. I want them to have the same kind of incensed posture for which the founders of our profession are accused—that muscle bound, high-mindedness that left a rich legacy of leisure agencies and research.

In my classes I invite students to critique their textbooks by pointing out ways of improving on the principles they teach. In the leadership class there is opportunity for structured peer review of each other's leading techniques. At the end of the semester they also do a self-evaluation using a form adapted from the teaching evaluation that they use to evaluate me. We share the results with each other.

I help doctoral students record their teaching for later critique with the consultants at our University's Teaching Resources Center. In my statistics class we critique the analysis sections of journal research reports, searching for better ways of analyzing and presenting data. In the research methods class we play with alternative ways of studying the problems found in the leisure research literature, as well as in their research projects. I incorporate them into strategy planning sessions for my own research.

For Camp Wocsom (that's Moscow spelled backwards), today is dacha day, so I am spending the day as a counselor too. A big green Embassy bus takes us all—four counselors, two Marines (the students had shared beers with them the night before at the Embassy club and recruited them to help), forty children, and myself—to one of the country retreats, or dachas, on the outskirts of the city. It is beautiful. A rustic lodge located on the banks of the Moscow River, the American Embassy's dacha is similar to those which many Soviet citizens have access to for recuperating and relaxing. For a day camp outing it is perfect. There are thick woods for nature projects and large open spaces for games, all within a very high fence. Later in the summer the camp program is scheduled to include overnights in the dacha dormitory.

Without realizing it in our advance program planning, these days at the dacha will be critically important for children who-are constantly cooped up within Embassy compound walls. Even though these children have traveled to many countries, simple recreation activities fascinate them. They can play the same game of tag for hours. And although I initially doubted the benefit of having the Marines along, I soon learned otherwise. It started to rain, and the following conversation ensued:

In efforts to occupy the youth during the downpour, the adult in charge chimed in, "Okay, kids, now we're going into the kitchen to make brownies."

The general complaint arose from the boys, "I don't like cooking; cooking is for girls."

To which a valiant corps officer heroically replied, "But I like to cook, and I'm a man; in fact I'm a Marine!"

After the rain we go out again to the large playground apparatus. Mark, a nine-year-old American, falls from the climbing bars and breaks his arm. The students quickly move into their rehearsed emergency procedures. After the Embassy doctor and two Soviet doctors look at the arm, Mark is flown to Helsinki to have his arm set. I feel kind of sick.

I wonder how I'll be after this teaching experience? I've been told that people who spend time in the Soviet Union are never the same afterwards. In only a few days I have worked harder at my teaching and thought more about my reasons for teaching than I had in many years. I have discovered my promise to teaching. I realize from this Moscow adventure that teaching even in the traditional classroom is not just telling and showing. It is revealing your thoughts, worries, hopes, fears, surprises, and loves. It is using yourself as an instrument to enable others to change. I wonder what else I can teach? I wonder what else I can learn? I wonder if my luggage will arrive?

The Joys of Doing Research

5

Roger Mannell

I was finishing breakfast in a casino in Las Vegas at a research meeting in 1977, and was suddenly assailed by an idea that I hurriedly transcribed onto a piece of paper littering my table—the back of a Keno card. The recent recipient of a Ph.D. in psychology, and the relatively new director of something called a Centre of Leisure Studies, I had been struggling to give form to an idea on which to base a research program to explore the psychology of leisure, and incidentally obtain tenure and promotion at some remote point in the future. The feeling of excitement accompanying the moment is *still* vivid. Obviously, for me, these lightning bolt insights are not daily occurrences.

That moment was the true beginning of my career as a leisure researcher. During the intervening years other phenomena and topics have attracted my attention; however, now, over a decade later, my work is *still* influenced by that idea. Whether it was a good idea or not, whether it will lead to work that will have a lasting impact or do some good, is difficult to judge. However, the challenge of wrestling the idea to the ground, translating it into a research program, and communicating whatever insights I have gleaned from the process has been very satisfying.

In this essay I address the research role of a professor from the perspective of a person who does research on a more-or-less regular basis, carries the standard teaching load, serves on committees, discharges administrative responsibilities, and meets those minor obligations outside the university associated with marriage, family, home maintenance, community, and yes, even leisure. However, despite these many qualifications, there are two additional criteria that I feel certify me to write this essay. First, I would not be a professor if the job description did not include doing research. Second, I actually enjoy, and think I am occasionally able to communicate my enthusiasm for doing research.

The Craft or "Craftiness" of Research

I think of research as a craft. It is a process that involves the ability to perform a wide range of tasks that by themselves, and taken as a whole, are resistant to automation and standardization. Research is a labor intensive and very human enterprise. Research is best learned by doing, and it is often of more benefit to the novice to initially take on this endeavor under the supervision of a journeyman researcher—that is, through serving an apprenticeship. By research I include the activities of thinking, theorizing and conceptualizing, making observations, analyzing, and communicating one's findings. Most of my research has had at its core the systematic gathering of information about the behavior and experience of people; that is, empirical social science research. I am not suggesting that secondary analysis, primarily theoretical studies, or even performance by faculty who are performing artists do not count. In fact, many of my comments apply equally well to all forms of creative and scholarly productivity. However, I consider myself a scientist, and it is from this perspective that I approach this discussion of the meaning of research to me in my role as professor.

My enjoyment of research has many sources and was influenced by parents, professors, and even favorite fictional characters I have encountered. As an avid reader of science fiction, I have always identified with characters who were scientists, particularly scientists who, because of their theoretical knowledge, were able to jury-rig a solution to whatever problem they encountered. My father, who had little opportunity for formal education and little understanding of what we mean by science, was strongly influential in my love of research. He has always been a great problem solver. If he wasn't solving a problem, he was dreaming up a new problem that he could attempt to solve. He was a tradesman, a mechanical supervisor in charge of maintaining hydroelectric turbines and generators, some of which had been put into service in the 1890s. He also supervised the maintenance of the only icebreaker on the Niagara River, and kept my cars running. These tasks provided him with some interesting problems.

I can still see him walking around with his ever-present and ever-sharp mechanical pencil and a piece of paper, talking to no one in particular, scribbling notes to himself on his latest project, whether it was how to mount a new and improved turbine runner or how to expand our house to accommodate a growing family. He enjoyed all phases of this activity: discovering the nature of the problem, planning a solution, getting his hands dirty in putting the solution into effect, and seeing the finished product of his efforts. Though now retired, he still finds new problems to solve. While I was growing up, I often got caught up in these projects, and, in fact, worked for my dad for several summers when I was an.

A large part of the joy of research for me is the similar opportunity it provides for involvement in all aspects of the enterprise. Planning and executing research is like designing a house, ordering the materials, and translating the plan into a tangible object with my own hands. I am happiest when I am involved in the whole process from conceptualization, design, execution, data collection, data preparation, and analysis, to reporting. In my research, I have for various projects over the years, built my own electronic equipment, created cartoons and artwork, and carried out the computer design and graphics work involved in preparing research materials. Earlier in my career, I carried out studies often funded out of my back pocket. Working usually by myself or with a single graduate student, I was by necessity involved in the whole process. For the past few years, however, I have been involved in some large and well-financed research projects where I have become more of a manager. Unfortunately, I don't have the time or opportunity to dabble in the same "hands on" manner that I have always enjoyed.

As a student, I was fortunate to have encountered a number of professors who themselves were enamored with research—a sociology professor, who had us do weekly 600-word "think pieces," analyzing social phenomena that she felt required our attention; and a professor who loved to talk about research, and could make it sound terribly exciting. He went out of his way to encourage me to go to graduate school. For advisors, I was fortunate to have had two highly dedicated scholars for both my master's and doctoral thesis respectively. The best part of my graduate training was the research apprenticeships I served with them both.

My master's thesis advisor could go for no more than five minutes in any setting without some attempt to analyze the human behavior occurring around him. He lived in a world populated more by ideas than people. While he did research, he was more fascinated with ideas. I often left his office reeling as his ideas came at me like sparks flying off a whirling grindstone. We got along extremely well. I liked the challenge of catching and transforming these sparks into testable hypotheses. We remain very good friends to this day.

My doctoral advisor was the archetypical eccentric professor. He invited me to study with him after I had extended, tested, and supported a theory of his during my master's degree work. I would often come into his office early in the morning and find him sleeping in his chair, obviously after having been up all night. He ate, slept, and, I am sure, dreamed psychological science. He would call me in the middle of the night—any night, even when I was miles away on holidays—to share an insight. He died prematurely. Right up to the end of his life, he continued to work on an epistemic logic on which to base psychological science. While I have no wish to emulate his eccentricities, he did impart to me a commitment to scholarship, and a taste for the excitement of the chase for research-based knowledge. While he exacted a toll on his graduate students and colleagues by virtue of his complete and utter commitment to furthering psychological science, he was wonderfully supportive. He subsidized my travel and participation at conferences, introduced me to active scholars, and through discussion and by example alerted me to the rigors and rules of scholarship in the university.

Playing with Research Ideas: Confessions of an Accidental Theorist

My approach to developing research projects has been primarily deductive. There are numerous mysteries around that need theories and theories that need testing. I enjoy the challenge of doing both.

With respect to the development of theory, I am, however, hesitant to suggest that I have created theories. Perhaps it would be better to say that I have made a few forays into theoretical territory, and these under some duress. In the field of leisure studies we often hear the cry for more theory development. Actually, I think there is plenty of theory out there in the social sciences that is highly relevant to understanding leisure phenomena. I do not believe that the leisure studies field needs more theory, but rather more studies that apply and test existing theory. Nevertheless, occasionally circumstances have conspired to force me to develop "theory."

A few years ago I was presenting a state-of-the-art paper dealing with the psychology of leisure at a conference. One of several concluding recommendations I made was that a potentially useful direction for theory and research might be to develop what I call "leisure-specific" personality constructs to help us better understand individual differences in how people respond to free time. I had no intention of developing such a construct myself. However, while traveling to the conference, an example of a possible "leisure-specific" personality construct occurred to me. I had even come up with a name for it. I didn't give it much more thought and during my presentation casually introduced the "Self-as-Entertainment" construct as an illustration of my recommendation. The consequences of this "ad-lib" were startling. I think the only thing remembered about this presentation on which I had worked so diligently was the self-as-entertainment idea. A large number of people came up to me after the presentation, and the only question that they raised was where and when could they get a copy of the measurement instrument. During the next few months I also received a large number of requests for more information about the construct. The irony was that here I was with a "half-baked" idea that had generated much more enthusiasm than any of my completed and published work had ever received. The result was that some months later a conceptual paper, a scale, and some test data were in hand.

I have also found that when predictions based on a theory are not supported, one is forced to be, if not an accidental, at least a reluctant theorist. The most difficult part, and perhaps the most fun, of waxing theoretical is not so much developing the conceptualization, but naming the theory—being descriptive without being pretentious, conveying respectability without taking the idea too seriously. In a recent study certain unexpected but interpretable results suggested a hypothesis that I was inclined at first to name the "Human Laziness Theory of Leisure." However, following more sober reflection, and to add an appropriate level of dignity, I downgraded the idea from a "theory" to a "principle" and named the idea the "Psychological Inertia Principle of Leisure."

For me, the most exciting aspect of the conceptualization phase of the research process is the challenge of finding a way of testing theory; that is, deciding which of the many studies that could be done, should be done. As my doctoral advisor was fond of saying, any good theory presents you with an infinite number of hypotheses and predictions and, consequently, any number of actual studies that could be designed and carried out. There are many dimensions to the question of which hypothesis you should choose to examine and which study would best test it. Support for any prediction derived from the theory adds to our confidence that the theory represents and perhaps explains the reality we are observing. Obviously, one very important concern is identifying where the theory comes to ground in the objective, empirical world—in the social sciences that means the stuff of everyday life and experience. But there are other factors that can be considered in selecting the most appropriate study. For example, will certain hypotheses and studies be more attractive to those who fund research? Do certain studies have what advertisers often call a "hook" that has the potential to catch the eye of other researchers, funders, or the public? I have always been fascinated by ideas and studies that achieve what advertisers look for—that ad that will firmly embed itself, and a product, in the buying public's mind, and which continues to be enjoyable and eye-catching no matter how often it is seen. I have often asked myself what makes a classic study? We all know of a study or series of studies that are continually cited by every researcher and scholar in an area of inquiry—even long after they are no longer read. I don't think I have achieved such a study, but for me part of the fun of research is the search for the elusive "classic" study.

What are the criteria? Getting there first? Showing that something that others felt couldn't be done, can be done? Looking at the problem differently than anyone else? Using a new or novel research paradigm or technique? Doing something everyone in the field has been thinking about, but being the first to actively do it? These considerations add spice to the excitement of playing with research ideas. My attempts to develop an experimental paradigm for studying leisure in the laboratory have been in part motivated by this type of playfulness.

I also find there is a perverse pleasure in making counterintuitive predictions or in demonstrating how a well-accepted theory is correct only under certain conditions. I think this tendency toward perverseness is what originally attracted me to social psychology. It is a very playful social science. In my doctoral thesis I was studying how and under what conditions people express aggression through the playful medium of humor. By converting my laboratory into a "playatory" I was able to demonstrate that earlier research findings were only valid under the serious conditions created by the "serious" laboratory environment unintentionally fostered by the experimenters. However, when a "playatory" or a nonserious atmosphere was created, the subjects' perceptions and responses to aggressive humor were quite different. In one of my more recent laboratory studies, I was able to demonstrate that under some conditions some people actually experience less "leisure" with increased freedom, rather than more. This perverseness encourages greater qualification and refinement in our theory development.

Leisure and Science: A Contradiction in Terms?

It has been argued that research, or rather the scientific research process, is only one way of knowing or coming to know about the world around us. I agree. Art and religion, for example, are other quite legitimate means of coming to develop an understanding of our physical, social, and psychological worlds. For me, however, that set of rules and conventions, that human enterprise that we call science, has always held a special fascination. I believe that as researchers of psychological and social phenomena we need to evolve our own "scientific methods" to study and understand human behavior, but I also believe that observation and the systematic collection of information, sometimes under controlled conditions, is of continuing importance. I am a firm believer that the basis of research in the social sciences, any science for that matter, is systematic observation regardless of the methods for doing this observation. It seems to me, however, that while many of us give lip service to a pluralistic research methodology philosophy, in fact, we are intolerant of approaches that differ from our own. I am intolerant of all kinds of fanatics, especially methodology fanatics—I am a fanatic about this.

In high school, I focused on math and science. I had expected that I would do the same at the university. However, once I got there, and had taken some introductory psychology and sociology courses, I was hooked. I ended up taking a B.A. in sociology before turning to social psychology in my graduate work. Of course, social psychology was the most "scientific" in its approach to the study of the individual—relying heavily on the laboratory experiment as a vehicle for understanding.

While well aware of the limitations of the laboratory, the elegance of the laboratory experiment in social psychology has always attracted me. In a tongue-in-cheek manner, I have often drawn the analogy between the social psychological experiment and the television program "Mission Impossible." Like the "good guys" on the original television show, the experimenter attempts to design a procedure that confronts the subject with a reality that catches them much as daily life does, and allows us to see if the behavior and experience expected to emerge in these circumstances occur as predicted. The greater the extent to which the experimental reality reflects the processes and influences specified by the theory that is guiding the study, the better the experimenter you are. The greater the extent to which the subject's behavior and experience conforms to predictions, the more confidence you have in your theoretical understanding of the phenomenon.

Today I feel that one almost has to be an apologist if one does experiments—constantly reminding colleagues that you are aware of the limitations of the methodology. Today, the global majority tends to blame the United States for almost everything; and like everyone else, I can blame Americans too. In my case, however, the blame is merely for my aberrant affliction with experimental methodology. I did all my psychological training in Canada—something that was atypical until my generation. However, in my studies at three major Canadian universities I had only one Canadian psychology professor. The rest were Americans trained in American experimental psychology. My doctoral advisor was an American social psychologist. However, as a student of Muzafer Sheriff at the time when he was doing the famous Robbers Caves field studies, he had acquired a strong concern for the limitations of the social psychological laboratory. So, while I have always loved the elegance of the laboratory experiment in the social sciences, I like to think that I have always been aware of its limitations as well. So much for my apology.

The opportunity to learn, practice, and acquire new research skills is what has kept active research fresh and exciting for me. During the past ten years as new research questions have presented themselves, and as the need arose to examine some of our laboratory findings in the context of daily life, I have enjoyed expanding my research technique repertoire with new methodologies such as the experience sampling method, and other more traditional approaches including field experiments, survey work, and interviewing.

If People Only Came in Beakers: The Joy of Studying People

There have been moments when I wished that the sources of the behavior I study were rocks or chemicals rather than people, and that the "entities" I study came prepackaged in convenient easy-to-use containers that could be put away and stored until needed for the next study. The amount of energy spent in the recruitment, coordination, and human-relations work usually required to mount a social science study seems overwhelming at times. No-shows, nonresponses, and respondents harassing my research assistants are enough to make even pure mathematics or chemistry look attractive. However, I find the rewards of doing research with people usually outweigh these frustrations. I have always tried, even in my laboratory work, to treat the subjects as collaborators, and I have been rewarded with genuine interest and appreciation for what social scientists are trying to do. In one of my early lab experiments dealing with the conditions that foster absorption in an activity, I remember going over and over the final results of the analysis, checking the accuracy of the coding and entry of the data into the computer, and finally sitting back with the realization that there was no mistake. The results of the study were statistically significant, but exactly opposite those predicted by the hypotheses! I went back to the subjects who were quite helpful and even enthusiastic about sorting out this unexpected turn of events. They enjoyed the opportunity to retrospectively examine their reactions to the situations I had presented them with in the lab, and they had some interesting insights as to what went on. A subsequent study using these insights proved to be quite successful.

We have completed a series of studies in which our subjects carry electronic pagers and in response to a signal fill out a questionnaire that allows them to describe their physical, social, and psychological circumstances at that moment in time. The subjects are clearly collaborators in the research and get the opportunity to examine the structure and experience of their everyday life. We have received some very moving letters and in our follow-up interviews our respondents have indicated that they have greatly enjoyed the opportunity afforded them to examine their lives. Our current research with workers in Ontario has also proven that the act of research can be a meaningful and stimulating experience to the subjects as well as the researcher. The study explores their assessments and feelings about the future of work, leisure, and lifestyle arrangements. The respondents have indicated time and time again that their involvement allowed and encouraged them to systematically consider issues important to them, but issues they had not clearly articulated or taken the time to think about.

My research has also allowed me to meet a variety of people in a wide range of settings. It has taken me from the laboratory down the hall to the bottom of a gold mine several miles underground. I have always tried to put myself in the shoes of my subjects. I have been a pre-test subject in each of my studies. In our studies using the electronic pagers, I gained some insight into what it was like to sit in a meeting and have the pager emit its beep, feel the self-importance of pulling out a booklet of mini-questionnaires, and the sense of conspiracy in surreptitiously completing one. However, the insights have sometimes been painful. In an experiment we conducted some years ago, we were studying how the development of group norms influences the perception of pain in competitive team situations. The pain took the form of a mild electric shock delivered by an electrode attached to the players during a laboratory experiment. In fact, the experience proved to be so "insightful" I never did another like it.

Of course, part of the ongoing wonder of studying people is the occurrence of the unexpected. In one case, the unexpected involved unanticipated but perhaps more important outcomes than the ones we were predicting. We had developed, implemented, and were evaluating a counseling program in a nursing home. The planning, design, and data collection had gone off with no more than the usual hitches, which just happened to be manageable in this case. Our program impact measures seemed to be sensitive to the predicted impacts of the program suggested by the goals and objectives. However, we were so caught up in the research process we failed to notice that we were on a collision course with reality in the form of the care-giving and management staff. The subjects had not only increased their recreation participation and the satisfaction they derived from their leisure as predicted, but they had decided that they needed to take more control of their leisure in the institution, including the formation of a residents' committee to plan and run their own programs. This development led to some interesting conflicts.

The Researcher as Dispassionate Observer

I do not think I classify as the dispassionate scientist. The most exciting part of doing research is seeing how the findings of a study stack up against my expectations. I can't help but feel that successful prediction is a victory over the forces of chaos and entropy. On the other hand, the failure to predict is a further challenge to refine my conceptualizations, improve operationalization of the key variables, get rid of methodological artifacts that distort people's behavior, or come up with a better way to tease out those elusive relationships lurking in a data set.

I can still picture myself and a/my graduate research assistant sitting in front of a computer terminal. At the prompt from the mainframe computer that signaled the statistical run was complete, I typed a command on the keyboard and entered the resultant file that held the analysis. We were hunched forward, eyes glued to the screen as we cursored through the file until we hit the analysis of variance table that, with elegant simplicity, told whether months of thought, debate, and hard work had paid off. We were oblivious to the stares of the co-inhabitants of the terminal room as we jumped up, arms raised, and did our end zone dance of victory.

For me the roller coaster of emotions resulting from doing research is critical to my continued enjoyment and commitment to the process. Of course, this ego involvement in a study's outcome is something that must be kept in its proper place. The excitement and desire to have "things work out as predicted" should be savored, but not allowed to influence the design, execution, and interpretation of results.

Communicating

I enjoy communicating not only the results of my research but the excitement of doing it. The excitement of doing is difficult to convey in the rather joyless medium of the journal article. Oral presentations, however, do lend themselves to this. One challenge that has become a bit of a game for me is the attempt to convince my undergraduate students that research in our field is useful, good for them, and even fun. I teach a required research design course, and one of the joys I get is to foster a realization (or delusion) that research makes sense and can be useful in our field.

Another perk associated with doing research and communicating the results is that the university is willing to provide recognition, the opportunity to travel to share one's insights, and of course merit pay. Research, more than any other activity that a professor is involved in, is the currency of recognition. Particularly the opportunity to travel and meet researchers to share and discuss my latest work and the work of others recharges my scholarly batteries. If you are not an active researcher, and you do not have this currency, that latest bit of data, these types of encounters can be uninteresting and certainly unrewarding. Membership in a research community, or community of like-minded scholars, is an important incentive for doing research. The common commitment and agreement as to what are important and interesting questions to be pursued, and what are the fruitful ways of looking at these issues, are among the rewards of membership.

I was presenting at a leisure research conference, and the leisure researchers in attendance were from varied disciplinary backgrounds. I was part way through the description and rationale of the experimental methodology I had used, when I noticed a member of the audience was vigorously nodding her head in what I interpreted as an enthusiastic manner. As I learned afterward, this individual, because her training was similar to my own, had suddenly realized why I had designed the experiment in the manner I had and anticipated where I was going next in my presentation.

In a multidisciplinary field like leisure studies, it can be difficult to find this feeling of community. There are disparate views on what are the important research questions, and since there are so few of us and so many issues, leisure researchers are spread quite thin. So thin, that it is at times difficult to find someone who is pursuing an understanding of the same phenomenon you are, and even more difficult to find one who shares your worldview in terms of methodology and theoretical orientation. I am reminded of this when I present my work to a group of social psychologists. There is a wonderful feeling of not having to defend or explain the paradigm or perspective you have adopted. A common social-ization kicks in that allows your fellow scholars to read between the lines and, even if they do not agree with what you have done, at least they are able to participate in the scholarly game, and enjoy the pleasure in antici-pating the unfolding logic. Of course, some might call this a group delu-sion, but it is a comfortable feeling.

On the other hand, work in a multidisciplinary field like leisure stud-ies is intellectually healthy because it forces you to confront the many assumptions that you make in the process of carrying out your research. Doing research also has provided the opportunity to be a performer. I enjoy "playing" to an audience other than my students. I come from a theatrical family. My brother is a professional performer in Canadian theatre, and my other siblings are committed amateurs. I like to present my research the way a good mystery novel is written, the research ques-tion being the mystery, the conceptualization and methodology being the unfolding plot, and the resolution occurring with the presentation of the results and conclusions.

Where is the Search for Truth and Beauty?

Where is the altruism, the desire to better the lot of people, the world, and the cosmos in my discussion of the joys of research? If the funding agencies that have provided support for the various studies I have com-pleted, or am currently involved in, were to read the above comments, they might wonder at my motivation. In fact, most of my comments have focused on the joys derived from the process of doing research. And while I feel that these joys are what enrich and sustain an enthusiasm for research, I have also derived satisfaction from being part of a group of scholars who have been trying to see if the psychological study of leisure-related phenomena can advance our understanding of how people deal with, benefit from, or have problems with leisure. In our research I think we also have been successful at providing funders with some answers to policy-related questions. My work of the past few years has taken a more policy-oriented focus. Our current research on changing patterns of work and leisure among Canadian workers is strongly policy-driven and the findings quite provocative. We are now in the process of working with the government funding agency to develop a strategy and means to com-municate these results to practitioners and policy-makers. Seeing that the results of the research have an impact has been quite exciting.

However, I would likely have "run out of steam" and stopped doing research if my primary motive was to make a great discovery or improve the lot of humankind. Mike Csikszentmihalyi and Jacob Getzel in their book *The Creative Vision* asked artists why they created their art. The common response was that they gave little thought to creating beauty or truth in some abstract sense. Rather, they were compelled to pursue their art to learn about themselves and to extend their personal understanding of the life going on around them. I guess my answer to "why I do research" is not too dissimilar to that of these artists—it's a very personal enterprise.

In fact, social science research is a lot like art. We deal with many of the same timeworn issues, such as love, power, hate, conflict, insecurity-security, and meaning in life. If you look at what we have discovered or achieved in the social sciences, it often seems that many of the same ideas are repackaged and emerge as "new" theories with each successive generation of scholars. Maybe one of our major roles, like the artist, is to reinterpret the feelings, events, and problems of the day in a form that can be understood from the always-changing "modern" worldview.

On Being a Whole Professor

Not infrequently I am overwhelmed with a feeling of nostalgia for the good old days—good old days I have never known. The good old days when professors had time to exchange views with colleagues, talk at some length to students, putter at their research, and yes, even think. I do not know if such a time ever existed or whether it is just myth, but I do know that I have not experienced it.

My doctoral advisor was fond of telling the story of how he finally realized how to become a good researcher. When he graduated with his Ph.D., he apparently read voraciously, and stayed on top of the many subfields of psychology. In a sense, he was a well-rounded scholar. However, he found that until he "stopped" reading, he did not find the time to theorize and become a productive researcher. I get an acute anxiety attack every time I enter the library to catch up with the latest journals. When I graduated with my Ph.D. I was much better informed than I am today.

I have found that like most of my colleagues I have had to become a "time management" expert to even begin to fit everything I must do into the available time. I find this constant feeling of not having enough time and of being pulled in several different directions by the various roles required of a professor, a major occupational hazard.

However, I have not pursued attractive opportunities for full-time research outside the university. For me the multiplicity of tasks that is part of being a professor is at the same time a source of great complaint and, yet, part of the attraction of the job. Perhaps this schizophrenic state of affairs stems from my "renaissance person" complex. I like variety and I enjoy trying to achieve competence in a wide range of areas. While research is my first love, my teaching and administrative activity can be challenging and enjoyable aspects of the job as well.

Following my master's degree I completed postgraduate teacher training that would have allowed me to teach in the elementary and high schools. However, I realized that just teaching would "wear thin" quickly for me. I am, I think, a good university teacher. I enjoy it. Over the years my students have even formally recognized my teaching efforts. However, I find the prospect of only teaching unattractive, just as doing only research would also tarnish the enjoyment I receive from it. I do not see any immediate solution for the feeling of being a pinball careening off the various roles professors fill. However, I plan to continue enjoying the opportunity.

On Reading and Professing: Recounting a World of Privilege

Geof Godbey

For some people, being alive is so incomprehensibly stunning that it demands an attempt at explanation. For such people, if it is impossible to swallow the prepackaged answers offered by some formal religion or other narcotic, the mystery, the longing, the hunger and celebration of your life must be addressed through learning. One way of doing this, only one, is to become a professor. The life of a professor, more than anything else, should be about learning. To get the privilege of leading a professor's life requires some luck, freedom, intellectual curiosity, and some role models. For those who want answers, or just the chance to see if there are any answers, the life of a professor is a joy. This is not to assume that all subjects studied ultimately relate to the big questions, but that all subjects studied will end in the question: Why? A professor's life is in some ways selfish since the desire to help others must be secondary to the desire to learn. The learning, of course, may strengthen the desire to help, but being a professor is fundamentally about learning.

Such learning, if it is to be professed to others, also involves the development of what Josef Pieper called "a point of view from which to take in the world,"[1] or, as we might say, a philosophy. It also involves the development of what Hemingway called "a good crap detector."

Being a professor also involves a strong sense of play. I have always had such a sense. I love the thrust and parry of debate, the theatrical pomposity of those who think themselves to have answers (and who occasionally do), hide and go seek with the truth, the endless knocking on the door of the unknowable, showing off with numbers and startling statistical techniques, the invention of arcane terms to develop taxonomies which knock the common sense out of what we formerly knew in order to "privatize" the truth, the cocksure pronouncement which, like intellectual Chinese food, somehow leaves your mind hungry an hour later. You can only play in universities if you feel at home in them. I do. I have always thought that universities were not only a part of the real world, but also among the better parts of that world. Feeling this way has given me an advantage compared to some of my colleagues in this field who do not believe the university is part of the real world but still take everything that goes on within it with deadly earnestness, as though it were. I am also, I hope and pray, not afraid to be a fool. The role of professor has always had this wonderful dialectic at work in which one becomes wise and foolish at the same time. Because professors have a captive audience who seems to assume that the professor knows something unique, it is easy to become pompous, to forget that a professor is basically someone who, as was once observed, talks in other people's sleep. The pompous professor is an indication, in some instances, of merely the exaggeration of play. At other times, it indicates the university's failure. Wisdom and recognition of ignorance are surely related, and that recognition leads us to see that we are both the playthings of the gods and, occasionally, the masters of our own fate.

A professor must have something to profess, and the academic pecking order must be based upon what one has to profess and how well he or she professes it. Universities are usually not democratic, nor should they be. They are, at their best, meritocracies, and the most important arena of merit is one's intellectual accomplishment. Parks and recreation professors have sometimes fallen prey to what I would call "the cult of niceness." That is, the establishment of criteria for judging each other that have to do with how nice a colleague is, rather than what they know and can successfully communicate. This cult has done great harm to our academic achievement, not because being nice is unimportant, but because it is, within universities, of secondary importance to seeking the truth. Sometimes the cult of niceness is a defense formed by those who are living out their careers in a foreign work environment. I have never felt that being in recreation and parks or, now, leisure studies, meant that I was an intellectual inferior or a foreigner within the university. Were I not a professor in this field, I would probably be a professor in some other subject, perhaps English, sociology, philosophy, or journalism.

The cult of niceness, while it has hurt us within the university, does seem to provide a basis upon which a prerequisite is established to become a good professor—the development of character. Professors must love freedom—dare I say leisure—and it has been axiomatic throughout the centuries that one cannot be trusted with freedom unless their moral character can be developed and perpetually improved with each increase in freedom. The granting of tenure, which in this country appears to have no relation to its original purpose of ensuring freedom of speech within universities, provides the ultimate testing ground for the responsible use of freedom. Tenure means, to a remarkable extent, that one no longer has a boss. If one quits on the university, the only sanction may be a small monetary one. Tenure makes the locus of control more frankly internal for the professor and sets the stage to judge what is important.

This is not to imply that professors will experience leisure in the Aristotelian sense, or that most of them want it. In particular, it is easy to observe that professors in recreation and parks or leisure studies often don't want freedom. We frequently exhibit the traits of our colleagues in other fields. That is, we study what obsesses us rather than what we have mastered as does the nutty psychologist, the economist who can't manage his or her money, and the professor of literature who writes terrible poetry or prose. We are a work-obsessed group. This also has a situational component. Professors of recreation and parks or leisure studies are suspect within the university and rightly so. We are lower-middle class residents of the university, and, as some sociologists like to tell us, middle class is characterized by a central life orientation toward gaining respect, rather than the orientation of the upper class which is toward graceful living. Our drive for respect within the university and our, at times, fuzzy sense of reform make us inventors of work. The practitioner backgrounds that many of us have cause us to form committees at the drop of a hat. There is irony here, but then the role of professor is filled with irony that, as long as it is recognized, can become one more route to self-understanding.

Being a Professor and Reading

You can't be worth a damn as a professor unless you read. If professors are supposed to teach, research, write, and serve, reading widely is indispensable. To be a good teacher you must read, even if you have lots of "practical" experience, since without reading, how are you to put such experience into broader perspective? How are you to determine the typicality of such experience? How are you to understand where such experience intersects with the development of our culture? How are you going to see the tiny dot of your life as part of the mosaic of the universe? How can you gauge the relevance of your experience in the confusing whirl of both the world's change and its continuance?

To be a good researcher, you must start with history, theory, image, methods of seeking the truth, and the state of knowledge bequeathed to you by other researchers. How can you do this without reading widely? How can you add to a body of knowledge without exploring the body?

If you are going to be a writer, Ben Franklin advised, find a writer you admire and imitate his or her style. Being an authority in some subject doesn't necessarily mean that you can successfully convey your knowledge in writing. While talent helps, practice is of extraordinary importance. To practice writing, you must first read. In particular, it is important to read a variety of materials in a variety of formats.

To serve well you must serve wisely, offering not only a helping hand but also an informed mind. Reading informs the mind and makes the impulse to serve one that is less likely to result in repaving the road to Hell, a road that is already the best-paved road in the universe. The combination of ignorance and good intentions has historically been among the most deadly to humans. Reading can help break up this combination.

Professors, of course, also travel. While this is an important learning device, for which there is no real substitute, traveling without reading to help interpret the significance of what one sees and hears may result in learning or worse. I wrote the following verse, or worse, to express this sentiment:

PROFESSORS MUST TRAVEL

Professors must travel,
the ultimate blunder,
the wandering into
the world out yonder
defenseless, worn down
by the weight of the strange,
they look back and ponder
the place they came
from. Never a tourist
since never at home,
they contemplate
wilderness, K-Marts, and Rome
and wax sociological,
ideological,
wax metaphysical,
wane pathological.
Ants which leave
a stomped hill in a hurry,
from chaos to chaos
they go without worry.
Explaining the difference
in customs and seasons
with certainty, jargon
and preconceived reasons.

Reading, hopefully, can make the process of travel a bit more enlightening.

Perhaps, in summary, it can be said that reading is the basis of every academic function. It serves, at the least, as preparation and more usually as the central medium of continuing learning. We may, of necessity, temporarily abandon it to do our research or teaching, but we will always return to it. We return to it less like the firehouse horse to the firehouse than like someone seeking out an old friend after a long trip.

How I Became a Pointy-Headed Professor

My father was born in rural Kentucky and ended up, against all odds, getting a doctorate at Harvard. He was a hell-raiser in his youth and, some would say, a late bloomer. Actually he bloomed many times, as we all do, and the various flowers were quite diverse. He taught me love of language, perpetually correcting my grammar, reading me poetry now and then, and conveying to me the passion and ambiguity he felt about formal education. A gentle but contradictory man, he has as good a general knowledge of the world as anyone I know. My mother, who had done graduate work in Journalism at the University of Kentucky, admired learning and put great stock in the opinions and findings of learned people. She was a Women's Liberationist but didn't recognize it until into her 50s. Her mother, who was a career woman, raised her in such a way that my mom had to grow up fast. She is idealistic, stubborn, and hard working. She was, among other things, a skilled debater in college. Both my mother and father taught me the love of debate. My mother critiqued me as a child to a great extent and also, perhaps, took out her unfulfilled aspirations by giving me lots of attention; talking to me about serious issues, seeking my opinion, and giving me the benefit of hers.

I was legally blind from birth, and this problem could only be corrected with glasses that were thick enough to make me a funny-looking character. I was ridiculed about this as a child and became sensitive about it. I was a show-off as a kid, perhaps as compensation. I loved sports and all forms of play. I also enjoyed reading. The arrival of a new magazine at our house was exciting to me. A rainy day with a new *Time* magazine and about three pounds of cookies was all I could ask for. I have read a newspaper almost every day of my life since I was about eight. In school I was an underachiever, and in tenth grade I was advised by my guidance counselor not to bother applying to college. I remember even then knowing he wasn't a very bright man. I hung around with a bunch of guys who almost lived in a poolroom. For a while, I was one of the world's worst street-fighters (primarily because there is not much hate in me). I had a great sense of innocence. After one year at the University of Delaware, I was dismissed for flunking Biology (the three-hour Saturday morning lab conflicted with the Soupy Sales show) and for a physical altercation with an ROTC Sergeant who appeared to dislike me intensely for no apparent reason.

I worked in a clothing store, played in a rock band, and learned a few lessons. I was in lots of amateur theatre and began writing awful poetry with great earnestness. I also discovered that I was interested in learning and wanted more from life than a paycheck, television, and a shopping center. During the summer, I took a job as a playground director, just to escape the clothing store. I loved it. I worked on a playground in a lower-middle class neighborhood and what we did that summer made an obvious difference in the life of that community. You could see it. At the end of the summer, Stan Francis, an outstanding recreation and park professional, and Kitty Hall Lang, a friend and my boss on the playground, both took me aside and told me about Cortland State College in New York, from which Stan had graduated and Kitty was a senior. I could have a career in recreation, they said. I was thunderstruck. It sounded funny—but intriguing. I liked recreation. I had been in YMCA programs, hung around teen centers and parks. I liked games. I liked children, generally preferring their company to adults.

With some help from these people and from an inspirational professor at Cortland, Harlan "Gold" Metcalf, I was admitted to Cortland on probation. Metcalf didn't warn me or threaten negative sanctions if I didn't study. He said he believed in me, and it was apparent that he did. So did my parents. So did Bonnie, whom I married when she was 19 and I was 20. I responded. Bonnie and I lived at a school for delinquent teenagers while I was at Cortland. She was a housemother to 28 delinquent males at the age of 20, and I was a recreation supervisor. We saw lots of tragedy, suicides, drugs, and mental illness.

I did graduate work at Penn State, was a research intern with Philadelphia's Department of Recreation, and spent the better part of four years heading an associate degree program for inner-city youth at a Penn State branch campus near Philadelphia. I was committed to what I was doing and collected data for my doctoral research in the ghettos of north Philadelphia.

There was a gap, it seemed to me, between doers and thinkers in the field. Not that the doers were dummies; they simply weren't interested in life in the abstract, in books, theories, or the play of ideas. I was.

Gradually I realized I was cut out to be a professor and took a post at the University of Waterloo. My dad never gave tons of advice but he did give me a bit of advice when it was clear I was heading, albeit uncertainly, for the life of a professor. The advice was highly pragmatic—don't chase the coeds, stay out of administration, and go for full professor as quickly as you can. It was remarkably good advice, and, except for serving one year as Acting Chair at the University of Waterloo, I have followed his advice as best as I could. There was also some cynical advice I received with which I also agree: "Immature professors imitate—mature professors steal." Finally, "Gold" Metcalf made me memorize "Stay consistently in the presence of the best in the sphere in which you seek attainment and make an honest response." In the main I think I have tried, but sometimes not hard enough.

Some Mistaken Ideas about Reading

For a year or two, I got the pathetically mistaken idea that, as a professor, I should read something only if it contained the words "recreation," "play," "leisure," "parks," or a few other familiar terms. This idea, while perhaps understandable, was immensely harmful to my continuing education because it denied me, by and large, the opportunity to make the leaps of connection that anyone who pretends to wisdom must make. As professors, I think, we must pretend to wisdom. Doing this means, to me, giving up what is sometimes called the Newtonian-Cartesian view of the world—that reality is separate objects existing in three-dimensional space. That time ticks off in a straight line. That the rational nature of humans makes us able to use logic and technique to meet our own ends. Rather, I think, we must be more spiritual or holistic, viewing reality as a series of relationships among all things that are part of some universal consciousness. Neither humans nor the larger system within which they exist are completely knowable through science. Nothing is understandable unless we understand relations between the diverse elements that make up the world. For many years I have felt that if leisure studies or recreation and park curricula were to become better integrated into the university, it was going to be necessary for us to learn more about the world in general, even if at the expense of learning about our specific subject matter. It would appear that leisure and recreation are rather complex subject matters that continuously drag in the rest of the world with them, like a friendly dog dragging in some smelly prize for us to figure out what to do with. Our subjects relate to history, for our little vocational programs are often merely echoes of the Rational Recreation movements of Western Europe in the 18th and 19th centuries. They relate to philosophy, not so much because Aristotle, Pieper, or Veblen wrote about leisure but because leisure, and to some extent, recreation, always imply an ideal. If you aren't prepared to consider the ideal, you aren't prepared to deal with recreation and leisure academically. Considering the ideal requires some familiarity with philosophy. Similar arguments may be made for sociology, psychology, geography, economics, ecology, and a variety of other subjects.

The dilemma we face, if we attempt to teach students about the content and meaning of the behavior that they may be leading, administering, planning, or otherwise attempting to facilitate, is that we must know a hell of a lot of stuff, since the subject is complex, dialectic in nature, and inherently interdisciplinary. We may not want to deal with this complexity but if we do not, why not turn things over to professors of public administration, business administration, or those who deal with areas such as sport, drama, or the arts?

From the time I was an undergraduate student, it was easy to see that the division among educators in our field was not so much based on whether they did research as opposed to teach, or whether they were in therapeutic recreation or recreation program leadership. The critical variable was, to a great extent, whether or not they read. Those who read were much more at home within the university. Those who read were usually more intellectually curious, more likely to recognize that, for a professor, having the right questions is as important as having the right answers. Those who read were also more likely to respond, "I don't know" when asked a question beyond their expertise, perhaps since they were not traumatized by the admission. Not knowing was a temporary condition which could, usually, be remedied by reading. Those who didn't read tended to have all the answers and to be threatened by different points of view. They tended to perpetually argue that our field was not understood within the university. They also tended to believe that the university was not the real world (the real world being, perhaps, a recreation center in Syracuse). I can remember feeling very early in my career that the university was a vital part of the real world. I still stop any student in my classes who states they can't wait to get out into the real world. We debate the idea. How terrible it must be to feel you exist in an unreal environment. Sometimes, just for dramatic effect, I step on the student's foot and ask if it hurts. If it does, I suggest perhaps the student, professor, and university may all be real. Real does not mean typical, but you and I are not typical; we are uniquely ourselves. Reading makes the university come alive; makes it real. Reading is a form of perpetual continuing education about many real worlds. In effect, I have come to believe, reading is a way of making a real place for yourself within the university, feathering an academic nest.

I also sometimes got the mistaken idea that I should read primarily that which confirms my beliefs. Doing this only increases your dogmatism or, worse yet, makes you a kind of religious zealot. One of the reasons that a university education is wasted upon a religious zealot is that, to him or her, the truth is unchanging and a priori. I tend to agree with Descartes that to know you must first doubt. That means, I think, reading that which does not support your prior beliefs. From our field, that probably means reading books which can tell us about the essentially tragic nature of life, the immense evil loose in the world, and our basic inability to change it.

Finally, during one brief period in my life, I got the mistaken belief that I should read only that which was directly related to the macrocosmic, that which explained the big picture. There are, of course, many big pictures since the nature of truth is multiple. There is also, as Doyle Bishop pointed out somewhere long ago, the duty of the reader to infer relevance. This leads to a kind of "read locally, think globally" strategy. Perhaps that's why I always read local papers in whatever town or city of the world I find myself, making sure to include the classified section, the editorials and letters to the editor. I also like finding out what gets defined as news. John Naisbett did this a bit more systematically and, largely as a result, wrote *Megatrends*.

The Link between Reading and Publishing

During one year of my life, although married and a graduate student, writing poetry became more important to me than anything else. The impulse toward poetry was always in me but, for many years of my youth, the discipline was lacking. Poetry, like play, is surrounded by rules. Poetry, like leisure, requires discipline if it is to amount to anything. With poetry, a central part of the discipline involved is to read widely. Although you must first be touched by the muse to become a good poet, you must then recognize, as Frost did, that the ten percent inspiration must be accompanied by the ninety percent perspiration for good poetry to result. Part of developing discipline as a poet was to make myself read other poets, whether I liked doing so or not. I began, one at a time, to buy books written by those commonly considered masters of poetry in the English language. I read contemporary poets, began writing to Robert Bly and, to my surprise, found myself in a correspondence that lasted several years. When my forced campaign of reading had ended, I found that in addition to owning about 150 volumes of poetry, I now loved to read many poets. Dylan Thomas, Robert Bly, W.S. Merwin, W.H. Auden, and a host of others spoke directly to me and, by reading them, my own poetry benefited immensely. Soon my poetry was getting accepted in some of the better literary magazines, *The Nation*, and even in a few high school textbooks about poetry.

The link between reading and publishing is just as direct, I believe, in leisure studies. Most of the professors who publish widely in our field have read widely and what they publish is usually shaped by what they have read. So is their vision. Vision and imagination appear to be the two related commodities that are the scarcest among professors, and reading is critical to the continuing development of each. Three years ago, I simply would have been incapable of imagining how decadent this country has become or of how deeply we are in trouble. Reading numerous analyses of facts and trends in the environment, economy, and society stimulated my imagination a step at a time until it quit taking those neatly numbered steps and suddenly leaped to a differing consciousness. Professors must read if they are going to publish—if they are going to contribute creatively. Writing creatively is like playing creatively. Let's recall the stages of play as identified by Bishop and Jeanrenaud[2] and see how they match academic writing. There is first an attention stage. Something in the environment attracts our attention, based upon its comparative novelty and intensity. If it is too novel and intense we are likely not to get to the stage of exploration. If we do get to exploration, it may be either specific exploration of some object to find a solution to it or general exploration of an environment to find elements that excite and distract. After such exploration, there may be assimilation—a repetition of the exploratory play behavior with minor modifications so we make the play more appropriate for us and develop a repertoire of responses, thereby mastering the situation. Finally, may come creativity—the development of novel responses that have an appropriate effect. These steps, crudely recited here, would seem to correspond to the process of creative academic writing. Some issue, theory, or problem gains our attention, based upon its subjective novelty and intensity to us as individuals. If not too novel or intense, we begin to explore it, either to find a solution to a technical problem or to see what is intellectually exciting about it. Certainly reading is a key component of these stages. Assimilation, repeating the exploratory play behavior with minor modifications to master the play, is likely to involve both reading and writing. For the academic, this may involve writing, teaching, or researching the subject matter numerous times with minor modifications, thus developing a repertoire of appropriate responses. Finally, may come the creative part—the novel but appropriate response to the subject matter that advances understanding. Extensive, directed reading is likely to be the basis for the early stages of this process—continuing reading is likely to provide the insight by which we separate the merely novel from the novel and appropriate.

The Dignity of Uniqueness

Professors, to succeed, must develop their own uniqueness. We are, after all, professionals, and professionals produce an unstandardized product or service. In some sense, this uniqueness makes folly of the great effort we often go to in order to keep the content of a given course identical from professor to professor. It is the uniqueness of the professor that historically counts within the hierarchy of the university. Instructors, it is assumed, will often function as almost interchangeable parts. As one moves up in the pecking order, however, uniqueness becomes increasingly more important until, at the highest levels, what the individual professor does cannot be replaced merely by hiring someone else. This process runs parallel to taxonomies of knowledge, such as Bloom's,[3] which begin with facts which almost anyone can obtain and end with educational objectives which require unique resources. Within the cognitive domain, lest we forget, the taxonomy of educational objectives is as follows:

1.0   Knowledge

1.10   Knowledge of specifics

1.20   Knowledge of ways and means of dealing with specifics

1.30   Knowledge of the universals and abstractions of a field

2.0   Comprehension

2.10   Translation

2.20   Interpretation

2.30   Extrapolation

3.0   Application

4.0   Analysis

5.0   Synthesis

5.10   Production of a unique communication

5.20   Production of a plan for operations

5.30   Derivation of a set of abstract relations

6.0   Evaluation

As may be deduced from this hierarchy, the higher one goes in this taxonomy, the greater the need for individual insight, vision, and judgment. This situation has implications for what academics read. The printing of books, magazines, and newspapers has, in many senses, "massified." In 1958, for instance, independent, one-store firms sold 72 percent of all books, but in 1985, 52 percent were sold by four large book chains, and ten publishers accounted for more than 85 percent of the mass market. In newspapers as well, there has been continual conglomeration, resulting in the ever-increasing development of a common worldview. Computers have sped up the process of standardization of communication via the written word, as have fax machines and other technological changes which rob communication of, as J.T. Frazer termed it, "the dignity of uniqueness."[4] Computers demand a way of talking to them which carries with it a way of thinking: This communicates itself to people's assessments of the nature of reality and to their scales of values. "In the co-evolution of people and their computers, the most significant step has not been that computers became user-friendly, but that people became computer-friendly." They have also become friendly with the mass medium of television. Only about one-half of the American public claims to have read two or more books a year, but almost everyone watches television. What we watch on television presents a rather standardized definition of what is important, what is worthwhile, and more fundamentally, what is happening. As Frazer observed: "...the book does not seem to be the appropriate method of communication for the emerging global order of vast, inert masses."[5]

Professors must avoid great dependence on this mass-produced, standardized picture of reality, and avoid becoming merely computer technicians who leave real thinking to a few academics in specialized "think tanks." To a remarkable extent, what we do as professors has already become standardized. The bean-counters have taken over, weighing our vitae, counting our articles and comparing them to arbitrary formulae which use words like "productivity" but don't usually consider or even recognize the relevance of issues such as truth, wisdom, or quality of expression. As many universities become merely profit-seeking corporations, productivity becomes more important than contemplation, and that push for productivity results in more and more standardization. We must resist this however we can.

Professors, to paraphrase Erving Goffman, must see beyond the front regions of knowledge, such as television and the mass produced books and periodicals, which exist for profit and to placate their clients, and go to the back regions where knowledge exists without regard to its economic value, social propriety, or its cultural assumptions.[6] Doing this involves reading a wide variety of unique, esoteric, eccentric, cross-cultural, and cross-disciplinary sources. Sometimes you must even read crazy sources. (If you read such sources, however, you will find that "crazy" may be an insane response to a sane world, but it may also be a sane person reacting to an insane world.) If everything you read starts with the same or similar assumptions about the world, your imagination and vision must surely get proportionately smaller.

For this reason, I am pleased that I was involved in the establishment of a tiny publishing company several years ago that can publish a bit outside the world of mass produced textbooks. Being a co-founder of Venture Publishing has been a worthwhile learning experience about the business of reading, the extent to which people in our field read, what they want to read, and how much they value it in economic terms. It has also convinced me of the need for a "mixed economy" in publishing. Some of the most valuable contributions to our knowledge in leisure studies, as in other subjects of inquiry, can't make a profit.

A Professor's Life

Sometimes, as professors, we talk something to death. Perhaps we have done that with the issue of intrinsic motivation, internal locus of control, flow, activity whose meaning is imbedded in the actual doing, authenticating acts, freedom, leisure, self-actualization, and other wonderful stuff. After we have talked and written these ideas almost to death, we must put them somewhere in a corner and let them sit. Only then, if we glance at them for just a moment, may we get the idea that they relate to us, or should relate to us, as professors. All these terms, of course, can only relate to us in a comparative sense. Professors are not completely free, but then who would want to be? Only the dead are completely free (although I know a few professors who are completely free, having died on the job several years ago but who are still collecting a check). Professors don't always act from intrinsic motivation but, along with artists, writers, and a few other occupational groups, they usually have a greater potential to do so than most. This comparative freedom is a gift that comes with the job but, as with most gifts, has a few strings attached. To the extent that others don't regulate or impose discipline upon us, we must do so ourselves (How wonderfully easy this is to say!). Many academics in our field, as in others, appear to want the discipline imposed from the outside. Leisure, as de Grazia liked to remind us, is a difficult life. It is not the same thing as a life of ease and abundance. Ease and abundance is preferable to freedom if you lack passion and conviction about what you do. The problems of freedom, while challenging, are higher order problems that are, historically, an extraordinary privilege to have. In comparative terms, our "jobs" provide safety, justice, material comfort, travel, comradeship, and the opportunity for self-expression. I confess I have little patience with professors who decide to sulk for the rest of their lives because an article was rejected or their raise was $400 less than the person's in the next office. This is not to say that the role of professor doesn't have problems. Many of our universities today send us such mixed signals that the answer to, "What is important?" appears to be, "Everything." Many of us are being pushed to become bureaucrats or small business people rather than professors. The cost of living often increases faster than our salaries. Some of our schools don't care about teaching. These are problems, but ones that can be resisted if you love the life—and if you don't love the life, make room for someone who does, for without such love you will never do academic life, or yourself, justice.

On Professing, Publishing, and Sometimes Writing

Tom Goodale

i never think at all when i write
nobody can do two things at the same time
and do them both well

archy

I like quotes, always have it seems, even when, as with the words of Don Marquis' archy, they seem so hauntingly directed straight at me. Amidst the flattery of being asked to write a brief chapter about being a professor and writing, and with a long "lead time," both seducing happy agreement, I had forgotten archy's observation. One thing done well is taxing enough, witness documentation in pencil and crayon of a pre-schooler's efforts to print letters without reversing them, keep them between the lines, and get the right ones in the right order to make words. There is a photographic record of intense concentration, tongue clenched between teeth, nose not two inches from the paper. After printing comes writing, which still means the letters in each word are connected. Everyone must learn to print and write legibly, at least, an illegible pen being a telltale sign of 100 character flaws. That is one of the things you need to know and learn in kindergarten.

The word "sometimes" in the title of this chapter hints of a distinction, penmanship aside, between publishing and writing, between being an author and being a writer. Most professors publish at least a little something somewhere, but even the most prolific do not necessarily write. There are many exceptions, Boulding and Bronowski, or Galbraith, Gans, and Gould, but they *are* exceptions. Second, the presumption that this is an example of writing is a burden that few of us can bear. Writing requires something worth saying, artistic talent, and a great deal of time. Having all these is uncommon; having them all when needed is more uncommon still. Thus, writing by professors is a sometimes thing. Lack of time is, of course, our only limit. In any case, both publishing and writing are germane to a discussion of "being a professor," a more general topic that probably should be discussed before much more is said about writing.

On Becoming a Professor

Among the many reasons for being a professor or, perhaps, making a career of it, are those influences which lead one to it in the first instance. Each one's influences are autobiographical, of course, but there is nothing unique about them. Except in detail, surely thousands have been influenced in similar ways. Besides, too much is said about uniqueness and too little about all we share in common.

Those of my generation are products of a period of post Depression scarcity and World War II rationing, sacrifice, and effort. We are also products of extended families that worked hard and lived frugally, partly of necessity and partly conviction that their *raison d'etre* was to build the foundation of a better life for the children. Faith in a brighter future was unquestioned as was the assumption that the sons, at least, would get a better job and be more prosperous than the fathers.

Like many of my peers, I was a "first generation" college student; in fact, a first generation high school graduate. Without television throughout the formative years of childhood and adolescence, time not devoted to school and an unbroken string of jobs was spent entertaining oneself, inexpensively. Library cards were free. Around home there was always the local paper, the *Cortland Standard* (not quite affectionately tagged the sub-standard), the thick Sunday paper from Syracuse was a weekly treat, and reading was part of everyone's day. Though just short of extravagant, each member of the family had one magazine subscription, not counting a family subscription to one of the weekly news magazines. Dad read *The New Republic*. Not until I began university study in earnest—the first two years notably excluded—did I see that publication anywhere else or meet anyone who had even heard of it, much less read it faithfully.

The printed word, then, was important early on. Reading was a way of keeping informed, educating oneself, stimulating thought and discussion, shaping philosophy, developing vocabulary, enjoying humor, and so much more. It is quite impossible for anyone to develop an interest in writing without having first developed an interest in reading and having read a great deal and great variety of material.

By a stroke of luck I had failed, by age 19, to appreciate or benefit from a two-year college degree in business with an emphasis in accounting.

By a second stroke of luck there was a state-supported university in my hometown which, moving back home, was affordable. By another stroke of luck, "Gold" Metcalf, Chairman of the Department of Recreation at the university, interceded on my behalf with the admissions department, which, noting the record of my first two, less than earnest years of study, denied my application for admission. (Just between you and me, Drs. R.B. Ditton and Geof Godbey were salvaged from less than distinguished early records in exactly the same manner.) From there, a combination of diligence and fortune eventually led to completing the doctorate and entering the ranks of the university professorate.

My becoming a professor of the university in the recreation field was the result of unquestioned assumptions of a culture, an era, and a generation. It was the result of wanting to make the family proud, wanting to make something of oneself, trying to live up to the expectations of those who had patience and faith, and, vanity will out, prove something to those who did not. It was the product of active support of various kinds, from family, mainly, and encouragement from respected teachers. It was the result of reading and appreciating its many benefits, of a liberal political and social philosophy acquired unwittingly, some application to schoolwork and modest success with it, and enjoying university life as a student. All that, along with happenstance and a bit of good fortune, led me to the professorate. Except in detail, that story is familiar to thousands of us who now find ourselves in these ranks. So much then for the biographical but not unique account of becoming a professor.

A Professor's Perks

Why one would want to be and remain a professor is another matter. Decidedly secondary if not entirely superficial matters, to me at least but probably to most others as well, are the status, the salary, a generally pleasant physical environment, and a variety of perks such as relatively inexpensive access to good theater, concerts, exhibits, athletic events and the like, and use of library and athletic facilities and other resources of the university. It is, in these respects, a good job. The test of how good, of course, is whether or not that is what you would do if you were free from having to do any work at all.

The answer is "yes," though never an unqualified "yes," and the reasons are not those secondary matters that make professing a good job. There are days of disappointment, discouragement and, for hopeless romantics, even after all these years, disillusionment. Parts of the job most could happily do without; the politics, some of the paperwork, most meetings, those periodic tasks that are routine, repetitive, and mundane. But most of the work most of the time is what I would choose to do. There are two categories of reasons: the work is important; and I enjoy doing it. Perhaps in any occupation or career (as opposed to job), thinking the work important may be prerequisite to enjoying it. But there are many careers and career fields, the importance of which is beyond my power to rationalize—advertising, for example.

The University's Purpose

There is, in my view, no work more important than the work of the university, though I may see that work differently than do some others. The university is responsible for the generation of knowledge. It does this through research of all kinds. But there are many public and private corporations and agencies that produce knowledge as well. The university is also responsible for the transmission of knowledge in all of the principal branches and disciplines. It does this through teaching its students and other constituents touched by its service activities. But again, the university is far from alone in performing this function. Through its research, teaching, and service functions the university prepares people to take their place in society. To a large extent that function is reduced to selling work skills in the labor market, an important function no doubt but perhaps not to the exclusion of so much else. Still and again, the university is not alone in preparing people to work or to perform other functions in society. In these traditional functions and activities, the university has a significant role to play, but not a distinct or a special one.

Of special roles the university has two. First it certifies candidates for a respected profession, teaching. Via the normal school, then teachers college, and now university departments (schools, faculties, colleges, etc.), it licenses elementary and secondary schoolteachers. While degree requirements for entry may vary by place and subject, it also certifies teachers for postsecondary educational institutions. The doctorate in most cases is required for university teaching and admission to the professorate. Certifying teachers is a unique function and an important one.

The Heart of the Matter

The major special function, the importance of which cannot he overstated, is to shape and maintain the conscience of humankind. The first and finest definition of a university is a community, a community of masters and scholars. I think of myself secondarily as a member of a department (school, faculty, etc.) or field (parks and recreation). I am primarily a member of the university community. That community, largely autonomous, self-governing, and structured around main branches of knowledge, is now nearly 1,000 years old. It has survived, largely in original form, because of its commitment to the truth and because it is, in fact, universal and open to all who come. There is only one university. It transcends boundaries of race, nationality, religion, and class. These parameters also shape and maintain conscience, but not universally, as they are responsible for most, perhaps all wars. War violates the conscience of humankind.

The work of the university is important to all of us in another critical respect. I believe the words engraved over the portals, "You shall know the truth and it shall set you free." Illiteracy is a literal prison. So is illusion. Dissimulation—rapidly becoming the only manner of speaking our government, business, and political leaders know—can only lead to an Orwellian slavery by destroying our language and thus the symbols that make thought possible. Money and mobility are important to freedom, of course, but not nearly as important as knowing. One cannot be ignorant and free.

To anyone interested in leisure, the nature and importance of freedom and its relation to leisure need not be belabored. But note that the discussion is about freedom, not perceived freedom. The lens of perception is seldom thoroughly cleansed. Knowing the truth is the best cleanser.

Another reason I find teaching at the university important is because I care about the subject and I care about students learning about it. These are also, a spate of methods courses notwithstanding, the secrets of good teaching, which is important not in itself but because learning is important and good teaching helps. Students are a source of continuous renewal and of purposeful, meaningful change. At worst and least, they are the fresh side of generational change and no generation can disclaim responsibility for the next one. We are all responsible for the life that unfolds after our deaths. Students who know and care about learning, freedom, leisure, and humankind are our legacy. So are those who don't.

Enjoying Professing

These are the principal reasons why the work of the university is important. Without a deep sense of the importance of the work, the second category of reasons for being a professor, enjoyment, would be more difficult to realize and, even if realized, would be less appealing in the long run. Life must be more than pleasant except as pleasure stems from meaning and purpose. Without them pleasures become boring.

The enjoyment of being a professor, from a personal standpoint, results from its importance in addition to three other characteristics. Foremost among them is the autonomy professors enjoy. To a certain extent, professorship yields a freedom that is generally uncharacteristic of other work, even in the case of self-employment. Professors are largely free to teach what they want, often on the schedule of their choice. And provided that the necessary work is completed, the freedom exists for them to schedule their time in whatever manner they decide, excepting, of course, the case of classes and the inevitable committees, which also means that professors also enjoy certain luxuries like being able to buy groceries when there are no lines at the checkout, or playing golf when there is no wait at the first tee.

There are, of course, deadlines along the way that must be met, but some of these deadlines are self-imposed within limits that are broad. What one works on, how one goes about it, and on what schedule is largely self-determined, though some negotiation and compromise is often involved in deference to collective work and the autonomy and rights of others. Though junior professors may not fare as well as those more senior and more established, they still enjoy a great deal of autonomy. Much of the work, then, is as varied, interesting, and challenging as one wishes to make it. There is no shortage of challenge. Teaching is a challenge, as is getting material published, speaking, directing workshops, conducting research, securing grant support, supervising students, and several other involvements in the work of a professor and university.

A second source of enjoyment is the fellowship of one's colleagues. This includes the sense of comparable qualifications, competence, commitment and ability to contribute to a shared mission. It includes also the fair and consistent use of agreed upon standards and criteria for judging performance, and sharing a number of values (respect, tolerance, honesty, etc.) essential to the welfare of self-governing communities. This sometimes breaks down. Realities seldom match ideals, but clinging to those ideals is the only way to prevent even worse breakdowns. The collegial idea is important and worth the effort to preserve.

Because there is only one university, one's colleagues can be anywhere. Working with those colleagues over whatever distance and period of time is one of the greatest sources of enjoyment. The collegial process probably works better among these informal, widely scattered and often quite large groups than among immediately proximate peers. Such groups provide camaraderie and support, but also criticism, enjoinders, and whatever is required to keep the collegial process alive. Respect is the key element, for others and for oneself.

Proximity, as in one's department or college, seldom leads to communities as strong as those based on ideas, principles, and common intellectual enthusiasms. These weave through a wider world: a world professors ought to inhabit. Departments and even disciplines can be too confining, and magnifying the petty and diminishing the grand can distort contexts and perspectives, including one's own. Besides, proximate communities are often accidental rather than chosen, and assumptions, values, and enthusiasms are not always shared. You cannot instill community among sparrows and sparrow hawks. They have different feeding habits.

That collegial process spans generations. Students are part of the community; we professors were and remain students. I am still trying to live up to the standards and expectations of the Metcalfs, Brightbills, Storeys, and a host of other respected mentors in addition to keeping up with respected contemporaries. It is always a challenge, and success is a sometimes thing.

The final reason I enjoy the work is that at this moment I am home and have in front of me about 30 writing instruments of different kinds. Yet I haven't bought a pen or pencil for years. The bargain for the university is, however, a good one. In exchange for allowing me to work at home with some simple and inexpensive instruments, the university benefits from my charges for phone calls, postage, a pick-up truck, the bills from working-lunches and dinners, and hours of labor by my wife and two sons. But the main point is that life is congruent and whole in that the part that is work is compatible with what else I do and what other roles I play. Work intrudes only to the extent that I allow it. What could be done is unlimited, so what is imposed is self-imposed. Often, I take nothing home but myself. A realistic sense of self-importance lightens the workload. I leave saving part of the world to others.

On Writing and Publishing

"No man but a blockhead ever wrote except for money," Samuel Johnson (according to Boswell) once said. Were that the only motive, virtually everyone in our field would have given up long ago. Among professors who write about parks, recreation, and leisure, my guess is that only four earn enough from writing in a year to buy an operable used car. None have shown any inclination to give up their day jobs.

Of those who have realized some financial return, money was surely but one of many motives and probably a decidedly secondary motive in most, if not all, cases. Still, writing for publication is not just intrinsically motivated, even for those granted tenure some time ago, because publications figure significantly in university reward structures.

Among those rewards is money via merit increases, progress through the ranks, and promotion. Extrinsic factors such as this come with the territory. There is, in addition, a tacit understanding and agreement, at the university level at least, that writing for publication is part of the job. It is done because it is expected by oneself as well as by others and by the institution. This, too, comes with the territory. No doubt much that is published is coerced in these ways, even among those who have tenure, and certainly among those who do not.

Writing for publication is usually hard work, which of course was Johnson's main point, and a bit of coercion may be useful now and then. It is hard work for reasons other than trying to do two things well at the same time. The creative and therefore most interesting part of research is the design, including analysis of data. The creative part of scholarly essays is the formulation. Much writing, then, is anticlimactic. The discipline involved in preparing material for publication is one of the marks of a true professional, who, like a stage actress in 427th performance, still manages the freshness of opening night.

Like most others, I have done more publishing than writing. Vanity insists, however, that I have done some. The difference, to me, is that writing is more than conveying information; it is conveying information in ways that would be difficult to improve upon, and in ways that elicit an affective response as well as a cognitive one.

Imagine Lincoln saying, "Eighty-seven years ago." Imagine Paine saying, "Gosh, these are tough times." "Four score and seven years ago" is writing, as is "These are the times that try men's souls." Who can improve upon these grand openings? Not me, certainly. But I have done a little writing. Many argue that one of the secrets of good writing is to write as though speaking. My best writing (so far, I hope) was done preparing formal speeches: one in honor of "Gold" Metcalf at a National Recreation and Parks Association (NRPA) Congress; one in honor of Charles Brightbill at Illinois; one an address at my alma mater, S.U.N.Y. at Cortland. How important Metcalf and Brightbill were and are to me was already noted. Cortland and Illinois were and are as well. So invitations to give these addresses were genuine honors and privileges, rather than mere polite words in an introduction. Hoping to do justice to their contributions and expectations in ways that could only be personal, the words and phrases expressing the content became part of the content, including appreciation, respect and love. To say that something is important is to say, in effect, that you love it. Motivation, then, as with these addresses, was almost wholly intrinsic.

Largely the rest of what appears in print, mine included, there is some good composition and in some respects good writing, even if the phrases do not stir. Among the most important virtues of academic writing are clarity and efficiency. The words of Strunk and White's "little book," *The Elements of Style*, must echo in all our colleagues' ears: do not overwrite; do not overstate; revise and rewrite; be clear; omit needless words. Most professors do these things well enough.

Eric Hoffer, the retired longshoreman cum professor of philosophy who wrote a series of thin books in the 1950s and 1960s, once told the story of an exchange with his publisher, who thought the first book was too thin and should be fattened up. Hoffer's reply was, paraphrased, that there were x number of chapters in the book. In each chapter the editor would find one original idea and two good sentences, and that was more than could be found in any other book the firm had published. Hoffer's claim always struck me as an admirable goal for all of us—one original idea and two good sentences per chapter.

Anyone who tries to write would be happy with that. And everyone tries to write. Anyone I have ever met has written a few poems at some point. We may not show them to anyone, but experimenting with words seems part of a creative drive that everyone has, and we all need to express ourselves. We use words to do that most of the time, professors especially. We all dance and sing as well, even if often out of view and earshot, and even if the only musical instrument we play is the stereo, we are all conductors. I, personally, have conducted most major orchestras in most major halls. The need to create and express oneself is no gauge of talent. However good one's eye, ear, or dexterity, the need prevails. One of the reasons for writing, or trying, is that it is an aesthetic experience, one driven by intrinsic motivation, by the internally compelling love which, Godbey argues, characterizes leisure.

Preparing material for publication is usually not an aesthetic experience, though a bit may be experienced in getting some phrases and sentences just right. Aesthetic enthusiasm may be more common in writing done outside of work but sometimes we manage some within it. Aesthetic enthusiasm is a motivation for writing George Orwell identified. He identified three others and I appropriate them as they ring true to my experience and observations. I will add one more of my own. Before noting these other motivations, however, a reminder of Orwell's powerful insight is in order. Orwell believed when the meaning of words is destroyed, thought is impossible. When you reside on the outskirts of the nation's capital—where euphemisms, pandering, and dissimulation overwhelm clear, honest discourse—you become anxious about the prospect for communication and thus the prospect for community in the future. Words and phrases become more and more precious. You become irritated when they are wasted and downright unpleasant when they are twisted. In matters of usage and style, I am conservative; as it seems to me, most professors are and should be.

Most professors are also vain, though perhaps not overly so, and a bit of ego involvement seems inevitable. Being invited to say or write something touches the ego. Writing to prove something to someone other than oneself is vain, as is anything touched by the desire for praise and compliment. Perhaps a few people are egocentric enough to be motivated this way. Most are humbled, as often as not, as rejections and sometimes stinging critiques are powerful antidotes to egoism. Those who publish also sometimes feel that their words, rather than garnering praise, fall into a vacuum, creating no sound or ripple at all. So I am pleased to discover that someone read something I wrote, and flattered to see my words quoted. It is the fledgling poet-conductor seeking sustenance, but reminding the professor to keep his day job.

The other two motives Orwell suggested can be grouped under the general heading of believing you have something to say. This is probably the principal motivation for most of what is written by professors; certainly it is the most legitimate one. One is not always correct in believing one indeed has something to say, but mechanisms in the publishing process are intended to serve as correctives for mistaken beliefs.

One form of this belief is the recording of facts. Its purpose is to inform. Publication of virtually all research is of this type. It adds to the record as with original research, replications, testing alternatives, and the like. It may also correct or complete the record. Some articles and books, by providing comprehensive reviews, summarize the record. Bit by bit the store of knowledge is increased. Giants fill shelves but we journeymen researchers and scholars are part of the record too. Few write for posterity, but all know they have their place in it. Miniaturized text, much as I dislike it, means less of our work will disappear. Microfiche is better than no fiche at all. In any case, much of what is written by those who have something to say is, in a direct sense, "for the record." Who we are and what we know, think and do is recorded for posterity.

The other form of believing you have something to say is, in the broadest sense, political. Its purpose is as much to reform as to inform. Much research is political, though it cannot be admitted without the taint of bias. But essays and commentaries are more likely than empirical research to be more directly political. Much writing, including that done by professors, is designed to change how a reader thinks about the world and make one see more clearly (i.e., like we do) what the world is and what it can and should be. Many who write about leisure are, in this broad sense, political. I am, along with scores of others. Most of what emanates from departments of economics, political science and perhaps a few other disciplines is political. Some disciplines spend much of their time proselytizing; parks, recreation and leisure is a piker compared to the business school. Even the purest researchers cannot resist the opportunity, when the chance arises and the reputation won't suffer, to write for the political purpose not of informing but persuading. Pauling, Boulding, Hardin, Sagan, and many others have been both informers and reformers. There is a bit of the politician in all of us, and a bit of the muckraker, too.

We write mostly because we think we have something to say. We want people beyond earshot to hear what it is, and we want them to hear it, if not today, then some day. So we write it down, publish it if we can, and hope it may make a positive difference, however great or small. "The underlying reason for writing," Auden said, "is to bridge the gulf between one person and another."

The final reason professors write is that writing is important per se. Due to its importance, many of us insist that our students acquire and demonstrate the ability to write well. Not doing so oneself, or at least not trying, would be too hypocritical. Professors who make no effort to publish are, in my view, academically suspect, regardless of the other virtues they may possess. While there are surely a number of indicators of an educated person with a disciplined mind, I believe developing the ability to write, a primary purpose of a university, is probably the single best indicator.

Writing requires identifying topics that are at once interesting, significant and "doable": problems to researchers, themes to essayists. It requires the ability to locate or generate information and to sift and weigh it so as to retain what is good and discard the rest. It requires the ability to organize. It requires the ability to communicate clearly what one wants to say. Unlike conversation, where one has the chance to clarify what may not be clear, writers have only one chance. The burden of understanding cannot be passed to readers with the retort, "You know what I mean." Writing requires attention to detail (not that grammar and spelling are mere details) and following rules, including those governing references and citations. There are good and important reasons for these rules, including the obligation, based on respect for self and others, to be honest and to give credit where due. Writing also requires at least a bit of the artistic and poetic so as to communicate effectively. As Jacques Barzum once said, "The person you address ... is like you in his capacity for being bored by dull writing and irritated by what refuses to make sense." Add to all these skills perseverance, and you will have defined pretty well a disciplined mind and an educated person, what everyone in a university should strive to have and to be. In a university, writing, per se, is telling.

Being a professor and sometimes writing result from a complex array of motives; most intrinsic, some not; most passionate, some merely calculating. There are moments when masochism drives us on. At their best, professing and writing spring from a love of students and readers, a love of knowledge, principles and ideals, and a commitment to nourish and protect them all. For most of us most of the time these are the compelling forces.

Part II

For the Good of the Order

The genesis for this section was in Dan Dustin's experience chairing an academic department. In 1984, having neither aspired to nor having been prepared for administration, he found himself at the helm of San Diego State University's Department of Recreation. It was an awkward feeling because Dustin had always defined himself as a professor. His interest in higher education was rooted in his love for a subject matter, not in a desire to oversee others. Yet there he was, thrust into the midst of everybody else's business with little idea of how to proceed. The faculty expected him to champion their interests while the administration expected him to represent the interests of the larger university. He felt lonely in the middle.

Dustin never overcame that feeling. Not only was he frequently pulled in opposite directions, he never quite figured out just what it was that an administrator was supposed to do. It seemed to him that if everybody did his or her job, there really would be nothing to administer. Indeed, 80 percent of his time was spent trying to get 20 percent of the faculty to do what they should have been doing in the first place. He found little joy in that deficiency work, so as soon as a capable replacement was ready, he gladly stepped down to resume his life as a professor.

His successor, as it turns out, flourishes in administration. He finds satisfaction where Dustin found none. He represents the faculty to the university and the university to the faculty in a way that is not personally dismaying. He runs efficient meetings and enjoys them. And, by all accounts, he has plenty of friends.

What gives? Why is administration an anathema to some and an attraction to others? What should one know about administration before taking it on? What does administration feel like to different kinds of people? What are the rewards and frustrations of program leadership? Must administrators sacrifice their own scholarship in their efforts to assist the scholarship of others? In sum, is being an administrator in higher education worth it?

To arrive at an answer, we invited a cross-section of administrators from recreation, park, and leisure studies curricula throughout the United States and Canada to discuss these issues in the context of their own administrative histories. Collectively, the authors present a variety of perspectives on administration as they pertain to philosophy of service, management style, and the place of scholarship in their lives. All told, the essays portray an increasingly complex array of challenges and responsibilities for anyone who, for the good of the order, is willing to don the mantle of academic leadership.

Caring for the
Alma Mater
Andy Young

8

This is a good idea. Although there are other books, newsletters, journals, and conferences for people in academic administration, there is limited published advice for persons contemplating a move there. If you are such a person, you are probably thinking of becoming a department chair. You will likely receive two kinds of advice. One group of people, those concerned with *your* interests, will encourage you to stay put. They rightly understand that becoming an administrator results in a loss of many of the most rewarding aspects of being a professor. The other group, usually looking out for *their* interests, will urge you onward. They will remind you of what a good job you will do. Such encouragement is often a blend of a genuine belief and confidence in your abilities and an acknowledgment of the fact that few, if any, people want to go into academic administration anymore.

Being a department chair at the State University of New York College at Cortland for seven years has required me to tolerate and overcome recurrent ambivalence about that career choice. Paradoxically, that choice has also been a source of great satisfaction. Contrasting the ambivalence and satisfactions of my first year with those of my seventh may be instructive. For after seven years, I am much clearer about some enduring reasons for becoming or not becoming an academic administrator.

I won't kid you about the circumstances under which I became chair. It happened, in part, because nobody else wanted the job. The word is out about chairing. The rewards are few; the hassles are many. In most departments, people are not beating down the door to become chair. Likewise, fewer departments search externally for new chairs. So the humble reality is that I and many other contemporary department chairs earned this office almost by default. Some get dragged into the job kicking and screaming.

I kicked and screamed a bit. But I would mislead you by not admitting that the possibility of academic administration had long been attractive to me. I grew up in the home of an academic administrator. My father chaired the Department of Medicine at the University of Rochester School of Medicine and Dentistry and was Physician-in-Chief at the University of Rochester Medical Center. Retired now, my father knows the satisfaction of shaping a great program and of developing much emulated models of medical education that also have improved health care and health care delivery. My undergraduate mentor, then professor of religion, Melvin L. Vulgamore, left teaching for administration and went on to be Provost at the University of Richmond and later President of Albion College. As a trustee of my alma mater, Ohio Wesleyan University, I had the privilege of seeing first-hand the beneficial transformations brought about by two skillful academic leaders, former president, Thomas Wenzlau, and his successor, David Warren. Exposed to these models, I confess that for a time, many years ago, I aspired to become an academic vice president. These days, I am content to serve my department as chair and, when the time comes, to return to being a full-time professor.

Partly because of that earlier ambition, I was more open to becoming department chair seven years ago than I should have been. In most respects, the opportunity came at the wrong time. In just my fourth year on the job, I had only begun my agenda in teaching and scholarship. Any thought I had previously given to academic administration had been based on the assumption that I would embark on such a venture from the rank of professor.

But I was also a frustrated junior faculty member. At that time in our history junior faculty came and went frequently. Beginning to see *why*, I understood that I would need to either leave, put up with the problems, or see if we could create better conditions for faculty. I chose to become department chair because I wanted to try to make our department one in which I would want to work as a professor. I felt our department had a great deal of unrealized potential. By becoming department chair, I could find out whether or not things could be better. Despite the doubters, it seemed to me they could be.

When I accepted the appointment, I did not fully understand that gaining a measure of control over one agenda, the department's, would require a loss of control over another, my own aspirations in teaching and scholarship. No one at Cortland warned me about that. But a few days before I became chair, Geof Godbey cast a huge cloud of doubt over my decision. "The best advice I ever got was to stay out of administration," Godbey said at a dinner our department hosted in his and Bob Ditton's honor following ceremonies in which both received Cortland's Distinguished Alumnus Award. I don't recall whether he knew then that I was about to chair the department at his alma mater. At that point I did not feel much like talking about it. Imagine yourself as a young, untenured professor who is about to become department chair. You are sitting opposite a professor's professor and finding that his best advice is "to stay out of administration and go for full professor as quickly as you can."

Godbey's words were an ample and accurate warning about what I would give up to become chair. I quickly learned that the job consumed far more energy and time than I had imagined. This introduced me to one recurrent source of ambivalence in my work—the needs of the department almost always take precedence over the pursuit of my own scholarly and professional endeavors.

In accepting the chair position, I was ambivalent about the timing and naive about the sacrifices. Yet the measure of ambivalence that came when I understood the sacrifices was more than offset by the novel challenges of the position and the satisfactions associated with succeeding in both mundane and substantive matters. Seven years later, the ambivalence and satisfactions are still there, but in different measures and for different reasons.

In these seven years it seems I've been successful. Twice since my initial appointment my colleagues and the administration have reviewed my work and affirmed their confidence in my ability to chair the department. I have also been asked to write two articles this year from my vantage point as a chair. Presumably, to both intramural and extramural evaluators, I am perceived as a successful, effective academic administrator.

I am pleased by their confidence because I find great satisfaction in the accomplishments of our department over the past seven years. We have achieved all the major goals that motivated me to become chair in the first place. An extended period of faculty turnover was replaced by a period of stability. Faculty desire to stay and have moved successfully through the re-appointment, tenure, and promotion processes. With faculty stability and better workload management, the scholarly activity of faculty has more than tripled. Students' satisfaction with their major is very high. Rekindled relationships with alumni have strengthened our program and prompted substantially increased levels of giving to the college. Despite our president's opposition to departmental accreditation programs, our department obtained long overdue accreditation from the National Recreation and Park Association (NRPA). We even managed to double the office space allocated to our department.

I cite these accomplishments not to boast, but to illustrate some of the rewards of academic administration. These are worthwhile accomplishments that make a real and positive difference in the lives of many people. Although I regard these as our—not my—achievements, I am pleased to associate them with my years as chair.

To have made a difference is a wonderful feeling. Why, then, in my seventh year, did I still feel ambivalent about being chair? There were two primary sources of ambivalence. One was an old, familiar struggle. The other was new to me and perhaps the kind that only comes to seasoned administrators.

The familiar tension was the one Geof Godbey warned about. When you move into academic administration, you give up many of the joys of being a professor. I love teaching. As department chair, I teach less. I love to read. As department chair, I read less. Despite this, my research agenda grows while my research accomplishments dwindle. I am embarrassed by the amount of raw data at rest on my computer's hard drive. As a student and as a faculty member, I celebrated the sense of closure and relative freedom that comes at semester's end. Now my months of January and July are spent writing reports and doing countless chores, the content of which I cannot recall even a few days after completing them.

Although stepping into academic administration did give me an added measure of influence over the affairs of my department, it diminished substantially my control over my daily, weekly, and even annual agenda. Almost daily, I attend to the needs, wishes, problems, and concerns of others. To a certain extent I succeed, survive, and enjoy this work only by seeing the harmony between meeting the needs of others and serving the interests of our program. Some days I see this harmony better than others. When I don't, I am ambivalent about my job.

The second source of my seventh year ambivalence was in two ways a product of my success on the job. First, many tasks that were once novel and challenging had become routine and boring. Some were downright annoying. Second, and more profoundly, I began the seventh year without a series of specific goals for the department. We had achieved all the major goals that motivated me to become chair in the first place. Without new goals to replace the old, it seemed all I had left were routine, familiar tasks. It is no wonder I felt equivocal about my work.

I write now near the end of my seventh year as chair. I feel pretty good about my work this year. I moved past the earlier felt magnitude of ambivalence in part by self-indulgence and in part by being mindful of some overriding good reasons for doing academic administration. Self-indulgently, I decided not to engage my colleagues and myself in pursuit of any major programmatic outcomes for the year. Instead, I devoted myself to more writing and other, non-departmental projects. When I suggested to the faculty that we could slow down the pace of programmatic improvements and attend more to individual goals, they seemed relieved. So we balanced several years of ambitious work on department goals by giving our own agendas more attention. I also countered the ambivalence by recalling four of my own imperatives that I would have guide all academic administrators. They are useful to me in setting priorities and in guarding against complacency and too much self-indulgence. I have had enough exposure to different institutions and different levels of administration to believe they would apply in most situations.

First, academic administrators must measure some of their success by the achievements and satisfaction of their faculty. Of course, the mix of the measures of faculty success varies from place to place. Still, administrators must create the kinds of conditions that facilitate faculty fruition. I am not suggesting that administrators be slaves to every faculty whim, but I strongly believe that administrators can remove impediments and provide enhancements to the work of teaching, scholarship, and service. Whether in a research or a teaching-centered institution, a capable faculty is the foundation for everything we do in higher education.

Second, quality institutions have not only a strong faculty, but also successful and loyal alumni. The alumni at Cortland have taught me that I am a guardian of an alma mater and of a program that was developed with care and has held meaning for hundreds and hundreds of graduates. In caring for our department, I remain cognizant that many of these people watch with deep concern the directions we take. Our shortcomings cause them disappointment; our accomplishments add to the satisfaction, meaning, and pride they associate with their alma mater.

Literally, alma mater means "learned mother." Academic leaders need to create the kinds of learning environments that nurture affection for the people and places where the learning occurs. Academic leaders also need to understand that they are caring for the alma mater of present, past, and future students. College students have a lifetime relationship to their college. By comparison, the relationship of faculty and especially administrators to academic institutions is much more short-lived. When you make a program better, all of those associated with it benefit. When you let a program slide, you affect not only present and future students, but you offend the many that in years past came to care about the place. As an academic leader, you care for an alma mater. You care for someone's "learned mother." Do not take that responsibility lightly.

Third, academic administrators are guardians of the academy which provides society with learned citizens and professionals. Department chairs in recreation and parks are also guardians of their profession. Recently, over a dozen recreation departments have been eliminated or radically reorganized. It is no secret that our profession and our fields of study are poorly understood and often undervalued within and outside the academy. As such, we are easy targets when it is time to trim the staff and budget. In such a climate, our academic programs need leaders who can demonstrate the coherence and importance of our programs to the mission of the university. If leisure services contribute to the commonweal, and if the provision of leisure services is better done by liberally and professionally educated persons, then academic programs in recreation and parks need to exist and need to do their work well. Chairs play an instrumental role in seeing to the continued existence of our field. They must keep this higher purpose before their faculty, and they must make the importance of this purpose clear to deans and provosts who almost always have no prior exposure to a recreation and parks curriculum. It is sometimes our shortcoming, not our dean's, when the value of our programs is not understood by others, especially decision makers on campus.

Fourth, academic administrators should make decisions that are in the long-term best interest of their departments, programs, and institutions. Unfortunately, increasing numbers of career administrators "make a move" every three to five years. This trend is dangerous when people impose a major programmatic shift that looks good on their resume and then leave before the adverse impacts of the program are known or felt. Equally insidious is the temptation to make decisions that are expedient or convenient in the short term, knowing that the long-term effects will be somebody else's problem. I would wish for administrators to act as if they would be around for 20 or 25 years.

In sum, I would encourage academic administrators to 1) create climates that are conducive to the work of professors, 2) create programs that contribute to students' loyalty to their alma mater, 3) build programs that are viewed as central to the mission of the university, and 4) act in the long-term best interest of the program and institution. I believe these aims to be in harmony, although the specific structure of the harmony will differ widely from college to college just as it does from song to song. If blending these parts is appealing, then academic administration has meaning and purpose.

Deciding to chair the department at Cortland was one of the best decisions I ever made. Despite the ambivalence and some sleepless nights, I have been greatly satisfied with what our department has accomplished and with the means by which we made those gains. To be sure, my life would be simpler were I not chair, but, given my makeup, also less satisfying.

This section is well-titled. My work is for the good of the order. Still, initially I became chair to create the kind of environment in which I would be happy to serve as a faculty member. The day will come when it is in my best interest and that of the department for me to enjoy the fruits of my labor. Timing is everything.

On Being an Administrator

Doug Sessoms

Some see administration as where the action is. They enjoy the feeling of power that comes from controlling budgets, personnel, and resources. Others disdain the role, preferring not to be encumbered with decisions affecting others, endless hours in meetings and having to play "the political game." Then there are those who find themselves being asked to act as administrators even though that was not their desire; yet their sense of obligation and responsibility had them say, "Yes," to the invitation.

This, of course, is an oversimplification but there are considerable data in the organizational behavior literature which suggest that those who are successful in administration tend to possess certain personality characteristics. They like being in control whereas those who are more concerned about maintaining pleasing social relationships or those who are highly self-directed and motivated tend not to be as effective as administrators. If you are one of those who enjoys or does not shrink from having to make decisions, then administration may be the right path for you.

I discovered this rather late in my career as an administrator. I was one of those who found himself involved out of default. We were a two-person curriculum and my predecessor was required by state law to step down from his administrative role when he reached the age of 70. Being a small unit, a program rather than a department, my duties were simple. There were no personnel decisions to make, no budget to handle, only the scheduling of courses and the maintenance of good relationships with colleagues throughout the university and profession. It was fun. I had a title, which I found to be a helpful entree into the profession. The fact that I also happened to be at one of America's more prestigious state-supported universities did not hurt either. The rewards and satisfactions were there for one who is basically self-directed and enjoys developing and sharing ideas, one who enjoys being a teacher even though he was now an administrator too.

Mine was an idyllic life. It fit my personality perfectly. Unfortunately, it changed. Or perhaps I came to understand that being responsible for a program involved certain duties and obligations which I could not ignore. Our university was growing, our curriculum was increasing in size (more students and faculty), the institution was becoming more bureaucratic, and the competition for external funding was becoming acute. If we were to prosper and receive our fair share of the resources so that our faculty could be professionally involved, our students could be exposed to current materials and resources, and our curriculum could achieve its objectives, I had to become more of an administrator. This was not my druthers. I would rather have been at home writing than in the office returning telephone calls. I would rather have been in the classroom sharing observations and leading students on the path of inquiry than in a meeting with other chairs or the dean. I would rather have been doing committee work for one of our professional organizations than completing forms developed by some university bureaucrat or competing with colleagues for limited resources.

It was frustrating. I had become a department chair even though we were still a curriculum; one, however, with all the autonomy of a department. We had a budget, faculty members with their primary appointments in our unit, membership in the social science division of the college, and an annual report I was expected to write. It was at this point I was given some valuable advice. If I were to survive and find satisfaction in my job, I had to find satisfaction in administration or else relinquish the responsibility. It came from one of my colleagues, an older man who had served in the military. Perhaps it was there where he learned it. He said, "Doug, you must learn that there is satisfaction and joy in helping others achieve as well as in your own achievements, that the goal of administration is facilitation, making sure that both individuals and the institution fulfill their destiny." I listened, but I am not sure I heard what he was saying, at least not to the point of internalizing the lesson. My modus operandi was couched in the past. I had my own agenda, which I was following, and I assumed my colleagues had theirs, leading me to believe that the best leadership I could provide was to let self-directing people direct themselves. It was an idealistic assumption, but perhaps a rationalization as well for my own unwillingness to become a full-fledged administrator.

Administration is a noble but demanding role. It is a necessary ingredient in corporate life. There must be those who are willing to commit their time and energy to the institution, its operations and structures. It is an act of leadership and one of the roles leaders must play is that of articulating to the group a philosophy to which all can subscribe, a sense of purpose. Without that, there is only individual action, no composite effort. If you are unwilling to accept the mantle of leadership, do not become an administrator.

Leadership has us play many roles, one of which is to represent the group. Who else is going to advocate and arbitrate with the dean for resources for the program if it is not the curriculum's administrator? Who else is going to promote alumni support and seek their contributions if not the chair? Who else is to create the environment so those who have grants and research skills can do their work if not the chair?

The title of chair carries with it obligations and expectations. The chair is the designated representative of the group and although individual faculty members may achieve recognition and earn respect for their individual performances and interact informally as representatives of the curriculum, the chair is the official spokesperson. That means attending professional meetings, being active in professional organizations, making time available to interact with colleagues locally and nationally, attending departmental chair meetings, being a member of the faculty council and/or seeking membership on one or more university committees. It also means making sure that other members of the faculty for whom you are responsible have similar opportunities, that the reputation of the program as being professionally involved and academically integrated within the institution is achieved.

Quality control is critical. What is done under your tenure is your responsibility. Good teaching, respect by campus colleagues, making sure that recreation and leisure studies is seen as an acceptable academic pursuit are essential. I felt that our faculty had to be more than sensitive and liked by students. They had to be good teachers in the best sense of the term, unafraid to establish and enforce rigorous academic standards. That was sometimes a problem. Periodically, I would discover that some of our faculty were giving a disproportionate number of high grades, even though their students were not the most academically gifted. To me an exceptional grade should be given only to those who are doing exceptional work, and when everyone in a class seems to be exceptional I wonder about the standards employed. Recreation tends to have an image problem on most college campuses; it is often viewed as an easy major, and to foster that image by grading students on effort and personality rather than on their academic performance, or by substituting volunteer work for academic requirements, does not do us any favors. It helps neither our program nor our students, especially when being energetic and liking people rather than skill and knowledge are used as a basis for grading one as exceptional.

Standards equal to those of other academic disciplines had to be met. I found that I was most often able to do that when I shared with my colleagues my concerns and reminded them of the expectations of the university. I had to get them to buy into the system. I also found it helpful to let our faculty know how we compared as a curriculum with other academic units on campus and how each of us was doing in each of the courses we were teaching. I did not wish to infringe upon the right of my colleagues to teach and grade as they wished, or to dictate course content and assignments, but it was my responsibility as chair to protect the quality and integrity of the academic endeavors of the curriculum.

For most of us, parks, recreation, and leisure studies is not a high priority of the institution, its board of governors, or regents. We have to fight negative stereotypes about our academic viability, but I found that when our faculty members were involved with various university tasks—committee work, participating in university activities, etc.—we did quite well. We were accepted as colleagues. One of the basic tasks administrators must assume is making sure that this type of opportunity and participation occurs. It is so important when university decisions are made. It is difficult to act on the basis of a stereotype when you know the people involved. I thought it was important enough that I not only tried to place my colleagues in places of visibility, I would often carry documents by hand to various university offices rather than sending them by mail to make sure that the personal contact was there, that those receiving the information knew who we were.

There is another aspect of this representative role that should not be overlooked. It, too, can provide satisfaction. As chairs, curriculum administrators represent their student majors and are seen by them as their leaders. What a wonderful opportunity to be in a position to advocate and interpret the values of your activity, to show students the importance of professional involvement, to serve them as a role model for when they become administrators, as most will as recreation practitioners. Some might not like the idea of being a role model, but leadership and being an administrator implies that obligation.

It is important to have a sense of where you want the program to go and it is ego satisfying to know that you are in a position to make that happen. Administration offers that opportunity. It is one of the benefits but it also requires the development of good communication and negotiation skills. You cannot run roughshod over colleagues. They, too, have visions of the future, where the profession is going, and what our responsibilities are as academics to facilitate that progress. I found that faculty meetings afforded a wonderful opportunity to spend time sharing viewpoints and working toward common goals, but only when I had enough sense to realize that I had to plan for this and make sure the agenda was not filled with "nuts and bolts" items. New course proposals, faculty hires, and accreditation self-studies were also ideal times to make sure we were on track, had a sense of direction, and were together. They were also times of high negotiation and compromise, two skills an administrator must have. It helps when you remember that your term as chair is an opportunity, not a mandate, and that your time in administration is temporal whereas the life and time of the curriculum is continuous. Yours is a stewardship, not a kingship. But when you win one or are able to achieve one of your goals, there is a regal high.

What helped me keep my head on straight were the rational arguments of colleagues and the discomfort of having to mediate disputes and conflicts. They keep administrators emotionally honest. I did not enjoy having to resolve conflicts between faculty and students, between colleagues, or between faculty and staff, yet they occurred and as chair I had to arbitrate them. Another lesson I learned was to listen and not become judgmental and, where possible, to have the conflicting parties work out their grievances without my interference. When that could not be done, I had to intervene. I found that when I was able to resolve the differences effectively, it was usually because we were able to move together to a solution that dealt with principle rather than some action based solely upon the specifics of the event in question.

Developing and nurturing contacts and relationships is another important role of administration. Participation in professional organizations, being a member of a university committee or attending student-sponsored activities are some of the things I did to foster those contacts and relationships. I also incorporated another behavior that I learned from Harold D. Meyer, my predecessor. I tried always to respond personally to inquiries and when possible to do so within 48 hours of receipt of the request. Graduate students entering into our master's program often commented that it was my correspondence that became a critical factor in their choice of institutions. They felt someone cared, that they would not be just another number. My correspondence activity was not limited to responses about our program or requests for information. I incorporated it into my professional activity, trying always to keep committee members informed, trying to set and adhere to deadlines. This sometimes created an extra workload for the secretaries, but I tried to space my work for them so as not to take a disproportionate amount of their time from the work of others. I did not always succeed but my colleagues generally forgave me for they, too, became aware of the value of that activity and my rationale for a somewhat compulsive correspondence behavior.

I felt the obligations of leadership and I tried not to ask my colleagues to assume tasks or assignments that I was unwilling to undertake. That meant I taught the same number of courses they taught, continued my professional involvements, and honed my skills as a scholar. At first I thought I could do it all but that was not fair to the curriculum. Administration required my giving up something in order to do the many things that comprise the role. Perhaps it was because I was failing to do some of the tasks of administration or maybe my colleagues felt my dilemma; whatever, they encouraged me to reduce my teaching load and to increase my time as chair. That was difficult because being in the classroom was my preference; it was my recreation center. Like most educators, I could do without having to grade papers but the thrill of teaching was something I did not want to give up. I sincerely believe that in order for one to maintain sensitivity to problems of teachers and the concerns of students, administrators should not leave the classroom. University administrators should be academics first, administrators second. Never the reverse. When you lose contact with teaching, the duties and responsibilities of being an instructor, there is a tendency to forget why the institution exists and what the problems are of those who fulfill its first mandate.

The homeostasis between being an administrator and being a professor was a difficult one for me to maintain. It required a balancing of self-interests with the interests of the corporate. It meant recognizing the selfishness within me—that we are all seeking satisfaction in what we do—but that in achieving my satisfaction I could also enable others to achieve theirs. The lesson of administration is the lesson of facilitation. It is the lesson of leadership.

In this era of political correctness, fear of suits, political scrutiny and exaggerated public accountability, it is easy for an institution and its administrators to succumb to the disease of bureaucracy. When that occurs, leadership is often sacrificed for clerkship. Decisions are made out of the need to protect the institution and those responsible for its operation rather than furthering its mission and supporting those who are its primary artisans. At the departmental level, this often means constant battles with the purchasing office, the legal department, personnel, travel accounts, and the student aid offices, places which seem to foster bureaucrats and bureaucratic procedures. The battles often seemed to place me in the middle, between the university with its regulations and expectations and the faculty and staff with their needs and expectations. One was saying,

"Do this, do that," the other was saying, "There's no money to do that," or, "You have to follow procedures. You cannot do it that way." To protect yourself, there is the tendency to withdraw, to not share with others the battles you are fighting, or to take out your frustrations on colleagues, thereby forcing them into patterns of alienation and conflict. Neither pattern is healthy.

In times of economic scarcity, these tendencies are exaggerated and administrators often find themselves having to become one of the "bad" guys, saying, "No," to faculty requests for travel, new equipment and lighter teaching loads. It is fun when resources are ample and flowing. It is frustrating when zero budget exercises become more than exercises and become the rules by which we live. Then administration is a drag with few satisfactions. Pity on those who have not known the joy of giving, only the sorrow of saying, "No." It is then that the lessons of good communication come to the front. If the administrator has been sharing with colleagues the satisfactions that come with the position as well as the problems, being in the middle is not so bad. I learned that was when the faculty would rally around you and give you a helping hand. It was then that being the unit's advocate and buffer between the faculty and the bureaucracy paid dividends, when my administration was appreciated. Administration, like leadership, can be shared although the designation of administrator cannot be. If one does not like that role, then one should not aspire to it.

I found it easy to be an advocate, to assume the position of role model, to make opportunities available for colleagues to advance their professional careers. I attempted to involve them in curriculum decisions, to reaffirm our mission and mandate of the institution and our responsibility to our students and profession. I tried to share some of my responsibilities as chair, knowing full well that one or more of them would someday assume that role. That was easy to do.

The downside of being chair was that I had to make decisions about salaries, allocation of resources, judge merit and administer rewards: activities which affected the lives and careers of colleagues. That was painful. When you know something about the needs of individual faculty members and their families, it is difficult to divorce that understanding from the needs and expectations of the curriculum. I feel that rewards should be based upon the productivity of the faculty in fulfilling the expectations of the institution, not according to one's personal situation. But how is that done? The aseptic decision to base raises totally on academic productivity may have negative consequences. It may hurt morale if one feels trapped in a hopeless situation with an insensitive supervisor. On the other hand, if the reward is perceived as unjustified by those who are more productive, and given to those who are less productive even though their need for financial assistance is great, that, too, may hurt morale. Trying to get a sense of equity and interpret that to colleagues was difficult and sometimes agonizing. I did not like that task nor the hours spent in meetings where the information and issues seemed so foreign to our curriculum's needs and concerns. Why was I wasting my time attending those meetings? There were more satisfying things to do in life. It was when these thoughts became more frequent than the pleasures associated with the role that I knew I should no longer be an administrator. It was also at this point that my appreciation for administration, for those able to do it, was heightened.

An institution cannot survive without administrators. They give structure and continuity. Fortunately, there are some who enjoy the role. It fits their personality. They do not mind making the difficult decisions. When they are able to do this and at the same time maintain their understanding of what it means to be a teacher, positive things happen. However, when one becomes too concerned about maintaining the institution's procedures, or finds the role of administrator no longer satisfying, negative things happen. Perhaps that is why we rotate the position of chair. I was delighted with the opportunity to return to teaching, but I did so with an appreciation I would not have had if I had not been an administrator. At times I even miss the action.

The Academic Animateur
Bert Brantley

I was one of those ABDs, involved in writing the dissertation and enthusiastically entering into my fourth year of teaching at North Carolina State University when college administration knocked at the door. My energies were spread among the dissertation, teaching, and activities of home life and fatherhood. At no point had I thought about university administration. I'm not going to suggest that mine was the perfect way to enter academic administration. It was not even the usual entrance.

In 1965, in the neighboring state of South Carolina, park and recreation leaders had begun a campaign to convince the state's university presidents that a curriculum serving the profession was needed. Dr. Robert C. Edwards, President of Clemson University, the state's land grant university, offered the only positive response. Dr. Edwards assigned the department-to-be to the School of Education informing the school's dean that he expected him to establish a program patterned after the one at N.C. State University. Through a mutual friend the dean learned of my existence and of my affiliation with N.C. State University. The call came, the visit followed. And in November of 1965 I became the head-designate of the Department of Recreation and Park Administration at Clemson University.

It was a great opportunity to develop a curriculum and forward it to Clemson for the necessary approvals. As you might expect, the curriculum represented a great deal of that which was present in the N.C. State program, a program which had been fine-tuned by Tom Hines and his staff of experienced and professional recreators. And it was liberally spiced with the philosophy of Drs. Harold Meyer and H. Douglas Sessoms at the University of North Carolina where my doctoral work had been completed.

The Clemson University faculty had expected the worst, a watered-down curriculum accommodating large numbers of athletes who were thought to be ill-prepared or poorly motivated for university study. I understand from comments picked up over several years that the surprised response to the proposed curriculum was, "Hey, this looks reasonably legitimate." The ultimate compliment came a few years later when Frank Howard, football coach and athletic director, in a speech to our booster club said, "I thought that Brantley was coming down here to look afta mah boys. First theng I know he's hiring them damn Hahvard professors." I never expected the affiliation to last 21 years, but it did. Those were good years, made more so because the state was small, the university was generally viewed as a resource, and university faculty and administrators often were accepted as people with good ideas and abilities. As the state's role in parks, recreation, and tourism grew, so did opportunities increase for the department's faculty to influence the direction of this growth.

Obviously, my decision to pursue administration preceded any preparations I might have needed for the tasks. There is no single explanation for my having accepted the offer to go to Clemson or for following the route of administration for these 25 years. Fleetingly, I harbored notions about good teaching as seen through the idealism of youth and had concluded that I could influence teaching more effectively from the vantage point of administration. Through 21 years as head at Clemson and five years as chair at Indiana I've seen many things being added which have diluted the emphasis on "good teaching." Not always are our claims that we value good teaching supported by actions that affirm our contentions. Further, I've concluded from these 25 plus years of experience that those who pursue administrative positions with the most vigor are often the least prepared to manage in the unique environment of collegiality.

There are several admonitions that I would like to offer anyone contemplating even a temporary sojourn into the arena of university administration. First, choose carefully the persons who are to be your supervisors. If you have reservations, then don't accept the assignment. Don't expect to be able to change the supervisor's style nor should you expect to change his or her view of the world, especially the corner which you would occupy as a subordinate. I've been blessed by the opportunities to work with honorable people. For the most part, they have used the processes of delegation and accountability, leaving much to my own initiative and judgment. In my zeal to do great things I really botched a few. In naiveté I talked when I should have listened. President Edwards, about whom I spoke earlier, provided inspiration for daring and a calming hand when I stood close to disaster. I still recall with great clarity having received a phone call at home which started with, "Bert, this is Bob Edwards...." I knew my days were numbered. This call became one of many which usually meant that I had crossed the line. One case in point was as follows. Dr. Edwards had accompanied me to a breakfast meeting of a civic/service club at which time we discussed the administration of a camp for disadvantaged youngsters. The club was interested in helping us build a facility to house the program. After the breakfast meeting, a newspaper reporter asked me about the scope of the project, particularly the cost. I've had some difficulty reconstructing the conversation but I think it went something like this, "I don't really know… one million dollars, two million, perhaps five million." The headlines in the evening paper read, "Clemson University to Build $5 Million Camp on Lake Hartwell." Dr. Edwards had not been privy to my conversation with the reporter but he was very interested in knowing how the headline came to be.

On another occasion I, and one of my recreation and park colleagues, had been assigned to a committee with equal representation from the Department of Forestry to study the feasibility of merging the two departments into a new school. Our conversations had not been too constructive and I had walked to the campus one morning, taking time to formulate an explanation as to why the merger would not work. Before I could schedule an appointment with the academic vice president to state my position, I received a phone call by which I was informed of a meeting in the president's office at 10:00 a.m. No agenda item was identified. Arriving at 10:00 it was obvious that the Committee to Study Merger was convened. The president began the meeting by restating our charge, by reminding us of the time we had invested in deliberation and by adding, "Gentlemen, we're going to merge these departments to create a new school. Anyone who doesn't agree with this action does not see the big picture." My visual acuity improved immediately and my reply went something like this, "Mr. President, you're the only one who's been able to explain the merger so that I could understand it." Thus, the College of Forest and Recreation Resources was created, a move that proved to be of inordinate value to students, faculty, the university, and the state. Ben Box, who became the second dean of the college, was a perfect fit to the admonition, "Work for honorable people." His view was that problems do not go away. We addressed them promptly and pursued their resolution with vigor. I've adopted this attitude in large measure, and, in my judgment, it has served me well.

The next admonition I offer those contemplating administration is to be a risk taker. No growth or progress is made by counting paper clips. However, the degree of risk is often dictated by circumstances. It would be foolhardy to dare when the objective is not attainable no matter how hard it might be pursued.

Third, know that there are several ways that objectives might be reached. Early in my career I could not understand, probably did not want to understand, why everyone did not see opportunities and solutions to problems from the same perspective, notably my perspective. Management became much more pleasant when I realized there were as many solutions as there were individuals considering them. I can't tell you when and why I came to this realization. I wish it had come sooner. My wife wishes it had come sooner. My view of the role of the academic administrator is one of facilitator. The French have a word, *animateur* that is even more expressive. Animateur means one who enables things to happen. The administrator is thus responsible for seeing that faculty and staff are positioned and supported in ways which contribute to scholarship, professional growth, productivity, and a sense of worth and well-being. The administrator must also be a salesperson. Support in higher education does not come to a field of study such as ours because of the "great" view of our relationship to the common course. It occurs because of an expressed need and it is sustained because the function of the department becomes central to the mission of the university. Having become essential, it must maintain its centrality. We're never free from the scrutiny of skeptics.

I've known no more than five or six administrators who have not had to sacrifice their own professional and personal agendas in order to do the things required by the administrative position. Any faculty member who believes that he or she can change that formula, can in fact maintain a research program and a schedule of professional writing, is in for a shock. In most cases it isn't done. The demands in even the small departments are constant and unrelenting. They generally require immediate action, thus upsetting the best plans for a given day. Few are able to turn on and off the creative switch so that productivity can be maintained over the long haul.

I've been fortunate in having made good personnel hiring decisions. In the early days the decisions were largely mine. Increasingly, faculty have been involved in hiring, which has improved morale and, hopefully, the selection process.

Tenure decisions have for a long time required a deliberative process involving faculty and administration. However, it's become far too cumbersome, too restrictive, too much dictated by arbitrary rules of the university rather than the needs of the department. Often the best interests of the university are not served.

Twenty-five years of management at the department level gives rise to several questions. One question is, "Why?" Let's say that I've had an agenda. It took 21 years to complete the agenda at Clemson. There was an undergraduate curriculum to be developed, two masters, a professional degree, an M.S., for which approval of the State Commission on Higher Education was required, and a Ph.D. degree, also needing Commission approval. The development of an outdoor laboratory was a part of the agenda. Likewise, my tenure at Indiana has been focused, perhaps more so than at Clemson, because of the time constraints. University policy does not permit one to serve in an administrative position past 65 years of age. Here there have been retirements and replacements, a few new positions added, curriculum revisions and expansions, developments at Hilltop Garden and Nature Center and at Bradford Woods, the department's outdoor laboratory, an expansion of the professional development program and a concerted effort for growth in external support, both for research and for training.

Another question is, "Why so long without aspirations to a higher calling, a deanship?" Seldom was I tempted for more than two days at a time. The departments in which I served were comprehensive and large. Deanships were often no more challenging than what I had, and such appointments would have removed me one step further from students.

Would I do it again? Of course I would, without a moment's hesitation. There are parts that I would prefer to change or omit, but for the most part it has been a career which provided for what I would view as a high calling. To see students respond to academic challenges, to follow careers, especially those which represented what some would refer to as overachievements, to view value systems which reflect ethical character, and to know that many who chose this field have come to realize its values to the communities in which we live and work have merged to provide a high level of satisfaction. To know that the field increasingly has been accepted as essential to our communities, our states and nation creates a good feeling.

In my judgment, too many educators are too focused, too specialized and too single-minded of purpose. I believe that much of the really creative teaching at the undergraduate level is taking place in the smaller programs, those which have not become a part of the publish or perish syndrome. Faculty of the comprehensive, Ph.D. granting universities have found it difficult to focus on good teaching in the face of mounting pressure to secure extramural funding, to publish in respected journals and to provide excellent graduate instruction and supervision. Faculty of small, less comprehensive programs are more likely to have had practical experience. During our first half-century one could assume that most faculty had, in fact, spent time in practical, experiential work settings. The new wave increasingly will possess little or no practical experience, little commitment to the field other than through theoretical, conceptual research. Most will be little moved or bothered by application. Thus, the comprehensive programs will have increasing difficulty relating to the field. The danger is that we aren't yet able to guarantee our survival on theoretical scholarship.

There are a number of things that stand out and make these years seem special. The opportunity to develop and nurture the program at Clemson, the completion of the academic agenda which I cited earlier, involvement in professional activities from the state societies to the national level and the opportunity to chair the established, well-respected department at Indiana University all combined to create, for me, a perception of success. No recognition or honor, however, had quite the impact which was felt when a former student's daughter was given the name "Brantley." Talk about pride! Talk about humility!

I'm not sure when I realized or accepted the fact that my chosen field had been good to me. I never felt cocky about the things of which I was a part. On the other hand, when the opportunity arose to serve as President of the Society of Park and Recreation Educators, President of the National Recreation and Park Association, Chairman of the Council on Accreditation, President of the Academy of Leisure Sciences, and a member of the South Carolina Commission for Parks, Recreation and Tourism, all came together in what seemed to be a natural succession of opportunities which followed hard work and a deep commitment to being a principal player. Each position, in its own way, affirmed that the things with which we were involved were important.

Twenty years ago I had the opportunity to host the inaugural meeting of the department heads/chairs at Hilton Head Island, South Carolina. I recall how optimistic the 65 participants were, individually and collectively. Last year I hosted the group at Indiana University. Participants numbered 28. Optimism was not nearly so evident. Yet, there was not a feeling of gloom and doom. Among the group were visionaries, more realists than were present at the first conference but visionaries nonetheless. I'm optimistic about the present leadership. I'm optimistic about faculty who, in large measure, continue the traditions of good teaching. I'm optimistic about the new breed of scholars. I'm hopeful about higher education, about its ability to provide an environment in which teaching and learning can thrive. I'm grateful to have been a part of this wonderful movement for more than 30 years.

Building a Program at MSU

Lou Twardzik

After a master of science degree and a director's degree in Recreation Administration from Indiana University, and after 10 years as the State Recreation Consultant in the Tennessee Division of State Parks, I spent the next 31 years as a professor at Michigan State University: 13 of them as the first chair of the Department of Park and Recreation Resources. It must be understood that MSU is a land grant university, and that most teaching appointments include research or extension time, and almost all faculty in the College of Agriculture and Natural Resources are appointed on a 12-month basis. My appointment was 50 percent teaching, and 50 percent extension, which I retained throughout my career at MSU. I believe I was the first chair ever to hold a 50 percent cooperative extension service appointment because I insisted on it and I'm certain I was the first and only chair appointed in the college without a doctorate. In a large sense my university appointment was quite similar to my work in Tennessee. At least half of my time was expected to be involved in educating people off campus. These experiences impacted my style and productivity as the chair of a university academic unit.

I have strong feelings about the role and importance of the chair. This person is uniquely positioned at the interface of the faculty and the administration. The chair becomes the most important member of the faculty and the most important member of the administration because the chair acts in the best interests of both. I consider all university administration above the chair to be adjunct to the purpose of the university; to discover the truth, teach the truth and extend the truth.

As an undergraduate at Notre Dame, I gained my first insight regarding the vast worth of a university through Cardinal Neuman's ideas about preparing "educated gentlemen." In *Xenophon* we read of the young Persian nobility being taught to ride on horseback and to speak the truth; both being among the accomplishments of a gentleman. Neuman's concept of educating the whole person seemed to fit perfectly a contemporary university professional curriculum, especially in our field where we have the obligation to produce both a competent rider of horses as well as a student dedicated to the truth in all matters. As I have written elsewhere, college and university park, recreation, leisure, and tourism departments should join with general studies in interpreting this philosophy. The product should be educated citizens and educated professionals. Ours is truly a field of study and practice without end. Those who have a hand in it are amongst the most fortunate.

In the early 1980s, the State of Michigan underwent a severe economic crisis. Detroit lost its world monopoly in automobile manufacturing to Japan and Germany. The universities, along with all other public and private institutions, agencies and programs dependent on state funding had no choice but to make extraordinary budget adjustments. The only time a university can legally dismiss tenured faculty is when it can justify that a condition known as exigency exists: extreme financial distress. This gives the board of trustees and the president authority to dismiss tenured faculty and terminate entire programs, which they did. Our department withstood the cut in faculty by dismissing our visiting and guest lecturer programs. As a result, we did not lose a single full-time faculty member.

In the College of Education, however, the Recreation and Leisure Studies Program, with three full-time faculty and a secretary, was scheduled to be terminated. This was noted in all the media along with other terminations of faculty and programs throughout the university. I called a meeting of the departmental faculty and told them that I thought we should attempt to save that program by having it transferred to our department. I felt that our field of study would be better represented in one department and college rather than the present situation wherein we were recognized as a "parks" department and it would also give us a basis for additional growth and professional acceptance. I either did a poor job of explaining my stand or they didn't believe it, but the faculty voted against the idea. I went to the dean and explained the situation, which I thought was a once in a lifetime opportunity, and told him of the negative faculty vote. I asked him to override it and he did. Then, sometime later in the 1980s, there was a significant drop in traditional job opportunities and student enrollments dropped accordingly. As a result, we would have lost our departmental status because of low enrollments except that the "new" therapeutic recreation majors provided us with respectable numbers.

During the early building years of our department, the faculty was young and untenured and very productive. I had strong feelings about the importance of an international dimension for our curriculum, partly because of the outstanding tradition and commitment of MSU in international programs throughout the world. The problem was that in the College of Agriculture and Natural Resources the major entry points were closed to us because we were not identified with crop, soil, and dairy production interests. As a result, I became active in the World Leisure and Recreation Association and was subsequently able to identify several attractive international study and research opportunities for our faculty in Europe and Asia. The reluctance of the faculty to respond was baffling and frustrating. I knew that faculty in other universities would be ecstatic with similar opportunities. I finally realized that in my zeal to move into a new program area I did not remember the primary interest of young faculty—tenure. In those days, tenure granting authorities did not consider international programs of academic significance unless journal articles resulted, and the faculty were fully aware of it. They continued to limit their interests to domestic issues. Today, much later, I am pleased to note that faculty, graduate students, and the curriculum are fully internationalized.

Any department that did not offer a Ph.D. degree in our college was suspect. That goal became our highest priority. It required years of concentrated work by the faculty and never has my temper been tested over so long a time. At that same time we granted a doctorate in Park and Recreation Resources through the Department of Resource Development and the Department of Forestry and it was recognized as being of higher quality than the Ph.D. program in at least one other department in the college. Our proposal to offer our own Ph.D. program was studied and modified by representatives of the other departments in the college for almost three years. I finally went to the provost to make my case. He told me that he would approve our Ph.D. program in half an hour after it arrived on his desk. That is when it became apparent that our problem was with our colleagues in the college and not the provost's office.

Within a month of my visit, the program was approved. The provost said something prophetic to me that day in his office. But, as usual in matters of prophecy, it was lost on me. He said, "In a way, your success is unfortunate. I've shared some of your M.S. theses with other chairs to show them that M.S. programs can be of high quality. But now you will undoubtedly resort to type; like the others, your M.S. program will suffer." I said never. He was right. Faculty tend to spend more time with Ph.D. candidates and usually reserve choice assistantships for them. All of this attention was formerly focused on M.S. candidates.

Chairs should understand the special interests of their deans and the provosts and focus on them in establishing departmental priorities. I enjoyed knowing an assistant dean who equated departmental achievement with quantifiable accomplishments. He, in turn, understood the need of the state legislature for measurements they could use in demonstrating the productivity of the various universities in Michigan and allocating funds based on the simplistic Student Credit Hours Per Full Time Faculty Equivalent (SCH/FTFE). By following this route, the early growth of our department was escalated beyond my expectations.

In the early 1970s, while discussing the teaching assignment of a new assistant professor, Paul Risk, who was appointed to develop and teach a program emphasis in interpretation, he mentioned his interest in teaching wilderness survival. I encouraged him to prepare a course outline based on environmental concepts. He did. I was pleased but told him to change the title from Wilderness Survival to something more academically acceptable. He did, but thankfully, I changed my mind and Wilderness Survival became a piece of history at Michigan State University.

Dr. Risk was the most charismatic teacher I have ever known. He took his students on field trips where they cried and cheered while carrying rabbits all day, and walking waist deep through swamps. At the end of the day they were required to build a fire and fix a meal with their rabbit as the entree (this later changed to chickens when parents complained). They needed to know more about their source of food.

The popularity of Dr. Risk's course was phenomenal. In a few years it grew to being offered every quarter term. He lectured to a full auditorium of 300. It was the largest available, while his video class presentations were available in a central location for individual student viewing, and for the off-campus students via TV. In the Spring Term, 1971, more than 600 students enrolled in Wilderness Survival. For ten years that course served our purposes, as it did Dr. Risk's. Even though we were a new department with a small faculty, we led the entire university in SCH/FTFE's. During that time I was able to demand the necessary additional funds to accommodate our record-breaking productivity and it was forthcoming. I gradually converted that soft money for teaching assistants, along with extension and research support, into tenure-track appointments. The university needed those SCH/FTFE's. It was a critical time in the development of the department and those extra positions provided the necessary boost to come on-line with a new research thrust, status and productivity as a department.

There is nothing immoral or disloyal in negotiating your interests with the university. This was true even before it was popularized by athletic coaches at Michigan State University. It was generally accepted around this place that I would be buried along with my desk. So, when the inevitable notices from the university arrived about retirement benefits, I demurred for an appropriate time, but eventually began to negotiate my interests. One of the most important was an unheard of agreement that my salary would be returned to the department in the form of two new tenure-tracked junior faculty. It was, and they are here.

There is a great difference between the attitude, productivity, and growth of faculty when they become the other family as opposed to teachers who complete their scheduled hours and escape to their first family at every opportunity. The collective faculty should be the other family, working together for the betterment of the department and each other without deterring from their primary responsibilities to the first families. The chair should expect that when it becomes necessary for a teacher to take an evening class that there is no grief forthcoming about taking time from the first family. An attitude has to be established that both families have responsibilities to each other. This essentially means that faculty do not approach teaching as an 8:00 to 5:00 job. There are other kinds of employment that feature those hours.

It also means the chair should nurture the family interests of the faculty, including occasional social events with the first families. In this type of recreation planning, the chair must be sensitive to the social lifestyles of the faculty rather than that of the chair; it will range from square dancing and "bring a dish to pass" to formal dinners and retreats.

If the college's mission statement is worth the effort required to put it together, it should provide considerable leeway for individual departmental growth. The annual program established by the dean for all departments within the college should therefore not be considered as the department's program. The department's future is based on its own needs and they are unique to the needs of the public, faculty, students, and alumni of that department, and they should not be mired by the college's mission. The chair and faculty have to take advantage of every opportunity to call attention to and explain the interests and needs of the department, to the point of creating "opportunities," traveling with the dean (preferably by car which encourages conversation), or inviting the dean and provost to speak at professional meetings.

Each department has to feel free to explore its future. A continued, vigorous program by the department to keep its mission statement current will help the college identify and pursue its mission. Besides, you can't ever be sure what college will domesticate the department next year. Don't interpret the college's mission to discourage chairs from innovation in management and program planning. Treat it, instead, as a series of guidelines, not as a risk-free justification for the status quo.

As a field of study we are either so insecure or introverted that we do comparatively little to keep the public and our markets informed about who we are and what we accomplish. Within each university there is a unit that has as its sole responsibility, extending information about the university to everybody else. If you wonder why certain schools are consistently covered by the media, it's not only the accomplishments of the students, faculty, and alumni; it's largely because there is a chair who is sensitive to the value of publicizing the accomplishments of individual faculty and the department and he or she has made the effort to know those faceless university publicists. They have a job to do and they appreciate a chair's assistance in doing it with information about the department. Interestingly enough, unlike the old departmental newsletters, there is no cost to using the media network.

A university has an absolute requirement to deal with the truth. As amorphous as the word is, there is, nevertheless, the commitment, at the very least, to critically inquire into all the interests that impinge on any issues before it. The university cannot confine itself to one path, regardless of its attractiveness. The university is required to explore the various interests involved in any issue before it takes a stand on what constitutes the truth. For instance, do we automatically teach that everything the environmental organizations propose and propound represents the truth and those who are against green are wrong? Or do we require a platform for the anti-green people and organizations for the exposure of our students of policy and management? Do we automatically perpetuate the notion that wildlife has to be harvested or do we expose our students to the views of PETA (People for the Ethical Treatment of Animals)? Are the interests of all the parties equally reflected in our lectures? If your answer is no, you are not a university. You are something else.

This concern often places university faculty in a difficult position in their relationships with agencies and organizations that have a commitment to advance their own values as represented by the interests of their members. University faculty have no such limited responsibilities. It is just the opposite. Everybody agrees that the university, when addressing an issue, is required to address its various sides. But how realistically do we work at it in comparison to our belief in diversity of gender and race? It is not unexpected that faculty in our field come down on the side of environmentalism, as espoused in the programs of national environmental organizations. Membership and literature in the "green gang" is most commonly available in academic and faculty offices. Seldom are those with opposing views. It takes a concerted effort by the chair and faculty to assure that students are not limited to a monocultural academic perception of their field of study. To assure that students have an opportunity to know the various sides of issues, it is incumbent on the chair to program these views into the academic experience and environment. It is an effort that is not always appreciated by the faculty, or the professional and special interests; nevertheless, one does not achieve diversity, nor fulfill the mission of the university about the truth, by listening to only one perspective on any issue.

When it became our turn as a department in 1985 to select the speaker for the annual Natural Resources Banquet, I felt that we should try to attract someone who could speak to both the public agency side of natural resources management and the side of the private sector. I chose the former U.S. Secretary of the Interior, James Watt. That, however, did not seem reasonable to the mainline environmental interests, who along with the Michigan Recreation and Park Association, boycotted the affair.

An interesting sidelight to Mr. Watt's participation in our week-long series of meetings, symposia, lectures and seminars revolves around my unsuccessful attempt a week earlier to entice a prominent, local TV personality to meet with my evening class on Park and Recreation Resources Policy. I wanted him to discuss the impact of communications and the media on policy formulation. He refused. I thanked him nonetheless, and told him that I looked forward to meeting him next week at the university news conference. His interest was aroused because he did not know about the news conference. When I told him that it was with James Watt, he became interested to the point of being agitated and he demanded that Mr. Watt do a half hour live appearance on his program. I told him that was not possible because of the demands on Mr. Watt's time, and I was scheduling his time. As a result, he changed his mind and agreed to make an appearance before my class and I promised to deliver Mr. Watt to his TV studio.

The most important part of all this is that it was an amazing TV program. The TV host and his select media colleagues were positively salivating while waiting to get the former Secretary of the Interior before them. Before it was over, though, the cool Mr. Watt walked away with his perpetual half-smile intact and left behind several demolished local news people. According to my further agreement with that TV personality, a tape of that performance was produced for my classroom use. That tape is now one of the best teaching aids I have, and I show it in every policy course I teach. Colleagues who teach other aspects of resource policy have requested a copy of the tape, and I have obliged. It shows students, first hand, the impact of the media on policy and how both sides pursue their own views. Many students were dumbfounded because, while they didn't admit it, they originally perceived Mr. Watt as the devil incarnate of the environmental movement while the media and national environmental groups could do no wrong. Where and when were those perceptions about policy formulation developed except in the classroom? Stewart and Vogt define the issue clearly, "As educators, we should model critical thinking about policy choices and their implications, rather than falling into the idiot's practice of empty advocacy."

In 1990 it was our turn again, and I invited Alston Chase. Dr. Chase was fortunate enough to publish his best selling book *Playing God in Yellowstone* just before the famous Yellowstone fires in 1988. Dr. Chase, a former university professor of philosophy, was recognized as the intellectual critic of the National Park Service. This time we did not have any boycotts and, in fact, we drew a record crowd. It is now generally recognized that this department takes its responsibilities for diversity seriously by not becoming a handmaiden to any piece of it.

There comes a time when an academic administrator has to calm down and look at a "favored project" that is not going anyplace, cut the losses in time and energy, and walk away from it. When I was appointed to the MSU Faculty Intercollegiate Athletic Committee, I was surprised to find that the conventional wisdom about the powerful role of intercollegiate athletics in the university were, if anything, understated. For instance, when Clarence "Biggie" Munn, former MSU athletic director and chair, Department of Health, Physical Education and Recreation, appeared before the committee to justify a change in the rule that prohibited freshmen from playing in varsity games until their sophomore year, he said "we should vote to remove that obstacle to assure good recruiting in the Big 10 because the other regional university athletic associations already have or are considering it, and MSU and the Big 10 could be at a serious recruiting disadvantage." Biggie then told a few more of his famous jokes. The vote was taken, it sailed through, and I was the only dissenting faculty vote. As most everybody knows, it is now the "law of the land," and with it my introduction to the imbalance of the university and intercollegiate athletics. I served on that committee for four years during the early '70s.

At a National Recreation and Parks Association (NRPA) meeting in Miami several years later, the Society of Parks and Recreation Educators (SPRE) past presidents met for their breakfast and the annual exhortation by the current president to use our "combined wisdom to continue assisting the profession and society." Then President Dr. David Austin of Indiana University advanced some priority projects and asked for assistance. I kept eating. Finally, the last concern he had was to address the emerging problems with university athletics since many athletes were enrolled in park and recreation classes. My old friend and colleague Dr. Leslie Reid of Texas A&M University commented loud enough for all to hear, including the waitresses, that I had not accepted any of the other responsibilities and suggested that the least I could do was undertake the one on the role of intercollegiate athletics. I spent a year preparing a report, "The Imbalanced University: Conflict of Values with Intercollegiate Athletics."

In the report I noted that the sad state of affairs in academics and athletics in American universities is due primarily to the inability of the university to face up to the problems and correct them. Special designation for being at fault were the university presidents and their trustees—not the coaches. I further claimed that the universities had demonstrated their inability to resolve this problem and because of the severity of the damage runaway athletics was doing to the country and its perception of the role of higher education, that the U.S. Congress had the responsibility to step in and order the National Academy of Sciences to prepare a report for them on the subject.

I sent the report to the SPRE president and received a nice letter of thanks. The NRPA Board of Directors refused to act on it. The MSU presidency was in a state of transition. I played it safe and sent a copy to both incoming and outgoing presidents. Never heard from either. At a social function several years later the provost mentioned that he appreciated my paper. Getting desperate, I sent copies to various national and local sports media. Not a word, not even acknowledgment. Another year passed. It finally occurred to me that I had become too emotionally involved in the resolution of the issue and I was spending too much time on it without adequate benefits returning to the department. I closed my file on the problem, late but wiser.

The role of the chair has usually been limited to the confines of academia. Today that role should be expanded to include a working relationship with local, state, and federal agencies, and the private sector. How these relationships are developed is not important. The objective is to create an awareness of the department's programs and needs with a wider circle of people and organizations.

The outreach linkages should never be considered the exclusive domain of the chair. In most departments some faculty have special interests and talents in outreach programs and they should be encouraged to develop them. However, it's not enough today to have faculty actively engaged with a variety of organizations with a heavy national and even international travel schedule unless there are substantive benefits returned to the department, including funding for special programs, institutes, and research. At MSU, several faculty and the chair have long-standing outreach relationships with a variety of power points. As a result, when it was decided that Michigan needed a travel and tourism center at MSU, we invited a group of state legislators, both houses, both parties, to dinner at the Kellogg Center on campus. We explained our rationale. It was accepted shortly thereafter and there is now a Michigan Travel and Tourism Recreation Resources Center, a separate, but associated, unit with our department headed by one of our senior professors, Dr. Donald Holecek. Funding by the state legislature is in the best possible currency, a continuing college budget item.

Chairs should always work at extending the mission of the department through the interests of the faculty, the vision for the profession, linkage with other universities and government agencies and legislative leaders, and upgrading teaching, research, and extension programs. Only with a constant exertion to better existing programs will the department remain relevant to the university and society. This places the department in a growth mode, always changing, but only in a controlled way. Mission statements are the rational approach to policy formulation, administration, and management but they are of limited use unless they recognize the value of opportunism. If both chair and faculty are immersed in their science, there is not much hope for a department of park, recreation, leisure, and tourism or whatever. Even if the chair is one of vision and understands the academic enterprise, it is doubtful he or she alone can pull a dead weight faculty of self-absorbed scientists into the necessary growth mode made up of several parts of creativity, opportunity, and the scientific method.

All this interest in change and growth is based on the fact that the university is comprised of two separate and unequal entities: the basic disciplines and the applied fields of study. The university is required to offer courses of study in the basic disciplines in the arts and sciences: Biology, Mathematics, Chemistry, Physics, Psychology, and the like. It is not required to offer any of the applied fields of study except those that it feels fulfill the function of the university and the changing needs of society.

The problem with some university programs in our field is that the current crop of faculty is programmed to publish only in refereed journals. This system serves the disciplinarians well but it can be self-defeating for the applied departments. When professors work through the publishing phase of assuring a future in academia, they often feel they no longer require exposure and involvement in the wonders of the ever

changing student body and public clientele interests. Instead, they are satisfied to measure it. The sad part about this is that the university is chock-
full of people who are experts at measuring everything and anything, and
some of them are knowledgeable about our field as well. And when the
national and state economies require severe adjustments, as is the case
today, those applied fields that are perceived as not being as relevant to
the public's needs have to bear the heavy sacrifices.

Above all, professors should not be left to their own devices. Only
the religious can stand the freedom of the cloistered. Others tend to become slothful with such an excess of pardon from the polity, such as in
tenure. As an isolated university condition from life, tenure can become
increasingly unreal without accountability and direction of some sort.
Continual and systematic evaluation of tenured and untenured faculty
by the faculty and chair is the answer. But that is not enough. Like the
religious, more is needed—a vision of good. That is the real role of
the chair—to instill into the faculty a vision for the department. When
this vision is accepted as a mission by the faculty there is no need to be
concerned about tenured or junior faculty slippage because a faculty, so
driven, is like a beautifully balanced machine made up of many different
parts. There is no need to tinker; get out of the way and provide only occasional guidance.

Don't consider accepting the extra work of a chair unless you have
an unmistakable desire to lead and develop the academic and professional
interests of your field. If you do, there is no problem with the extra work
and time. It simply becomes a part of what you very much want to do.
As Dustin continues to remind us, being a tenured professor is as good
as it gets. The question is begged, why get involved in administration
where you take leave of the best for what is obviously not, where there
are uncertainties and pain is guaranteed? When a professor takes on the
role of department chair, it's because there is a personal fire, unknown to
anybody else, to accomplish something greater than the usual academic
satisfactions and challenges. It has to be the fulfillment of leading into
better ways of doing things, carte blanche to part the waters, the excitement
of creating new opportunities unseen by others, and the satisfaction of
watching them develop into awareness and acceptability as policy and
eventually programs and benefits to students, the department, the professional field, and the larger society.

12 Thoughts from a Green Twig
Phyllis Ford

Translated from Greek, my first name, Phyllis, means green bough. The old saying, "As the twig is bent, so grows the tree," is very relevant to my life and today. As a retired college administrator, I am pretty well-bent yet still green. I spent half of my professional career in college administration so I have seen quite a few changes in the professional preparation of recreation and leisure service personnel, but I still have much to learn.

How did I become an administrator in higher education? The answer will be revealed. I've been chair at four universities and the interview processes are probably good examples of the evolution of college hiring practices from the 1960s to the 1990s. Taken in order, they went something like this:

"Oh, there you are. I thought I'd see you. We're interested in having you as chair of our Recreation Education Program and would like to spend some time discussing it." What a greeting! There I was, walking through a hotel at the American Alliance for Health, Physical Education, Recreation, and Dance (AAHPERD) National Convention in 1969, and was thusly greeted by Lou Alley. I knew there was a vacancy at Iowa because Swede Scholar was leaving there to go to New Mexico as Ed Heath was leaving New Mexico to go to Oregon State University. So I thought, "Why don't I try to go from the University of Oregon to Iowa and complete the circle?" Needless to say, I weighed all the pros and cons, submitted my application, attended a brief interview at the University of Iowa, and subsequently accepted the position. Why?

Two of the Iowa faculty had been students at Oregon so I felt pretty much at home. I was interested in the challenge of curriculum development as were all three of the faculty. Besides, they had that marvelous MacBride Field Campus where I could continue my work in outdoor education. (I think seeing two deer cross the road at MacBride was the culminating push.) I had been frustrated with lack of trust and respect for recreation in our two person department at Oregon and felt the change would do me good. It seemed that curriculum development for recreation at Oregon was an uphill battle with boulders falling all around, but I didn't burn my bridges. I left with the understanding that should they need someone in five to ten years, I would wish to be considered.

After being in Iowa for two years, I received a telephone call at 11 o'clock one night. (11 is only 9 in Oregon.) Would I return that fall to assume the chair of the Department of Recreation and Park Management (now up to four faculty) as Lynn Rodney was to be acting dean? So, against my professional ethics—never leave a job before three years—I agreed and left to return to Oregon. After all, an Oregon position in the present is worth two jobs that might materialize in five to ten years. No interview, no application, no other candidates. I just went back. That was actually the second time I went to Oregon without any other applicants.

About 13 years later, Roger Wiley at Washington State University asked me, "Why don't you apply for our university? You have spent some time on our campus, given lectures here, and are known by the faculty. This is the second time I've suggested it." So I applied, complete with forms this time. There were also three sets of interviews. The first was at the annual AAHPERD Conference in a room on a lower section of the hotel reached by a flight of steps off the lobby. On my way, I slipped on the tile floor in my new "proper for interviews" shoes and fell flat. I knew that everyone in AAHPERD must have seen me, especially the search committee. Of course, no one was in sight and the committee was downstairs waiting as I hobbled in trying to appear cool and nonchalant.

The interview in the hotel was mild and friendly; however, the second interview, held on campus, was more like doctoral orals. I had no idea what to expect and was asked to present my administrative philosophy extemporaneously. That served me right. For years I had asked students to explain the values of recreation without notes. The hardest question they asked me was, "How do you feel about antidisestablishmentarianism?" There was a good reason for the question, but I had to think for a moment before I replied. Then I was asked to interview the secretaries. Or were they interviewing me? I never figured it out, but through the process I was able to glean that they were very loyal to the university, and they wanted to know what kind of standards I had for maintaining university policy. The third interview was in June with the dean who had been out of town during the second interview. I had been told I would be offered the position if he approved. I guess I wasn't nervous, as this time I didn't fall on any floors, and he approved of me. If there were other candidates, I never knew of them.

Why did I go this time? At an Oregon post-tenure review, the committee asked me what I had planned for the rest of my career. I had taught, written, been department head, been on many university committees including the Graduate Council, Faculty Personnel, President's Advisory, and Academic Review and had spent a total of 23 years at Oregon. Still, there were a few years left in my career so what did I plan to do next that would make a contribution to the department, school, or university? I had no plans so I decided to try a new venture—chair of Physical Education, Sport, and Leisure Studies at Washington State. I was pretty tired of teaching a full load, advising graduate students, and being department head in a small department with hundreds of majors, so I tried a new job.

Two and one half years later, another phone call came from a former Oregon student. "Hello, Dr. Ford. We are developing a slate of applicants for the position at Michigan State University and would welcome your application."

"Hi, Dan. Thanks, but you probably want a known researcher. MSU is a big research university. I am more interested in curriculum development."

"That's what some of us think we need. We offer everything you can think of but it needs to be coordinated."

MSU is a major research university and it did offer recreation and park resources courses in about six different options. What a wonderful place with which to be affiliated. So I applied, filled out forms, updated what had become a rather extensive vita, and forwarded all to the search committee. By now things were really advanced as far as applications and faculty searches were concerned. I spent three days in interviews. I met with the search committee, the entire department (twice), the dean, three associate deans or their representatives, the provost, chairs from other departments in the College of Agriculture and Natural Resources, and some students.

Because of slow mail, I had not received the interview agenda, including the fact that I would be asked to give a presentation on administrative styles. Since I didn't know I was to have prepared anything, when the request came I spoke extemporaneously again, being very glad I had kept up on my reading and had recently done some writing relating to administration. Evidently, whatever passed my lips was acceptable, for soon thereafter I was offered the position. At this point, I had the advantage of being in a minority class (female) and the university was committed to increasing the ratio of female administrators.

Incidentally, when I was applying for the positions at Iowa, Washington State, and Michigan State, I had also applied for three other chair positions. In one case, I was told forthrightly that I couldn't handle the job because I was a woman and would have to work with a particular man. I thought that was ridiculous because I knew and respected that person and wished other universities offered the type of program he directed at that time. I didn't know a woman couldn't possibly "handle" him, and withdrew my application. Another university informed me, "You are not qualified," and dropped my name from the list with no explanation. In a third case, the dean chose his favorite candidate. That was a real modern case of violation of affirmative action. I was told I was one of the top three candidates but was never invited for an interview nor informed in writing about the final selection. I learned about the appointment from reading a magazine, and later the search committee chair told me that I had been the top candidate until favoritism took over.

Those instances probably sum up the history of applying for an administrative position from 1969 to 1990. It may be the history of getting any faculty position in a university. Even my first job as a university assistant professor came about when a dean drove across the country looking for a person (preferably a woman) to add to his one man Recreation and Park Management faculty. He told me later that he never sent out job announcements. If he and his cohorts didn't know of anyone qualified for the position, there wasn't anyone. Lucky for me he was seeking a woman and I was the only new female doctorate with a background in outdoor and general recreation in the country at that time—at least the only one of which he and his colleagues were aware. So being a woman and being somewhat known helped me considerably in the positions I acquired and worked against me in the positions I did not get.

Today, we hope the process is more objective. However, I know that is not always the case. I am not bitter about the three "put downs" because, while I have been discriminated against three times, I also benefited three times by that same, "We'll hire whomever we already know and want," system that we trust is no longer practiced. Open applications, screening by objective committee members including those from other fields, carefully orchestrated interviews, and affirmative action reports and approval are a better way to go.

Some of the things I really enjoyed about administration were: seeing young faculty get their first publication; mentoring a young faculty member through the years until he or she reached tenure; the interaction with other administrators, especially concerning the functioning of the college and university; directing a department self-study; and meeting the National Recreation and Parks Association (NRPA) criteria for accreditation. This last activity was accomplished at three universities and was always different, challenging and rewarding in seeing the faculty work together toward a common goal remote from personal research and service interests.

On the other hand, I always regretted having fewer classes and less contact with students. I had directed over 50 theses and dissertations as a faculty member and had worked with literally thousands of students. I know I missed teaching the most, particularly as the administrative positions became more complex and time for students disappeared.

I disliked annual reviews of the faculty. It is difficult to point out a person's weaknesses when you know they haven't changed in years and won't change in the future. What can you say to someone who just does the minimum while attempting to give him or her enough motivation to, at least, not do less? How do you tell the best teacher in the department he or she will probably not be granted tenure because of the paucity of writing? How can you reward the top researcher who is also the worst teacher? How can you motivate the lazy or direct the overly ambitious?

With shrinking budgets, how many ways are there to say, "You did a marvelous job this year. Next year do more, but do it with less money."? That was probably the most onerous task I ever had. A close second was having to let secretarial staff go because there wasn't enough money to pay them. On the seniority system, it may have been the best secretary whose job had to be terminated because that secretary had been there the shortest time. Also difficult for me was firing "inherited" secretarial staff for inefficiency—particularly since the union regulations demand evidence of every error. How can you convince the union that a secretary who eats garlic and orange juice for breakfast and drives students away with her breath is not efficient? Or what do you do with a secretary who tells everyone she is a recreation major and aspires to teach belly dancing—then demonstrates a bit? It is hard enough to document every error but to complain about those other items gets into personalities and one doesn't terminate union employees because of individual idiosyncrasies.

At one of the universities, one of my busiest and most varied days consisted of interviewing a candidate for university president, helping a mentally disturbed male adult who had wandered in from the other side of the state to find a place to spend the night other than the university swimming pool, and dealing with a peeping Tom in the women's locker room. I have had to deal with a manic depressive faculty member who disappeared from town, an employee accused of sexual harassment, claims of incompetence because I failed to support a faculty member for tenure, student drivers who were reported to the governor's office for consuming beer in a state car, and many other equally bizarre tasks that are never mentioned in texts on administration.

Because of my administrative status, I could intervene for students who were having problems with registration or graduation requirements. I was always able to convince the "powers that be" to listen to the student's side of the story, and I was able to help students overcome some administrative "red tape." That was always both frustrating, in that I could never tolerate inefficiency when it came to fairness to students, and uplifting, as I could help students understand how to resolve conflict by rational behavior. The day a young man brought me a rose because he had given up on solving his problem until I helped him resolve it to his satisfaction will remain in my memory as verification that it is worth the time and effort to help one person solve one problem—no matter how many other challenges there are to meet.

While I usually enjoy writing, I came to dislike writing reports again and again, each on a different format and for different time segments. Annual reports for academic years sometimes included summer school and sometimes did not, or the request came from one who hadn't thought it out. Some annual reports meant the calendar year, but there was also the state fiscal year, the federal fiscal year, and once the period of new salary raises (March). These constant requests for different forms of data made computerizing records futile as they could not be used to add later data. It was start from scratch time after time.

I didn't like working with faculty who did not maintain standards, especially for student papers or for quality course content, or who didn't follow university policies. I had a hard time accepting the point of view of faculty who were more interested in research than students. I was concerned with faculty who thought academic freedom meant being able to teach only what and when they wanted to teach, and that it was perfectly correct to advise students in ways that were against university curriculum requirements. It is difficult to handle a case where the student can't graduate because the faculty member "waived" a required course or credits. I found it hard to motivate faculty with no ideas and faculty with set ideas. "We don't care, you decide," and, "We've never done it that way and can't see why we should change now," are great challenges for any administrator.

It was hard not to have time to teach, to serve, and to write. I wasn't smart enough to give up some of those things and worked far into the night and on weekends trying to continue to be "productive." I know that human beings like challenges and puzzles. If we didn't, the multi-million dollar businesses of jigsaw puzzles, crossword puzzles, the Rubik's

Cubes, and the card and board games would all go bankrupt. I love puzzles and always thought of problems as challenges or puzzles to be solved—something I now do in the leisure of retirement. I never had administrative "problems," just lots of different types of challenges and puzzles.

But I sat too much. And I found it is lonely at the top, particularly for a single woman. As an administrator, one must seek friends who are not part of the faculty or not with the university. I joined hiking clubs until I was 55 years old. Then I joined natural history societies, and spent a lot of money telephoning friends and family just to have a "sounding board."

I am a bit of a coward. I like to do what I think I can do well and had given up marriage years before because I wasn't sure I could handle two important roles equally well. I believed that old quotation, "Things excellent are as difficult as they are rare," and I didn't want to stop trying to be excellent in academia. It is often difficult to be a single woman administrator, particularly in a college where all the other chairs are men. It is difficult at socials, dinners, and meetings to be in conversation with a male colleague until another man comes along and then be spoken across as if the men were embarrassed to be conversing with a woman while their wives talked together across the room. I can't talk about children and grandchildren and prefer to discuss natural resource policy issues or topics related to higher education. I developed a reputation as a good cook so I could fit in with the wives but only as an outsider. After all, I was, to some, that woman who worked with their husbands.

One failure, I think, is that I have never been able to convince many people that natural resources is a necessary component of recreation and leisure services. Most department chairs and even most faculty seem to be interested in the theory of administration, and the budgetary challenges of recreation, without concern for all the ramifications of the field.

One thing that made my career both unique and fortunate is the cadre of excellent administrators with and under whom I served. I had some of the country's best and most well-known professionals as deans. I studied under Art Daniels at Indiana University, worked under Art Esslinger, Lou Alley, and Celeste Ulrich, and worked with Roger Wiley. Each of these had been President of the American Alliance for Health, Physical Education, and Recreation. Each had high personal and professional standards, understood the profession, was held in high esteem nationally, demonstrated sincere interest in professional service, and understood more than one type of research. What role models!

So, in addition to the positive things mentioned above, what was so great about administration? Certainly the income is a bit higher than for faculty—but the hours are longer and the responsibilities greater. Still, administration offers one the chance to get involved, and make things happen. What might be the big pluses? I learned a great deal and watched myself change. I think I became an administrator by virtue of the fact that I was a caring, organized, and relatively good teacher.

In my first year, someone asked me what was the most important trait of a good administrator, and I replied without thinking, "To be well-organized and to handle lots of things at once." The questioner gave me a strange look but made no reply. Today, if I were asked the same question, I would reply, "To be able to help each faculty member do the best possible job in keeping with the goals of the department and university." I have learned that administration is the direction of human effort, and it should be to help that effort go in the best direction for the good of all. I have also learned that there are many paths to the same goals. Several of us may want to accomplish the same end and there are many ways to get there other than mine. I worked with one person for a while and realized that if we each wanted to go west, she would start out going south while I would start out going north and we would each end up at the same spot at about the same time.

Would I do it over? I don't know. I missed the teaching and the students and the feeling of being a member of a team. (The administrator is more of a coach than a member of the team.) People don't necessarily like authority figures. I took early retirement mainly because I was sitting too much and sitting is not good for one with arthritis. But the bottom line was, it became increasingly difficult to work with less and less money. Cutting productive programs and good faculty and secretaries hurts teaching, research, and service and denies students what education purports to be. When I first started in the field, research was not given as much importance as teaching and service. Today, we seem to be fueled by a plethora of research to the detriment of the students and the profession. Faculty seem to come from fields other than leisure, have little or no experience in professional employment in the field, and are devoted to cranking out articles. But they can't relate their findings to the reality of the profession. I think the pendulum has gone too far in the direction of "publish or perish."

Perhaps in the future there will be a way to recognize the excellent teacher, the servant to the larger community, and the researcher who writes meaningful articles that can be utilized by the profession. I hope we get away from our historic pattern of jumping on bandwagons because we feel being in leisure services isn't quite enough. Now we are joining business and its affiliation with economic growth. Leisure services is and always has been concerned with what happens to people in their discretionary time regardless of how much money they spend or generate for others. We need to get back to that value. We need to serve the low-income population again and develop some sense of accomplishment among the participants no matter who or where they are, where they go and what they spend. We need to get back to values about the quality of the environment, particularly how it is altered by recreational pursuits. Perhaps it is for future administrators to rekindle this spirit. If they don't do it, recreation and leisure services curricula may well disappear into the sunset as do old administrators.

13 Advancing a Social Agenda

Jim Murphy

Why would anyone in his or her right mind want to ascend to the department chair? In most universities it is largely a stressful, low paying, resource strapped position. Oh, I suppose a few "eager beavers" might jump at the chance. But others would probably judge such people to be crazy. After all, how can anyone engage in scholarly pursuits or find the time to carefully develop lesson plans, or have an opportunity to think and ponder the multitude of questions that ought to rightfully occupy the mind of a professor when beset by the demands of being department chair?

Actually, my assessment of serving as department chair at a comprehensive four-year state university is that it carries almost no authority, little glamour, some resentment from colleagues, and a crisis every other day to confront with which I have had little or no previous experience. I do believe, however, that being able to put into motion ideas largely developed at faculty meetings or in articles from years past provides a certain amount of satisfaction. In that regard, I have seized the opportunity to exert what little influence is available to me. The position has given me an opportunity to pass along ideas, insights and suggestions to my colleagues. And I have been able to collaborate with them at a new level on a variety of curricular and scholarly projects.

As I reflect back on my early writings, I urged colleagues to be more egalitarian, sensitive to diverse populations, create flatter, more flexible organizations which would be more accessible to constituents, and develop interactive styles of leadership that serve to empower people. Being department chair has given me the opportunity to practice what I preach. And, over the years, I have learned that effectively managing a curriculum in a college or university requires a number of other qualities as well.

Perhaps most importantly, the department chair must have vision, a thought-out perspective about the future of leisure as well as the role of the program within the academy. With such a vision the administrator can help cultivate thinking among faculty about the implications of the curriculum. Maybe even more important are the implications for society and the place of leisure within the broader context of our social, ecological, cultural, physical, and familial milieu. The curriculum must be viewed in its entirety; how the overall program prepares students for a professional career in leisure services; how students can be educated to better participate in a society characterized by change; and how a value system can be nurtured which equally embraces all of our citizens and community members.

In every organization, communication is important. Certainly the chair must listen to the needs and issues of faculty and students. The chair must develop rapport with each faculty member in the program, designing a comfortable context for each person in which communication transpires. Obviously, the chair's own demeanor should serve to inspire, not repel or deter faculty or students. Just as critical for the leisure studies chair are his or her interactions with university administrators. This role may be essential to whether the program is viewed as central to the mission of the university. In fiscally tight times, the department chair has a key role to play in articulating the merits of the place of leisure as both a professional preparation program within higher education and as a fundamental component of general education. I have had to be well-versed in both the meaning of leisure and its benefits to individual and community life. Every day I am confronted with questions of the relevance of leisure, both within the academy and outside. How I treat the questions is essential to gaining respect for me, my department, my faculty, and my program.

In this regard, it is critical for the department chair to interact with the entire academic community. I have seen this role as being essential to forming coalitions and to building support for projects, research, courses, and curricula. Moreover, it cultivates trust through meaningful social participation in work activities. By working to build a sense of community, I strive to develop a sense of belonging and a moral sense of our involvement. My view of fostering a sense of community within academia reflects my similar posture about how leisure is intertwined with human expression. The essence of community life becomes more significant and symbolically meaningful to people if individuals are encouraged to engage in personally fulfilling activities and feel they have a stake in what they do. I believe it is my responsibility to help create a work environment in which faculty work together to establish an environment in which we all are able to experience work that is challenging, interesting, socially significant, and uplifting.

I have found that I must try to foster this type of cottage industry within my unit and articulate its relevance to the larger university structure. By doing so I am helping to mold and foster both an organizational form that is more amenable and responsive to personal expression and one that holds a collective sense of quality living. It is my hope that this approach will more likely lead to colleague satisfaction and improved service to students.

People appear to have a higher degree of commitment in the workplace if they are given opportunities to engage in personally meaningful and interesting work assignments, full appreciation for work done, promotion and growth opportunities, the best possible work conditions, sympathetic understanding of personal problems, and a feeling that they are invited to be in on things. This list of employee needs, often corroborated in a variety of workplace settings, reflects a common desire by employees to be respected as individuals. In my experience this respect is gained through an interactive style of management in which colleagues are encouraged to pursue scholarly activities, teach courses representative of scholarly and professional interests, be a full partner in planning the direction of the program, and be recognized for their contributions and efforts. In a word, faculty colleagues want respect.

There are times all of us have to serve on seemingly irrelevant committees, teach mandatory core courses in which we have little interest, and are asked to set aside personal projects for the mandates of a department or university program. However, these intrusions into our personal workspace can be tolerated if we believe that our needs are recognized, and efforts are made by administration to provide a work structure that will support faculty so they can engage in more creative and personally fulfilling academic assignments.

Perhaps one of the most important roles of a department chair is mentoring faculty in their daily assignments and in helping them make progress with their professional growth activities. This latter area is particularly critical for "junior" faculty. This responsibility is best carried out through modeling exemplary good manners, professional knowledge, openness to change, ethical conduct, sound approach to deliberation, excellence in teaching and scholarship, and perhaps most importantly, support, assistance and guidance for faculty in their teaching and scholarship. Some of us have had wonderful mentors, others have not. If our discipline is to survive, indeed prosper in academia, it will necessitate bold, visionary, and astute leadership. A critical catalyst in this regard will be the ability of department chairs and their unselfish commitment to assist their colleagues to find a secure and challenging workplace and by providing careful guidance in their development as teacher/scholars.

This mentoring role does not necessarily mean the department chair is the most gifted teacher, researcher, or scholar. But, it does mean that the chair is able to move outside himself or herself and stand in the place of his or her faculty. It means that the chair needs to transcend his or her own bias toward teaching strategies, research topics, professional interests, and/or political preference. This is no easy task. Leisure studies is in its youth in the academic life cycle. In order to make a successful transition to adolescence, it has to learn to feel comfortable in its independence as a full-fledged discipline. At the same time, knowing its uniqueness and special contribution to the human condition, our discipline must begin to understand how it fits with other fields of inquiry and meshes with a more complete human, physical, and metaphysical interpretation of individual well-being. As mentors, chairs can make a significant contribution toward maintaining our discipline's presence within the university and strengthening its role as a locus for human development in community life by guiding faculty to view leisure as a fundamental form of human expression.

If specialization and complexity cause us to lose sight of the common elements of our field and their relationships to each other, we will have lessened our ability to provide the most effective and relevant leisure services. The chair's role as a mentor may be the key link to the full maturation of leisure studies, and this is balanced with the chair's important role as a visionary leader to ensure our future presence in the academy. Professionalism, a cornerstone for all fields, requires an expanded interpretation within the academy and the community. In my view it must progress beyond representing a code of conduct, body of knowledge, and specialized training.

Professionalism for leisure studies educators and leisure service personnel has come to require that department chairs and leisure service managers model an interactive style of management that encourages constituent (employee and participant) involvement, decision-making, and choice of leisure options. To ensure that individual faculty and students meet their needs, department chairs must become activists and champions of human expression within their work environment. This new dimension of professionalism suggests that department chairs learn to collaborate more fully with participants, colleagues and clients, rather than pre-assign teaching and committee responsibilities for faculty and/or curriculum for students. By establishing a collaborative relationship, not only will faculty be respected and supported, but an appropriate model will be exhibited to students who will be entering not only the leisure service profession but community life as well.

Much of my exuberance over serving as department chair lies in my conviction about the importance of the immense responsibility of increasing the livability of community life through leisure expression. If such an exalted opportunity is the result of what we do in preparing students for a professional degree, then I believe that those of us who elect to ascend to the position of department chair must take on such responsibility with a full understanding of the contribution of many of our field's past leaders—Charles Brightbill, Mary Wiley, Jackson Anderson, Al Sapora, Lynn Rodney, Harold Meyer, Serena Arnold, Edith Ball, Gerald Fitzgerald, G. Ott Romney, Ardith Frost, and David Gray. These former department chairs were gifted visionary leaders who were recognized as articulate, knowledgeable academicians, and spokespeople for leisure studies in higher education. Indeed, such recognition carried with it an acknowledgment of the rightful place of recreation and leisure in community life. Since leisure studies curricula have served primarily as professional preparation programs, these educational pioneers had communicated the significance and relevance of recreation as an integral part of the fabric of our society.

As I reflect on what I do and what I have accomplished as a department chair, I'm proud of having cared for my faculty colleagues, for having assisted them in facilitating student learning, and for having encouraged them to seize the opportunity to serve as facilitators and advocates of leisure expression and the improvement of the quality of community life. However, I feel uneasy about the future. Looking back on the civil upheaval in south central Los Angeles following the Rodney King verdict of 1992, I am still trying to make sense out of what transpired. What went wrong? Why did people of south central L.A. feel they had no hope to be full participants in society? What was the role of leisure in this regard? There are those who say we had no direct role or concern as leisure studies faculty or leisure service practitioners, that it was a police matter, that it was purely and simply an economic issue, or that it reflected racism out of control. Yes, we live in a two class society—the haves and the have-nots. And leisure, as espoused by most leisure texts, speaks essentially to the white middle-class and seems to eschew any relationship of leisure expression and social responsibility for our community recreation programs. In my role as department chair I can serve no higher purpose than to challenge the demagoguery that is represented not only in our society but also in our discipline and profession.

Leisure has reached a stage within the academic developmental cycle in which our discipline must be socially committed to ensuring the right to leisure expression for all members of our communities. While much has been achieved in leisure studies (most notably professional accreditation), we are not generally viewed as being a critical, fundamental and integral discipline in academia. Even some of our nationally accredited programs have been either severely downsized or eliminated. I believe this is the case because leisure studies is not recognized as a socially relevant field of study or perceived as a discipline of inquiry within higher education that makes a substantial contribution to the improvement of the human condition.

Yes, I believe leisure studies does the aforementioned noble things, but unless we speak to such socially significant issues and articulate leisure's contributions to the human condition, we'll likely be "dethroned" someday from the list of degree programs. Our early leaders articulated the necessity for urban dwellers to be accorded respect and gain access to opportunities for leisure expression. They were visionary in their beliefs and convictions and competent in their actions.

Serving as department chair of a leisure studies program can't be viewed as just a typical job. Leisure represents the positive experiencing of freedom. Leisure's earliest roots were tied to civil rights. While only granted to a relative few, this cherished right of an individual to be able to exercise his or her full capabilities as a human being must be assured for all citizens. Leisure offers the opportunity for hope. Leisure studies curricula should provide leadership within academia as a discipline that explores the full dimensions of perceived freedom and intrinsic motivation, the bases of leisure expression. These critical factors contribute to a person's ability to develop resistance resources and a personality predisposition toward wellness—being psychologically and physically healthy. Many of the dispossessed who vented their frustration and despair in Los Angeles in late April, 1992 did not perceive that they had any hope or that positive freedom was within their grasp.

To ensure leisure can be realized in more people's lives and enhanced in others, I believe we must strive to raise people's consciousness about constraints to leisure expression—racism, sexism, handicappism, ageism—and serve as role models to ensure that leisure becomes not just a field of study within an accredited university program, but a right available to every member of our society. By respecting the people I work with, and by creating a workplace and learning space that promote individual expression and achievement, it is my hope that as department chair I can make some small contribution to that larger end.

14

A Day at the Office
Nick DiGrino

Join me at the office this Monday morning and I will share with you
some of the ordinary, and not so ordinary, experiences of a department
chair at a moderately sized recreation, park, and tourism administration
department in the heart of the Midwest. I assure you that the day's events,
planned or otherwise, will not be particularly dramatic or glamorous. It
will not be a condensed version of several years of experience forced into
a 30-minute sitcom or melodrama. The events of the day will reveal that
while I put in my share of long hours, I am not a work-centered person.
In fact, I prefer to work in the company of colleagues who place a high
priority on family and/or significant others. I am also pleased that my
colleagues maintain a balanced lifestyle and that they respect the role of
faith as a guiding life force. Is this reflected in my day-to-day decision
making? Perhaps not on this day, but a profile of the highly productive
Western Illinois University (WIU) faculty members with whom I have
had the pleasure of working provides strong evidence for the benefits of
balance in one's life.

Like most people, I have a "to do" list for this Monday morning.
Actually, I have two of them. On my office computer is a list of scheduled
activity for the day that should have been updated last Friday during my
regularly scheduled end of week meeting with my secretary. My second
list—the famous "magnet on the refrigerator list"—reminds me that I will
be sticking around the house until my first and second graders catch the
school bus, as my wife's job will require her to be at the other end of the
county by 8:00 a.m. Fortunately, I live within walking distance of my office and the school bus arrives at 7:30 a.m. I am also reminded that our
second grader will need to be taken to wrestling practice at 5:30 p.m.—
gear will be next to the door and a sandwich is in the refrigerator.

Along with two scheduled meetings with department faculty members, a meeting with the dean of my college, and a meeting with the

director of an on campus institute, I have a number of tasks that require telephone contacts and written correspondence. I also have two one-hour periods of time set aside this Monday to do project work—a local service effort involving safety assessments of local play areas and a research manuscript. While scheduled with the best of intentions, you will see why I do over 90 percent of my project work between 9:00 p.m. and midnight. A frustrating part of my job as department chair is the lack of available time for project work during the day.

A little pre-planning allows us to arrive at the dean's office for an 8:00 a.m. meeting prior to stopping at my office, which is in another building. This morning I am meeting with the dean and his associate, along with fellow chairs from the Departments of Health Sciences and Physical Education. A specified level of cutback has been designated by central administration for each of the colleges on our campus based on efficiency factors such as "student credit hours generated per full-time faculty equivalent" and "cost of instruction per student credit hour generated." We are meeting to assist the dean's office in establishing a response to the proposed cut. It is obvious that all three department chairs will also be prioritizing and defending the need for existing resources in our respective departments. While the dean is soliciting input from his chairs, it is incumbent upon me to articulate accurately the priorities of the Recreation, Park and Tourism Administration (RPTA) faculty and staff, protect departmental resources that are directly related to current and projected levels of service, and remain a team player within the dean's cabinet. Being a team player means understanding that "all decisions must be in the best interest of the college."

The words of a dear friend and former WIU colleague echo through my mind as the meeting progresses. Dick Westgate, a former deputy director of the Philadelphia Recreation Commission, reminded me that the ability to compromise is one of the most important, yet most difficult, traits for an administrator to acquire. What he described and practiced so well as a public administrator and as acting chair at WIU went well beyond the art and science of negotiation. I am slowly learning that it involves a level of objectivity that segregates departmental goals from one's personal investment of time and emotion. It involves active maintenance of professional trust and sense of community. It keeps the organization moving at a brisk pace with the emphasis on many "good" decisions coupled with a few that may have burned your britches, rather than prolonged unyielding ego-driven efforts to win the battle or arrive at the perfect decision.

The dean obviously has a set of priorities relative to resources within the college. He chooses to utilize a management style that discourages end runs and maximizes participation. It was my job to walk into this 8:00 a.m. meeting with an understanding of what our department can afford to give up with the least damaging impact on current as well as long-term levels of service. I am not surprised that my counterparts from Health Sciences and Physical Education focus on external funding success and teaching quality in their appeals to prioritize and protect college resources. It is my position that efficiently operating programs should experience less cutback than their over-funded counterparts. This position might be stated differently if we were not the most efficiently run department in our college. As a department chair one must be thoroughly familiar with the various efficiency ratios maintained by his or her academic unit. It is not a substitute for quality performance, but at WIU and most other institutions it is tied closely to funding formulas and it serves to remind us just how many are benefiting from the quality services provided.

We emerge from the meeting at 8:55 a.m., having reached consensus regarding projected departmental cutbacks. One adjunct faculty position in the RPTA Department was flagged. It could have been worse. We have between now and next fall to get it back. What a way to start the day.

It is 9:05 a.m. when we arrive at my office. I purposely avoid the morning mail, for I have a 9:15 meeting with a member of the RPTA faculty who serves as chair of the Department Personnel Committee (DPC). Since every department chair on our campus originates a set of criteria for tenure and promotion evaluation (subject to approval by the college dean and the academic vice president), the DPC chair and I are holding a preliminary meeting to discuss constructive changes that will go into effect with the new collective bargaining agreement. Since I am considered part of management and not a member of the bargaining unit, an uncomfortable level of protocol and formality sometimes results. For instance, this meeting to discuss changes in evaluation criteria could not be formally held until a specified date was arrived at through formal negotiation. Have informal discussions been held between me and members of the faculty regarding this issue? Do I have a relatively good feel for faculty sentiment regarding the evaluation criteria? Of course. I have been working along with the DPC chair on a regular basis to acquire an accurate perception of the faculty's positions. If I am not a strong advocate for the faculty, their support would be quickly lost and I would find it difficult to maintain the respect of central administration. The folks in central administration expect me to fulfill my responsibilities as a representative of management by administering the contract. However, they have little patience for a chair that lacks the confidence of his or her faculty. A department chair quickly learns to transcend this paradox by maintaining an open and honest relationship with the dean and central administration as well as members of the faculty. I spend considerable time explaining central administration's actions and positions (which are sometimes distorted or misrepresented by the union) to members of the departmental faculty. Yet on most issues involving differences of opinion between the faculty and central administration, I find myself representing the position of faculty.

Since our current set of evaluation criteria was established with considerable faculty input, there were minimal concerns expressed by the DPC chair and our meeting was primarily reduced to a work session aimed at tightening contract language to avoid misinterpretation of performance criteria. Future work sessions with DPC members will result in an improved set of evaluation criteria.

Project time is from 10:30 to 11:30 a.m., but first comes a quick review of the morning mail. Had there been something of major importance I would have been notified by my secretary prior to the 9:15 meeting. After signing several purchase orders and a travel request, I hit a detour on my road to an hour of project work. A second travel request had been submitted by a faculty member who was invited to present a paper at a prestigious conference in several months. The request exceeded the amount budgeted for this person's travel by several hundred dollars. The situation was addressed immediately but it did not culminate for several days. For me, it is one of the more enjoyable and rewarding aspects of being a department chair. While the faculty member in question was prepared to personally finance the speaking engagement, I strongly believe it is the chair's responsibility to maximize support for professional contributions by faculty and staff. Depending on the nature of the contribution, up to a dozen different sources of funding exist on the WIU campus. By the end of the hour I had met with the faculty member who submitted the request and made several contacts for funding consideration, which eventually resulted in full funding for the speaking engagement. An understanding of the campus system and the various, and changing, personalities represented is an important part of the chair's job. It takes considerable time, cannot be forced, and requires regular maintenance. Chairs must be willing to invest in this aspect of the job.

Well, it's 11:30 a.m. and no project work was completed. Why do I even bother to schedule the project time? Actually, a couple of times per week I do productively pursue project work. If I didn't keep the project work on a front burner it would lose priority and not find its way to my briefcase at the end of the day.

For the next 15 minutes I will make routine calls and write one or two letters of reference for graduating students. At 11:45 a.m. I will join a group of faculty companions for three or four quick games of basketball. (Notice that I am not using the noon hour to work on one of my projects.) By the way, one of those sources of funding for the travel request made earlier this morning is a regular in our basketball group. At my age, the twisted knees, bruised shoulders, and sprained ankles outweigh any aerobic benefit achieved during the hour of basketball, but I sure have fun playing, and my head is clear as we trudge up two flights of steps to my office with a cold soft drink in hand.

From 1:00 until 1:30 p.m. I just do some visiting. I try to do this every day and at random times. Often it is initiated in the early morning by a colleague before I ever make it to my office. I may join some students studying in the lounge, but most commonly I will visit with one or more faculty members. If I am at a loss for pertinent questions or comments regarding their work, family, or position on an issue at our university, then I really need to know them better.

At 2:00 p.m. we attend another meeting on campus to speak with the director of a newly developed state-funded institute. The institute is pursuing programs and projects while responding to a set of priorities from the governor's office. It is obvious that the institute must demonstrate effectiveness along with associated visibility. It is my responsibility, along with the RPTA faculty, to explore cooperative opportunities relative to the goals of the RPTA Department and the College of Health, Physical Education and Recreation. Demonstrated effectiveness and associated visibility are also important to academic departments. As we discuss the viability of two joint projects it is imperative that all parties understand and agree to resource commitments and risks associated with short- and long-range benefits. It is also important to establish agreement, contingent upon "buy in," by those faculty and staff members instrumental to the projects' success. Today's discussions with representatives of the institute involve the commitment of resources and discussion of preferred outcomes, but do not reach beyond a conceptual level. A series of meetings will be planned for the near future to involve selected faculty and staff in the assessment of project feasibility and probable formulation.

Have I been focusing unreasonably on organizational benefits and outcomes to the exclusion of personnel implications? I ask myself that very question several times a week. Normally, that which is in the faculty member's best interest is also in the department's best interest, but there are exceptions. As department chair one learns to gauge short- and long-term benefits relative to the level of resources invested. There is a significant but sometimes subtle difference between long-term investment of departmental resources and leakage of departmental resources. When a faculty member utilizes his or her talents to provide professional service to a legitimate client, institutional affiliation cannot be ignored. A challenge to today's department chair is to develop a creative entrepreneurial spirit among faculty and staff, while capturing for the university the return on investment of their contributions. For example, by minimizing bureaucratic red tape and compensation penalties, academic departments could gain tremendously from the technical assistance and applied research that its faculty provides under the heading of consulting.

We are back to my office for a 3:15 p.m. meeting with the coordinator of the department's graduate program. We will spend approximately 45 minutes finalizing the assignment of graduate assistants to faculty members for the next academic year. Based on expressed needs among the faculty and their overall work assignments, for which I am responsible, graduate research and teaching assistants will be appointed. Assignment of duties and development of course schedules are usually the responsibility of the department chair. It is a coordinative function that is much more complex than it would appear on the surface. There is a factor in the scheduling equation that the chair must consider, and that is the number of students served, or student credit hours generated. As mentioned earlier, this productivity measure significantly influences budgetary decisions on many campuses. It influences the number of high-enrollment general education (non major) sections of classes that we offer each semester and it also results in the scheduling of required courses at unattractive times (while professional elective courses are usually offered between 9:00 a.m. and 2:00 p.m.). As a chair responsible for scheduling and assignment of duties, the challenge lies in optimizing student and faculty satisfaction, overall effectiveness, and student credit hour generation. The approach commonly leaves everyone tolerant of the chair's actions but firmly convinced that with a few more brain cells and a lot more sensitivity the chair could have done a much better job. The department chair is definitely in a people-pleasing business but this is one part of the job that requires a clear articulation of your rationale (and a thick skin).

It is now 4:00 p.m. and I conclude that any project work completed today will take place tonight after the kids are fast asleep. My secretary scheduled time for me to meet with a prospective student and his family visiting campus without prior notice. Even though they have spent considerable time with our departmental advisor, who also introduced them to a number of faculty members and students, it is important that we meet for a few minutes. Along with answering any questions they might have, I want to contribute what I can to their positive perception of WIU. If, through preliminary information, or in this case during the course of discussion, I am convinced that the person is an outstanding prospect and that his needs match well with our department, I will shift on the fly from "information" gear to "recruitment" gear. My approach will be situational, but the person will leave knowing that the faculty, staff, and students would value his presence at WIU. Our success as an academic department is directly dependent upon the recruitment and retention of good students. And it is usually done one at a time. Just as a politician needs votes to put his or her ideas into practice, an academic department ensures its future with qualified majors. Most universities believe that once a prospective student visits the campus, the likelihood of their matriculating increases significantly. I am convinced, and that's why I view today's 4:00 p.m. meeting to be one of the most important of the day.

A freshman RPTA major has scheduled an appointment with me for 4:15 p.m. to discuss a classroom concern. Satisfied with his courses and life in general at WIU, the student is concerned with his level of progress and performance in several classes. A quick discussion of his class schedule and study habits reveals that he could probably benefit from peer tutoring and study skills orientation and training. Rather than make the referral, I delegate this job to our department advisor. After walking the student to the advisor's office and seeing that he schedules an appointment with her for the following day, I return to my office to make several calls, write a letter, and respond to an undergraduate internship report. It is 5:15 p.m., the secretaries are gone for the day, and several members of the faculty are enjoying their quietest and most productive time. And, as you know, a 60-pound family obligation will occupy the next few minutes of my time.

I have reflected a little on the various aspects of today's involvements, but I assure you that tomorrow's activity will be considerably different. I will be covering a colleague's class while she is away at a conference, and I will also be teaching a senior seminar. There is the summer rotation of faculty assignments that must be developed according to the collective bargaining agreement, and the letters of nomination for graduate faculty that must be prepared for two new members of the faculty. A hearing for a newly proposed undergraduate course in research and evaluation will be held by the faculty senate, and a planning session with selected students and faculty is scheduled for an upcoming recognition social event. Then there is that project work that must be completed on schedule.

The role of a department chair is not dramatically different from the requirements of most managers. The focus of much of the chair's energies is on developing a more responsive system. This involves improving the quality of service to students and other publics while maintaining efficiency.

It also involves the establishment and maintenance of accurate and positive perceptions by those recipient publics. With that comes realization that change, for the most part, occurs slowly. Just as an aircraft carrier gradually reverses direction as the wheel is turned and the course is adjusted, organizational change takes time. As you communicate change within the organization and to the publics served, keep in mind that the department's reputation, earned over a considerable period of time, tends to lag by at least a couple of years.

Much has been written in recent years about the need for leaders, not managers. While the chair is in a unique position to provide direction and inspire faculty and staff to focus their creative energies and talents in a cohesive manner, someone had better be conscious of the managerial functions. Granted, the department chair that sets out to "manage" his or her people is dead in the water. In fact, the chair who profiles faculty and staff in order to adopt a management style appropriate for his or her staff will learn quickly that an academic department is comprised of individuals.

I view my role as department chair to be one of managing resources effectively in order to serve the unique needs and capabilities of each member of the faculty. Our clerical staff, academic advisor, caretaker of our field campus, internship coordinator, and graduate coordinator, while serving students directly, also function to support the work of the faculty who are the direct providers of our department's services. I will lead the charge and provide a high level of visibility when appropriate. More often I am behind the scenes facilitating the efforts of highly qualified experts. This "service leadership" approach can be highly effective, but the chair must maintain an excellent perspective on the faculty members' individual and collective contributions toward goals of the academic unit. It is up to the chair to see that the aircraft carrier remains on course. Within the broad spectrum of personal ambition and academic freedom, faculty members are recruited based on their willingness to accept ownership in the mission and responsibilities of the university and the academic unit. The chair's efforts should be geared toward creating an environment whereby faculty members have an opportunity to improve the system which subscribes to this purpose. The faculty member who chooses to pursue a course of professional activity that contradicts the aims of the institution and academic unit should be encouraged to join the team or find another work setting. However, the chair must be sensitive to academic freedom issues as well as issues of diversity, and capitalizing on opportunities to move in exciting directions based on the recognized strengths and interests of the faculty.

Chairing an academic unit involves supplying the individual faculty member with a unique set of resources and assistance, depending upon his or her background, experience, expertise, preference, and, to a large extent, confidence level. Levels of confidence in a field dominated by highly successful self-directed Ph.D.'s would appear on the surface to be a factor of minimal proportions. Experience tells me that self-doubt and low levels of confidence accompany most of us in higher education at points throughout our careers, particularly prior to earning tenure. The department chair should systematically meet with each faculty member to review performance and provide constructive feedback and support. However, such actions are not a substitute for building a team of faculty members who genuinely care about and support one another. It took me a few years as chair to realize that I was not Henry Kissinger, and it was not my job to resolve every little squabble between faculty members. However, it is my job to remind faculty and staff that they are responsible for speedy resolution of individual differences through open communication, particularly if the conflict is detrimental to functions within the department.

As department chair I find the "service leadership" approach to administering the academic unit extremely satisfying. The inverted relationship between faculty and chair seems to work effectively, but only because we are capable of inverting a larger portion of the organizational chart. For this model to keep the chair from being stretched to unrecognizable levels of deformity, the dean must see himself orherself as serving the needs of the chairs. Loyalty must travel in all directions. For instance, my supervisor, the dean of the college, sees his role as one of assisting each of the academic units in carrying out their respective functions. He maintains the same level of concern, support and advocacy for the departments that I try to direct to faculty and staff. Likewise, faculty and staff must be comfortable with their role in serving the best interests of our students and other constituents.

Before our visit comes to a close I would like to comment on the importance of autonomy for the academic unit. Prior to becoming a department chair, I served as coordinator of a leisure studies division within an institutionally defined academic unit. Fortunately, my supervising department head was an outstanding administrator who delegated both responsibility and authority. Even with such support, attempts to establish a university-wide identity were hampered significantly. The pool of resources available to faculty within our larger academic unit was frequently distributed based on factors other than our designated divisional goals. Departmental goals represented a parochial focus slanted toward the division with the largest number of faculty members. Being located one additional administrative layer from the college dean's office did not lend itself to development and implementation of strategic initiatives. Our effectiveness as a division, while contributing to the overall performance profile of the academic unit, had no official statistical relevance. Politically, the head of our academic unit had to be sensitive to popular reaction to efficiency-related reallocation decisions between divisions. I am convinced that a number of fine parks, recreation, and leisure programs throughout the United States with division or program status would flourish if granted departmental status.

There is no question that within the university system competition exists for limited institutional resources. Oftentimes, those internal resources are instrumental in the academic unit's efforts to marshal external support. The autonomy associated with departmental status does not guarantee the academic unit success, but it does result in an established identity that normally extends to the state-wide governing body. There is no room for complacency when you know that you are being compared with various departments on your own campus as well as other departments in your discipline at sister institutions. Comparatively large contributions to the institution's goals and objectives usually serve as a major criterion for favorable review. During the best of times, favorable reviews translate to increased tenure-track faculty lines, travel funding, equipment, and even enhanced support for added depth and/or breadth of levels of departmental productivity and a recognizable consistency with the institution's central mission can spell the difference between status quo and major cutbacks. Keep in mind the "short-term profit long-term failure" syndrome. It's one thing to know that you have excellent ratios of "student credit hours generated to FTE" and "number of majors to cost of instruction." Achieving such statistics while maintaining quality instruction and accessibility to faculty is the real challenge.

In building and maintaining a quality faculty, I have comfortably maintained that long-term productivity is generally enhanced by employing scholars who place family and faith above their work. I choose to define both family and faith in the broadest and indiscriminate of terms. In my early years as chair, departmental productivity drove most of my decisions regarding the employment of faculty members with lifestyles that reflected professional stability resulting from breadth and balance. Since then my colleagues have helped me appreciate that the journey is as important and often more satisfying than the destination. As we strive to accomplish our goals as an academic unit, it is the colleagues with whom I share ideas, strategies, talents, and dreams that will remain dear to my heart and clear to my memory. That is one of the unparalleled benefits of chairing a department—the relationships initially developed around common professional goals that evolve to a great deal more.

First Among Peers
Mark Searle

What is the task of an administrator in higher education? What are the joys, the rewards, the challenges and disappointments? After much thought, I believe the role is best described as a privilege which must be handled with great care and sensitivity. Why is this a position of privilege? The seventh edition of the *Concise Oxford Dictionary* states that privilege is a "special advantage or benefit." I believe it is a special advantage to be able to lead others and to engage actively in the establishment of the direction and focus of a group. To lead, one must be concerned with action. The goal of the leader is to ensure movement toward the achievement of the unit's goals and not simply to bask in the status of holding a position. To lead in an academic environment means to have the privilege of addressing the concerns and ideas that flow from students, peers, professionals, and senior administrators within the institution and from the field.

Why did I accept this "opportunity" to be program head when it was offered? My colleagues would likely tell you I was the only person willing to take it on. There is some truth in that statement. However, my willingness to be the *first among peers* was rooted in my belief that I could effect positive and substantial change. Moreover, I believed the circumstances were ripe for the kind of initiatives I had in mind.

Did I jump into this naively? Possibly. However, I am an optimist at heart moderated by a reasonable amount of pragmatism. I do not believe I was captured by the compliment inherent in being asked to assume the unit's leadership. Indeed, one of my greatest concerns was what would happen to my scholarship? Here I was in the final throes of my doctoral dissertation and assuming the role of program head. Was I sacrificing my personal academic future for some greater cause? No, I was not that much an innocent. However, I did realize that I would have to put in an extra effort to sustain my scholarly productivity. Moreover, I was caught in a certain trap with respect to scholarly production. My personal view has always been that all members of the faculty should contribute to both teaching and scholarship and that it was not acceptable, especially in a small program, to have one or two people "carry the ball" with respect to research. As the leader, therefore, what could I do to sustain my productivity and not claim a lack of time due to administrative duties? There was one thing—work harder than I really wanted to or imagined was necessary. In retrospect, that may indicate more naiveté than I thought.

I assumed the post of program head with a particular perspective and sense of purpose. My perspective was rooted in the need for a strong professional curriculum which would build upon theory, research, and practice. This ensured that students possessed a sound understanding of leisure and the associated service delivery system, while sustaining a solid core of liberal education upon which the original curriculum had been established. More specifically, this translated into an agenda associated with curriculum change, new thrusts in program promotion, better liaison with junior colleges, the development of a graduate program, and the development of better links with the provincial government and other recreation and park organizations. I also had the challenge of maintaining scholarship. (Indeed, I believed I should increase it as leadership by example is important to me.) Further, I believed that a curriculum should have as few rules as possible. A good friend of mine who had served as an academic administrator for a lengthy period of time observed that rules create unnecessary problems more often than they solve them. They also seem to run counter to the notion of treating situations and students individually. To make the situation more muddled, I believed that my colleagues and I had to bring a more cogent structure to the degree program in terms of my aforementioned agenda.

The adventure began. At first I kept a relatively low profile, not volunteering to take on any tasks or suggest ideas I knew would end up back in my proverbial lap. In fact, I invested heavily in writing in order to set my priorities straight and to establish the importance I placed on scholarship for those around me. I cannot comment on its effects on my colleagues, but it made me realize that to be successful in this position I had to be successful in scholarly writing. The result was the first building block in my approach to being an academic leader. Be a scholar first, an administrator second. This was, from my perspective, being true to the notion of the university.

Having been educated in administration, I reflected on a comment offered by more than one observer of managers, administrators, etc. That is, there is the need to separate the functions of leadership from those of administration—the need to lead the organization toward greater achievement of its goals and objectives and the need to keep the paperwork flowing. While each has an effect on the other, it seemed to me a hollow effort to provide the administration without the leadership.

The second component of my leadership approach was not to react too quickly to crises or problems that were delivered to my doorstep in my capacity as administrator. I would generally seek out the best solution for the problem and then suggest that we, as a faculty, consider the issue again at a later date. This allowed me to maintain my minimalist perspective on rules and, at the same time, address the concerns presented in a way that was comfortable to faculty members.

My third rule of effective leadership was to develop a positive relationship with the dean, founded on trust. Being a sycophant is not the answer to either a good relationship or a satisfying experience as program head. A good relationship is one wherein the dean is kept informed of achievements by students and faculty members in the program, and where problems or potential problems are addressed without delay such that the dean does not become the problem solver for the unit. In my case, I have been fortunate to be able to work with a person of great integrity who could be relied upon once he gave his word. He is a true person of honor. Nonetheless, I have often expressed my criticism of some of his ideas and he of mine. This has led to a frank and open relationship wherein the winner is the program.

Finally, my fourth rule of effective leadership was to be honest and open with my colleagues. The phrase, *first among peers*, served as a constant reminder of my role and position. I was and am neither superior nor inferior. At most, I hold a temporary position in which the functions performed are those associated with a super ordinate. This does not mean one must not proceed with their ideas. It means building support from your colleagues. It means sharing information about the administration of the unit if it is likely to affect them or may simply be of interest to them. An open approach has resulted in my colleagues telling me what information they want and what they would just as soon I handle and keep to myself. One corollary of this style has been to circulate the materials that cross my desk as an administrator that may not cross my colleagues' desks. In this way they can read it if they wish or simply pass it on. With these basic principles of leadership in mind, I began my term.

I would now like to reflect on some of the rewards of the position. First and foremost, I have had the opportunity to play an influential role within the faculty. This has ranged from decisions on staffing and curriculum to building relationships with other academic units in the university.

It has also allowed me an opportunity to meet more students than I would otherwise, know more about them, and keep in touch with many fine alumni.

Second, being program head has given me the opportunity to play a role in shaping provincial recreation policy and programs and to participate federally on some of the same issues. Third, I have learned about the complexity of administration in a university environment. As a professional who worked for ten years in government prior to beginning an academic career, I can safely say that the government's decision-making processes and decision rules are less Byzantine than the university's. Nonetheless, after a number of years I have learned to appreciate the unique manner of peer review, the concept of academic control of the curriculum, and the oversight role of the central administration. In our university I have come to appreciate decentralized budgeting, as cuts are a local faculty decision and are not imposed by more senior levels of the university hierarchy.

Fourth, I have been rewarded by my colleagues through their support of my ideas, and their willingness to work on behalf of the unit. While many programs have individuals who may be ineffective or "on-the-job" retirees, I have had the good fortune not to have that circumstance. I have had a collegial group who share a common vision for the degree program, enjoy each other's company, and willingly work together. As program head, I have discovered the satisfaction of working with people who demonstrate daily the meaning of the word commitment. They are productive with respect to their research, excel in their teaching, and contribute in many different ways to the community.

Fifth, the role of program head has given me the opportunity to think about curriculum in a way that I have not had to or, quite frankly, ever sought to consider. I am more sensitive to the pressures of students and the need for the curriculum to be sensitive to students. More than that, it has crystallized the struggle between specialist and generalist approaches so often debated. I have realized that despite the continual job pressures, pressures from professional groups and others interested in what we teach, we have a duty to educate students for the long term. Most will not return to the university. Most will not seek another degree. We must ensure that they have a balance of liberal arts education with the necessary skills to perform as a professional in a wide variety of possible tasks. I am reminded of something John Farina was fond of saying: "We prepare students for careers, not jobs." Career education must be founded on the need to have a broad understanding of numerous aspects of life and living. It also requires some specific skills and knowledge to perform the tasks associated with an individual's chosen field of endeavor. Part of the struggle, as pointed out to me so well by one of my colleagues, is the demand for specialists in entry-level positions and the demand for generalists in the more senior positions. Thus, I am firmly committed to a strong undergraduate education in the arts and sciences. It is the role of graduate education to further refine the focus for those who seek such a narrowing. It is clear that I have developed some strong views on curriculum as a result of serving as program head. This has been a positive result for me. Better to have a position to debate than to be on shifting soil.

Finally, the position of program head has given me the opportunity to work with a variety of people I might otherwise not have met and to promote actively and effect change as I believed necessary. These things cannot be done from the back benches. Having said that, I believe the program head should not be a permanent appointment but should have a definite term of office and should be, as a matter of policy, rotated through as many faculty members as feasible. This assures many have the opportunity to understand the struggles of the person assigned the task of *first among peers* and at the same time provides an opportunity to others to lead by sharing their vision, beliefs, and ideas.

In considering the disadvantages of this position it would be easy to focus on struggles with personnel decisions or faculty politics. But these, in fact, have not been sources of disappointment for me. Rather, most of my disappointment is in the personal belief that much has yet to be done in both scholarship and leadership in our program, and I do not have the energy (and sometimes patience) to get all of it done in the manner I would like. Coming to grips with the desire to achieve excellence in the program and understanding the need for limits on involvements is increasingly difficult because of the external pressures placed on the university.

One change that has occurred over time in the name of greater productivity and efficient use of resources has been the use of technology for student registration (telephone registration systems), the addition of a nonacademic staff person to advise students on matters pertaining to registration and course changes, and the introduction of various print materials to assist students in their decision making: on everything from career focus to available electives. This has effectively reduced my contact with students. As a result, I often feel less in touch with the students, with who they are, and with what they seek from their educational experience. This is troublesome for me, as student contact is a reward I identified.

While the advances described above save time, which can then be devoted to research, it nevertheless changes the nature of the role of the academic leader. It concerns me, because the greater the distance from the student, the more dangerous the threat to the relevance, quality, and significance of the curriculum we teach. The result of these administrative advances is to further isolate the administrator from the students. I find this frustrating, as I am already distanced by less teaching, and the increased contact I have tends to be more issue-centered rather than pedagogical. While these could be addressed in part through structured experiences, they would not replace the contact lost. The meetings with students for reasons surrounding registration, course changes, etc., provided a forum for discussions on a wide range of issues and created a closer connection between the students and myself. I miss that, yet I know the demands of time are such that the process cannot be reversed without wholesale changes in the way we teach at the undergraduate level and the concomitant demands we place on faculty members for promotion and tenure.

Some other disappointments are in the constant struggle to sustain the academy when governments seek accountability. Yet, how does one account for time to reflect? How does one justify the development of knowledge to persons who care little for your field of endeavor and care less about "ivory tower" researchers self-absorbed in their activities? How do you assert that teaching six hours a week is enough for faculty members in an era of accountability? While often a disappointment, these matters also present challenges that need to be met head-on and addressed. If not, given the current milieu, we may find ourselves relevant from our perspective and out of the degree granting business from the university's perspective.

Yet, some of my disappointments have come in the form of watching talented young people leave our field because the opportunities are too limited. With a relatively young professional field and one that is organized according to traditional professional roles, there is the added responsibility to act as an advocate for our students and for recreation professionals generally. This is a disappointment, because it is something for which there is precious little time. It is something that should be done by and for the profession, and it is too important to be ignored.

I believe that on balance the rewards associated with the position are far greater than the costs. Nonetheless, it is an unusual person who can sustain the energy necessary to maintain scholarship, academic leadership, and administration for a long period of time. For those in our field who have done so I have great respect. From my perspective, I am looking forward to completing my sixth and final year as program head and returning to the role of professor. I will have gained substantially from the experience, and I will have something else to offer in my role as colleague to a new program head. I will have an empathy I did not have before, I will probably have some overbearing perspectives I will need to rein in as I will no longer be doing the job, and I will be able to take on tasks with a greater appreciation as to how they fit in the overall success of the unit, the faculty and the university.

I want to reiterate a point I made at the outset; that is the need for ongoing leadership in the realm of scholarship. We are a small field of study. We also have, in my opinion, too many individuals who abandon research and writing too quickly either in the name of administration or because teaching loads are excessive. In the latter case, I regret this and can hope it only reduces productivity rather than eliminating it. However, if academic leaders are going to assert that the field needs more good researchers and needs more productivity, then those individuals need to be sure they are making substantive contributions to the literature themselves. This may be in the form of textbooks or articles in learned journals, but they must contribute. My preference would be that each individual always makes at least two contributions to scholarly journals each year. If heads of programs would accept this as part of the job, we might be able to set a better standard of performance for the staff. I realize fully that leadership by example does not have an impact on all persons. It does, however, influence the extent to which I feel comfortable challenging a colleague to be more productive or encouraging a new faculty member to emphasize scholarship as something more than a means to tenure and promotion.

In the end, I have come to believe that the role of an academic administrator is one of privilege. It is an opportunity to lead and promote the interrelated fields of recreation, parks, and tourism, and to contribute to a greater understanding of their significance in modern society. To view the role of leader as one which is a burden is to do a disservice to your peers, your students, your institution, and ultimately yourself. We must be prepared to advocate for the vision we have and build a consensus around it. We must be prepared to be an active participant and not a backseat driver. Administration may not be the career calling for all faculty members. However, for those who assume the role, it is imperative that they engage in it with the vigor and tenacity necessary to achieve the mission of the unit.

16 Managing in Times of Retrenchment

Bob Rossman

The role of department chair has changed dramatically over the past fifteen years. Previously, the chair was elected by the faculty of the department. Universities were operated as a loose federation of discipline-based, academic programs. There was a club-type caste system of professorial ranks to which faculty were admitted by elections of those currently holding the rank sought. Since those occupying the same rank were seen as equal, it really did not matter much who occupied the chair's role and it was routinely passed around among the professors in a department.

Today, universities have a much more defined organizational structure and the chair's role is a supervisory, middle management one. Chairs are often appointed by a dean and continue to serve at the dean's pleasure with the consent of the faculty. This change places chairs in the classic dilemma of middle management—satisfying two masters who often have mutually exclusive goals. So you must have a thick skin if you want to be chair because you will often not be able to please both masters concurrently.

A department is also the primary organizational unit of a university with accounting, personnel, and curricular responsibilities. Through departments, a university produces its primary products of research, teaching, and service. Therefore, almost all university organizational functions must be dealt with at the departmental level. For example, a department has an active file and an ongoing relationship with almost every staff office in the university in addition to all line function offices.

You will be expected to respond and represent your department to many internal and external parties. You will need to play a major role in filtering and directing information to the appropriate parties in both directions: that is, from units across the university to individuals within your department and from your department to units across campus. The number of opportunities presented for action will exceed your ability to respond to every request, and the pace is often rapid. Although your education as an academic has taught you to be methodical and deliberate, administration is most often neither. Decisions frequently must be made in a short time with only partial information. The amount of time you can spend on most issues is small and the number to be handled is great. You must master multiple task management.

Therefore, a major role of the chair is helping the faculty sort out and choose what to respond to, what projects to undertake, and with what campus-wide programs to align. These are important strategic decisions, and the faculty will be more dependent on you to guide them in making these decisions than they will be willing to admit. It is not that they are not wise enough to decide; they simply do not have the time to read all of the data you have read to prepare for making these decisions. This is why chairs get release time—so they can prepare to exercise strategic planning and other responsibilities of the chair.

In most universities today, the biggest challenge is to maintain a quality program during a period of financial retrenchment. Terms for describing the situation abound: "cutting the fat out of the budget," "operating leaner but meaner," or "doing more with less." It seems we need to revisit E. F. Schumacher's *Small is Beautiful* to relearn that devotion to unbridled growth is not possible in the long run. To maintain quality in this day and age requires that we truly understand what is required for both students and faculty to achieve it. In a climate of retrenchment, there is less margin for error, and the chair needs to keep the faculty focused on what is necessary for excellence.

The practical outcome of retrenchment is for faculty to reassess what are the essential elements of educating for leisure and educating leisure service practitioners. One reason curricula grow is because of the "knowledge explosion." However, some new discoveries replace or invalidate previous findings and not all knowledge is applicable to leisure studies.

The department chair is often left with faculty who are very much invested in a curriculum that has evolved for several years which now must be reconceptualized and downsized. For faculty, this often means there may no longer be the resources to teach their favorite elective courses—the ones they enjoy but that are not essential for program maintenance or quality. For students, it may mean that each course is no longer available each semester or even every year. Therefore, successfully completing a curriculum requires more careful planning in order to fulfill sequences. Consequently, faculty must devote more time to advisement. It may also mean that students do not get a completely customized version of a marketing, planning, or budgeting course from their leisure studies department and, as a result, they may have to do some transitional application. Practitioners as well may need to invest more heavily in job orientations and on-the-job training to move students from more theoretical, general education about leisure studies to the specific training of how the job is accomplished in a given agency. Thus, retrenchment leaves the chair with a major role in redefining and refocusing the curriculum and the task of interpreting the need for and implications of these changes to faculty, students, and practitioners.

One principle of management suggests individuals should be given the authority necessary to discharge their responsibilities. In universities, chairs have many responsibilities and little direct authority to carry many of them out. Often, the chair must work through faculty committees, deans, or other staff offices to accomplish anything of significance. Although negotiating this organizational and procedural labyrinth is frustrating in its own right, the most frustrating part to me is the time famine it creates. Too often chairs must spend a great deal of time getting permissions and approvals to make changes they and their faculty have recognized as being necessary for months. Although there are many checks and balances in universities, my view is that there are so many checks that they have gotten out of balance, and the shortfall is in the amount of time chairs have to get things done.

There are rewards, however. The chair is the figurehead of the program, and with this comes respect and deference. When you speak to parties external to the department, people assume you are knowledgeable and consider your opinion. Such moments are refreshing.

In addition, your role as chair places you in a position of power. Two kinds of power come automatically—role power and the power created by a superior knowledge base. Even though your faculty may not agree or realize it, the chair does have some defined authority and the power that emanates from the exercise of this authority. For example, the chair has authority to allocate travel funds, make teaching assignments, assign offices and other space, and make personnel recommendations regarding tenure, promotion, and merit pay. If you are not willing to make decisions and differentially distribute the rewards available based on performance, you will not be exercising your authority in a manner that will build the power base you need to succeed as chair. In addition, your position as chair will provide you access to much knowledge about what is happening in the university. This superior knowledge base also gives you power.

These two types of power come with the job. However, and this can be the most rewarding part of being chair, if exercised properly, these two kinds of power can be used to build a third power base—charismatic power. Many think of this type of power as having to do with good looks and/or the charm of a nice personality. But more typically, charismatic power involves people being drawn to your leadership. It is built over time as the chair exercises the first two types of power in a democratic fashion, with good communication, thereby building credibility with the faculty that the chair's decisions are well-tutored, in the best interest of the department, and fair when examined from a broad perspective. Success at building a charismatic power base is one of the best rewards of being chair.

I believe it is best to think of the chair's role as seasonal work or even day labor. You do the job as long as you believe you are being effective for your program and have the support of both the faculty and dean. Once you lose the trust of either of these entities, it is time to return to being a faculty member.

Since even the most skillful chair will eventually fall out of favor, it is critical that you maintain your own scholarship while serving as chair. Too often, chairs administer their departments for many years at the expense of their scholarship. A deposed chair with no ongoing record of scholarship is in a very bad position. To avoid this, I personally schedule two mornings a week at home to write. It takes something of monumental importance to get me to change this appointment with myself and for myself. Thus, I devote one day a week to scholarship. I take a very cavalier attitude about this. If some other things don't get done, and people are upset as a result, I am completely willing to resign from the chair's role at any time. In addition, this active role in scholarship enables me to lead by example. Even under the best circumstances, however, you will not be able to maintain your previous level of scholarly productivity, and you must be willing to take a longer time to get things produced.

You must also know when it is time to quit being chair. Administrative roles are broad, and even the best administrators bring a limited set of skills and abilities to a specific job. Eventually you will have solved all of the problems your set of skills and abilities will permit you to solve, or the organization's needs will change and your skills and abilities will no longer be applicable. In either case, it is now time to move up to a deanship or even further up to the most prized and esteemed appointment—a tenured professor with no administrative assignment.

Many days I ask myself, "Am I having fun yet?" The fun part of the job for me is networking on the department's behalf across campus. The chair must be keenly aware of campus politics. This requires frequent contact both horizontally and vertically within the university's organizational structure. The chair must maintain a good line of communication with the dean of the college. The dean is the primary conduit of information to and from central administration. But nurture other contacts too, so you have additional checks on what you are being told is going on in the university. Your dean has several departments and priorities of his or her own. You may not be at the top of the list.

You have a responsibility to keep your dean informed of what is going on in your department. No one likes surprises, especially your dean. He or she should always hear about newsworthy items from you first, even if it is bad news. You must also nurture contacts horizontally with other chairs and departments throughout the university. You must constantly be receiving information. The norm of reciprocity operates here. You will likely get about as much information as you give. When this is done socially we call it gossiping, but when we do it in organizations we call it networking. By any name, having good reliable information sources is essential for keeping on top of what is happening in the university.

Finally, you must keep your faculty abreast of what is happening. It is often difficult to determine at what point to involve them in the information loop. Some of what you learn will be just rumor. Other information will be trial balloons sent up by central administration to get feedback from department chairs and deans. And still other information will be the real stuff. In the initial stages it isn't always possible to know what kind of information you actually have, but you cannot constantly keep your faculty in turmoil and on edge with rumor. You will make some mistakes on this one. I guarantee it.

The hardest thing for me to do as chair is to tell faculty about adverse personnel decisions. Denial of tenure or promotion strikes people in a very personal way and involves the welfare of their families. At these times, faculty are almost always very emotional and angry, and the chair receives the brunt of their wrath.

The only advice I can offer to mitigate these occasions is to give honest and forthright evaluations each year so there are no surprises. Remember, the probationary period is six one-year appointments, not one six-year appointment. If an untenured faculty member is not progressing toward the award of tenure, release that person as soon as possible. It only makes it more difficult for all involved if you continue to reappoint such a person year after year. Regardless, these are still the hardest moments for me.

What you do or don't do as chair in today's universities does make a difference. The stakes are high. Positioning the department to be a visible, contributing member of the college and a good citizen in the university community is an important job and one that is very time-consuming. Too many scholars see the chair as little more than a nuisance, the same as all administrators, because they do not realize the importance of the role.

Every organization has a structure, an agenda, and individuals placed within the organization that control its resources. No program can survive without resources and often the decision to keep or eliminate a program is irrational and based on false impressions. I sometimes believe chairs should have training as magicians since we are often involved in illusion management rather than rational management of the department's infrastructure. Whatever the magic employed, in this era of dwindling resources it is absolutely essential for a chair to be able to convince the powers that be of his or her department's centrality to the mission and purpose of the university. Otherwise, the only effect achieved will likely be a disappearing act.

The Changing Proportions of My Life
Peter Witt

In one sense, I have always been an administrator. I have always had responsibilities related to conceptualizing, organizing, and directing certain academic activities beyond my own teaching. Early in my career, I had a research grant from the Canadian federal government. This meant that I had to hire, train, and supervise a group of research assistants, while taking care of all the financial duties associated with stewarding the government's research moneys at the same time. A bit later, I worked with a group of five other people to create the *Journal of Leisurability*. As the first managing editor of a privately produced journal, I undertook all responsibilities associated with advertising, editing, producing, and distributing the publication.

In reality, probably every professor administers some activity, whether this includes being responsible for career day, the activities of all of a department's teaching assistants, or being responsible for preparing the department's accreditation report. However, few of these activities earn one the endearing label "administrator." That label is usually reserved for the individual who serves as department chair, in some capacity at the college level such as dean, or perhaps "occupies space" within the central administration of the university. Although individuals in these latter positions may undertake nothing more than a series of the activities listed above, we label them administrators, pay them more than we would if they were full-time professors, question whether their involvement in furthering the academic enterprise justifies the pay, and immediately assume that each of us could do the job better. Within hours, one of "us" has become one of "them." So, although the extra pay is nice, and while the opportunity to earn extra money in the summer is appreciated, why would anyone want to become an administrator?

Without being facetious or representing the job on too grand a scale, I believe many of us become administrators because we believe we have the capacity to help organize, staff, and direct the activities of a particular unit, and have a set of ideas we would like to see advanced. Thus, being an administrator is the best way to further an agenda. On the other hand, it may simply be the progression of things; we may fall into the trap of believing that organizations are arranged in a vertical manner and that the higher the position, the more status and power one has to effect change or make sure that things happen. While this is true in some organizations, in others the assumptions linking verticality, power, responsibility, and monetary reward are tenuous at best. But that is another story.

All of this begs the question of why I "volunteered" to be labeled, first by becoming a department chair, and then through a series of jobs in the central administration at the University of North Texas—with the last title being "Assistant Vice President and Associate Dean." (If longer titles indeed describe lower status, I am in trouble.) Department chair is easy. I had the arrogance to believe I could do the job better than any of my colleagues. Besides, I thought I would rather work in a department run by me than one run by them. But enough for modesty.

Moving into the "big house" on the hill was another matter. One day an announcement was circulated that the university was looking for an associate vice president for research. The job met all of my criteria: it paid more than I currently made, it allowed me to move up in the pecking order, and it contained the fundamentals of challenge, newness, and mystery (the latter because I had no idea what the job really entailed). Besides, how many times can one teach the same course or try to convince administrators of the correctness of a particular path of action? If you can't win with ideas, it is time to move on to a more powerful position.

It is now 11 years since I first became a chair and 9 years since I moved my office to the administration building. On reflection these have been the best of times and the worst of times, or paraphrasing Casey Stengel, "I've won a few, lost a few, and the rest have been rained out." Even as one of "them," I am still expected to teach one class a term, and I still find time to be involved in service activities such as editor of the *Journal of Leisure Research (JLR)*. I have even been able to sneak in a little research and writing, although there is no internal university reward for doing so.

In reality, I have a full-time job as an administrator. Thus, I have a parking space in Lot 1, two rows from the chancellor. I am frequently quoted in the school newspaper as someone with knowledge about current university issues. My advice is sought by a variety of persons from deans and chairs to "ordinary" faculty. And, if the truth be known, I have affected policy and the direction of certain activities within the university.

However, again paraphrasing, "Am I better off than I was eleven years ago?" Maybe no, maybe yes.

No, I am not better off, because I have not fully utilized the investment made in me by my teachers and research mentors at Illinois and elsewhere. I am not investing in a full-time career pursuing in-depth research questions that have the potential to further theory or improve practice. No, I am not, because I have been unable to keep up fully with the literature in the field (except that I do get to read every article submitted to *JLR*, accepted or not). No, I am not because, while I remain devoted to my teaching, it is something that is over and above what is my full-time job.

On the other hand, yes, I am better off, because I find the opportunity to be exposed to issues on a university-wide scale to be both interesting and exhilarating. Yes, because in my own small way I have been able to effect change which not only impacts my own field but the variety of disciplines that make up the university as a whole. And yes, because I probably would not have been happy only dealing in the limited frame of reference that a single department entails.

The good news-bad news about being an administrator centers on the challenges and frustrations of the job. For example, it is challenging being in a position that is not secured by tenure. While I still hold academic rank and can return to my department as a tenured professor, administratively I serve at the pleasure of my superiors. In itself, this is a humbling experience. I am not sure I work any harder or better than I would with a lifetime job guarantee; however, the threat is real and invasive depending on the chances one is willing to take. On the other hand, there is always a tenure-track position to go back to; thus the risks of creativity or failure are not as great as they are for some of the other administrative staff.

The ultimate irony of being an administrator is that I am far less prepared for a "life of the meeting" than I was to undertake the "life of the mind." We complain that few of us learned much about the science and art of teaching while we were in school. Yet, we are asked to stand before a class and impart knowledge or somehow manage to run a seminar. (It is fascinating that we are, in most cases, best prepared by our university training to undertake research, but few of us pursue this activity much beyond tenure.) Hopefully, search committees (also not trained for what they do) are skillful enough to identify individuals who can rise above their backgrounds to become successful administrators. In my case, I hope my selection to undertake administrative activities was not a fulfillment of the "Peter" principle: "Those who can't do, teach; those who can't teach are promoted to the highest levels of administration."

So my daily challenges have involved an 11-*year* struggle to understand how best to administer. I have tried to balance efficiency and effectiveness. It is easy to become too rule-based. It is harder to learn to analyze, assess, plan, and see a problem through with a degree of flexibility, insight, and humanity. It is easy to exercise control. It is harder to understand the value of leading by example; how to set the parameters for action while not having to determine all of the specifics. It is easy to be negative, find fault and blame others. It is harder to be a cheerleader, value incremental progress, and see at least some good in everyone and every situation.

The challenges have also included dealing with the administrative styles of those "above" and "below" me. While being a faculty member also entails getting along with those around you, including those in positions of power, the very nature of the responsibilities in the "big house" seem to magnify the challenge of getting along. Office and university politics need to be mastered; one becomes a general fighting strategic battles (especially when the president is an ex-general), complete with a plan, acceptable casualties, and a ready fallback position. In addition, I have had to gain a whole new perspective on the university, how it is funded, how and to what degree state politics impact our decisions, and short-, medium-, and long-range issues affecting higher education. In other words, the substantive knowledge I gained studying leisure behavior is not of much value (except to the degree social psychological principles of motivation, attribution, learned helplessness, etc., can be applied to the work setting). Thus, all in all, I am involved full-time in a job for which I had neither the knowledge-based education nor the management training. Ah, the rewards of being a self-made administrator.

Of course the job has not been without its frustrations (i.e., challenges that weren't opportunities). My schedule is more externally driven than I would like it to be. Gone are the leisurely hours in the library trying to keep up with the latest knowledge in the field. While we try to avoid crisis management, what needs to be done is too often driven by somebody else's agenda: an urgent "to do" from someone above me who has to have feedback "yesterday."

Then there are the joys of dealing with decision making in an era of retrenchment or, at best, a budgetary stasis. While creative ways can be found to move the university forward, my job contains too many episodes of squelching someone else's creativity or expansionist ideas. While there are opportunities inherent in trying to be "lean and mean," some days I go home only having experienced the "mean."

The bottom line for any administrator could be seen as the results one is able to bring about. But, in reality, success should not only be judged on the basis of results, but also on the basis of process. For example, programs can be eliminated with the brutal stroke of an ax based on unilateral, top-down decisions. Or, a process can be implemented to help impacted constituencies understand the choices and trade-offs involved and the consequences of alternative decisions. The former is often more expedient, with the latter better able to build a basis of support for the chosen outcomes and preserve long-term relationships. In the end, however, once process has had a chance, administrators are often challenged to make tough decisions in circumstances where there is no clear right or wrong answer and where someone will always feel that you haven't done a good job.

There is also the challenge of not letting one's own biases intrude on judgments or decision-making processes. Administration usually requires a broader perspective than viewing the world from the narrow base of one's own discipline or subdiscipline. Thus, at the department level, it was necessary to "see" the whole field of recreation and leisure studies, not just make judgments based on a therapeutic or outdoor recreation perspective. In the same way, administrative responsibilities at the college level require one to have a vision that encompasses a variety of disciplines.

In my case, the vision has to encompass every discipline that makes up the university. I have had to learn the language and expectations of them all. There are vast programmatic, teaching, and scholarly differences between the sciences, music, business, and the humanities. The challenge is to learn to appreciate the perspective which each field takes when dealing with a particular issue and to try to make judgments that take account of these differences. On the other hand, there is a critical need to develop and enforce a university-wide perspective: one that recognizes similarities or needs of the whole versus the parts.

All things considered, it has been quite a ride. The number of "wins" has been greater than the number of "losses" and "rainouts" combined (at least that's what my annual reviews say). Besides making some small difference, I have also learned a lot, and occasionally had a good day. The question of going back to my department on a full-time basis arises occasionally, but after considerable thought, I continue to opt for the kind of responsibilities I am currently undertaking. In fact, at this point I don't know if I will ever resume full-time teaching and research. At the moment, I am having too much fun dealing with colleagues from across the university, trying to play a role in developing the university of the twenty-first century, and learning how to be a good administrator.

My friend Tom Goodale, a writer extraordinaire, once had the humility to note that he was just learning to write a good sentence. I am still learning to make a good decision. Luckily, my research and analytic skills are of use in this process; however, the reviewers seem tougher than those who have judged my journal articles. In the final analysis, administration is just another university job. It takes knowledge, ingenuity, perseverance, tact, energy, and patience, among a hundred other skills, just like teaching, research, and service. As long as I am happy and of use, I will remain an administrator.

18 A Once and Future Chair

Steve Smith

Les, a newly promoted and tenured associate professor, is seeking counsel from Steve, a former chair. The scene is the University Club over a bottle of Chilean cabernet sauvignon. (Les has good taste, but a junior faculty member's budget.)

Steve: Thanks for the wine. This is a good label and a good buy at the liquor store, although the Club's markup is appalling. Be that as it may, let's have a toast. To hard work recognized and rewarded. May you not only have success, but happiness, a career, and a life.

Les: I'll drink to that! I don't know why the administration drags out tenure and promotion decisions so long. It must be nine months since I first submitted my materials.

Steve: Yeah, I know what you mean. I had the same frustrations. All the damn paperwork. Canada can make a decision about hiring an entire Parliament and a Prime Minister faster than this place can make a decision about a simple promotion. I understand that it's getting worse. Every year senior administration comes up with new forms, new information summaries, new pieces of evidence for the candidates to assemble and the tenure committee to read. By the way, did you know your promotion to associate professor has absolutely no practical implications for your salary? You don't get a raise. I guess the maximum you can earn is higher now, but I suspect you weren't anywhere close to the maximum as an assistant professor. Oh, I forgot, there is one financial implication. Your dues at the Club go up.

Les: Humph. I feel so honored.

Steve: Since I'm paying a full professor's dues, I should feel even more honored. Speaking of your tenure decision, as annoying as the paperwork and the long lead time are, there is a reason for it. The university wants to ensure that a fair decision is reached, and that due process and natural justice and all those touchy-feely ideals we hear so much about on campus these days are respected. It's easy to be cynical, but the motivation is good. If a negative decision about promotion or tenure is made, the administration wants to make sure it is the right one.

Les: So they can defend themselves in a lawsuit.

Steve: Granted, but don't trivialize the threat of litigation. I've been threatened with several lawsuits, and I've had to help a couple of your colleagues defend suits. It's not fun. Fortunately, we've always won, but it's still something I'd rather avoid. And I can understand why the administration wants to protect itself.

Les: Steve, let me ask you something, and I hope it doesn't sound mean. You keep speaking of "the administration" like they were someone else. You were part of the administration for a long time. And you weren't just a chair; you served on the University Senate and the Senate Executive. You were even the representative from Waterloo to the Council of Ontario Universities for two years. You are one of them! Or at least you were. Why did you do it? And why did you get out? You see, I've been thinking about getting into administration. I think I might be good at it, but I don't know. How much do you have to compromise your principles? How bad is the bureaucracy? I saw the kinds of hours you had to put in to keep up with your research. I don't know if I want to do it that bad. But, I have some ideas about where this department should go, and I like to think I could get us there. Should I? Would I be any good as chair, or even a dean some day?

Steve: That's a lot of questions. Fill my glass and I'll try to answer them. Let me begin with your basic question. Why did I, why would anyone, want to become department chair? Arrogance. Stupidity. They both play their parts. However, I think there are three basic reasons. They vary in terms of their inherent dignity, but they are all real. First, some people want to become an administrator because they want power. In this university, of course, they are kidding themselves. The only power a chair or dean really has comes from the trust and respect of colleagues. You might be able to force a few small things once in a while, but there are so many checks and balances, and so many bright and obdurate people watching and second-guessing everything you do. An administrator doesn't have power—he or she has trust, and speaks for his or her colleagues—and that's it. Watch out for anyone who goes into administration because they want power. They aren't only dangerous—they're fools. The problem, of course, is that no one admits they do it for the power, but you can often tell. It's hard to hide your true personality very long from your colleagues.

Others become chairs because they worry that if they don't, someone else who wants it for power will make a grab for it. That's how David, my predecessor, talked me into serving as acting chair. He pointed out who the logical choice would be if I said, 'No.' He knew that I knew that person would be in it for the power. My original motivation was thus not terribly noble and was based on David's appeal to my ego. With time, I began to realize one of the other legitimate appeals of being chair—the opportunity to build something.

This is the third reason. And it's the reason why I allowed my name to stand for consideration for election. There is a real intellectual challenge in making sense out of a department as eclectic as ours, in trying to get it to run smoothly, and in helping it develop to its full potential for the students and faculty. You really have to stretch your understanding of what recreation and leisure studies are all about in order to lead this department effectively (not to mention stretching your human relations skills to manage the department's human resources). Maybe there is a fourth reason as well. It's probably a combination of the first three; administration can be a career choice for some people. As you know, university, departmental, and faculty administration is temporary and rotated here. It's a good way to get to know how the university operates and to strengthen your network and reputation on campus and off. If you have the aptitude and interest, it can be valuable professional experience and lead to who-knows-what sort of contacts. You can use your departmental experience as a springboard into more senior administrative positions at other institutions where administration is a permanent career.

Les: I'd like to think the reason I would become department chair is to help lead the department into some areas I think it needs to move. But how do you do that? We've got some pretty strong-willed people in this department and they don't always agree with each other.

Steve: Well, first, I don't think you lead this group of faculty anywhere. I don't need or want to be led. I want my job facilitated. I want resources, support, and somebody to protect me from senior administrators who want to lead me. I suspect that none of us in this department need to be led. I know that a lot of contemporary management literature extols the virtue of managers being leaders, but I don't buy it. At least not for faculty.

Les: Okay. That tells me what you want and don't want. But what should a chair be? A paper pusher?

Steve: No. A chair needs to be a lot of different things to different people. I guess the jargon is "situational manager." There may be a time for a chair to be a leader, but that is not the primary role. Basically, I think a chair is the collective consciousness of the department. He or she needs to spend a lot of time listening and thinking, not talking and doing. You, or any chair, must try to divine why people are doing what they are. What are the faculty teaching and why? What are they doing research on and why? What sort of jobs and co-op positions do our students get and why? What are the staff doing and why? How can you help everyone do their jobs better? At crucial times, which may or may not be obvious, you need to ask questions or pose ideas. You have to become the department's consciousness and conscience. This does not mean you go around telling people what they should do. It means, instead, that you get your colleagues to ask themselves what they should do, and remind them of their obligations to students and to their craft. A good chair manages by getting the department to manage itself.

Les: But how do you do that?

Steve: I don't know. At least I don't know how to tell someone to do it. I only know you need to do it. Maybe it's intuitive. Certainly it requires that, as chair, you put your students, faculty, and staff first. And it requires that the faculty be committed to the department and its mission of teaching, research, and service. If you have a faculty member who doesn't share those values, you are going to spend a lot of time trying either to convert them, or to clean up the messes they make, or in trying to motivate them to find a career elsewhere. None of those three options are pleasant or easy.

Les: What kind of person can be a good chair?

Steve: That's a difficult question. Certain things are obvious and constant, like integrity and respect for other people. In practice though, a department will need different types of chairs at different times. Sometimes you want a builder and visionary. At other times you need a diplomat or healer. Despite the fact that many different types of people can be good at administration, not everyone is cut out for it. One cannot be taught all the skills one needs as chair. An honest, self-reflective, and committed individual can recognize her or his weaknesses and strive to improve on them. But deep down inside, I suspect the best academic administrators—like the best teachers and researchers—are born, not trained. Training can improve your abilities. And, to be sure, without proper training, even a natural administrator is going to be a disaster. Nevertheless, I think there is an inherent talent for administration like there is talent for music or painting. By the way, one of the important skills any chair should possess is the ability to recognize those individuals who have that talent, and to encourage them to think about taking their turn in administration. The ultimate responsibility of a department chair

is to groom his or her replacement. I think you've got what
it takes for administration, and I am pleased to hear you are
thinking the way you are.

Les: Thanks. I wasn't fishing for a compliment.

Steve: I know. I won't joke around about someone's fitness for academic administration. It's too important for them and me.

Les: Okay. Let's assume you're telling me the truth. Should I do
it?

Steve: [sighs] I don't know. You'd be good, and I could work under you, or with you, or whatever is the proper preposition.
There are a lot of neat things about administration. But times
are changing, and I don't think the job is as much fun as it
used to be. You know, in the "old" days when I did it.

Les: What do you mean?

Steve: Alright, lecture mode. First, let's summarize the positive aspects of administration and then the negative ones.

Les: Let's not get pedantic.

Steve: Sorry. On the positive side, a department chair can help build
a department. You can make a difference in how well students are educated, and in how well faculty work together.
You have to have the instincts of a parent, and learn to take
pleasure in your "children's" successes rather than your own.
That pleasure, though, can be real and deeper and more satisfying than many other forms of gratification. Next, you know
that this field is under attack. Politicians and senior university
administrators are always looking for ways to cut budgets.
An academic program with the words "recreation" and "leisure" in it is a tempting target. One of the first challenges I
had to deal with was to justify the existence of this department to a new dean, a new academic vice president, and a
new president. You weren't here then, but things were pretty
tough, and pessimism abounded: not unlike now.

I'll spare you the boring details, but we prevailed. We met the challenge. The biggest problems were to retain our sense of optimism and self-worth, and to find the vocabulary to communicate our message to the administration. It took a conscious decision, but we refused to give up; we refused to doubt our own worth. We believed then, as we do now, in the fundamental importance of this field in higher education, and we formulated rational, objective arguments to support that belief. It was then a matter of finding the words to communicate those arguments to the administration. Fortunately, engineers largely ran Waterloo, as they do today.

I come from a working class family with a father who had worked his way up into senior management in a power plant by sheer willpower and native intelligence. He used to eat young engineers for lunch. Dad taught me how to speak with them. Or maybe I should say "argue" with them. Although dad never graduated from high school, he taught me a lot. Fortunately, my mother was around to help correct and polish a lot of what dad taught me.

Les: Excuse me, but where are we going with this?

Steve: Oops! Sorry. I guess my point is that a chair can fight for the very survival of a department. That's one helluva gratifying experience if it is successful. It's not so great, I guess, if you fail.

Les: No, I don't suppose it would be.

Steve: So, where were we? Oh, yes, building and protecting. Another major joy of being chair is helping your colleagues succeed. You play a role in tenure and promotion decisions like the process you just went through, but as chair, your work begins long before the formal decision process. You have a role in selecting which applicant is hired, in teaching assignments, in committee assignments, in providing fatherly or motherly advice, and in setting the tone of the department. Helping young faculty get a good start is especially important. At Waterloo, and I suspect it's true elsewhere, the faculty workload gets worse every year. There is growing pressure to raise research money, to conduct research, to publish, to provide service to the university and the profession, to get involved with practitioners or industry, to spend more time offering independent studies to students, and to do committee work. I'm glad I'm not a new faculty member. I don't know how many of them will survive emotionally or scholastically. As chair you will have to find ways to protect them until they develop some survival skills and an academic track record.

Les: I know what you mean. I can see an increase in pressure on new faculty who arrived just a few years after I did.

Steve: Yeah, and you had it tougher than I did when I began. Somehow we have to reverse this trend and allow faculty to concentrate on the essential things like teaching and research. You and all the other new chairs will have to find a way to let us take care of the basics first. Then we can succeed. The ironic thing you need to be prepared for, of course, is that when a department is successful, when the faculty work well together, when students are successful, and when the staff are supportive, productive, and happy, the credit goes to the faculty, students, and staff. If, on the other hand, there are faculty cliques, the students are disenchanted, and the staff is bitter, the chair is to blame.

Les: Sounds like a win-lose situation. They win and you lose.

Steve: Well, between you and me, if things are going well, you should give public credit to everyone else. But, as chair, you can take personal pride in the fact that you set the proper tone, create the right environment, and serve as a good role model. You know you share some of the credit, but it is bad form to claim it publicly. It's sort of like a parent taking credit for their child's success. That probably sounds paternalistic, so please don't repeat a word of this.

Les: Okay, it's our secret. Tell me about the flip side. Why don't you think being chair is as much fun as it used to be?

Steve: Well, to start with, the bureaucracy is becoming horrendous. One of the first things I faced was survival of the department. The fight was exhilarating and we won. By the end of my term though, the issue was not making tough decisions or fighting the good fight, but documenting that every move I made was politically correct. Correctness was defined by a variety of faculty, university, Council of Ontario Universities, Ministry of Colleges and Universities, and a wide range of other provincial and federal agencies. I don't disagree with many of the ideals these organizations espouse, but the operationalization of those ideals is something else. At times, I almost fear that my undergraduate dreams have come true."

Les: What do you mean?

Steve: That a philosopher king is running the world. That ideology has vanquished common sense. That form supersedes function. That it is more important to be seen as fair than to be fair.

Les: Aren't you getting a little cynical?

Steve: Well, maybe. But seven years of administration in this current economic and political environment can make you a bit jaded. As I mentioned, I really got my teeth into the job of wanting to help the department progress. As time went along, though, I spent less time on strategic planning and dreaming and more time listening to complaints about why professor x had a smaller office than professor y, about parking, or even about the brand of overhead transparencies we were buying. And if I wasn't listening to complaints, I was attending meetings to discuss problems we wouldn't have had if we hadn't held so many meetings. As chair you will need to deal with some pretty unpleasant situations, such as problems between faculty and staff, accusations of racism, and sexual harassment charges. You will also become privy to some very personal problems. Even if you can help solve the problems, the emotional costs can be high. And if you can't solve them...

Les: So the job of chair has become more complicated, and a lot of it has very little to do with the reasons you became chair in the first place?

Steve: Right. And as I suggested, there is also a much higher degree of accountability. I have no problem with a manager being accountable. The issue is how accountability is defined. In practice, it means an ever-growing volume of paperwork and reports. You will spend much more time reporting what you do and why you did it than you will spend actually doing it.

Les: You sound weary of it. Are you sorry that you spent those years in administration?

Steve: Absolutely not. But, I was ready for a change, and the department needed some fresh blood in the chair as well. I hope my successor, Roger, has the same sense of contribution and accomplishment I had. That position was my vocation for seven years. My fear is that being chair is becoming less of a vocation and more of a job. The political, bureaucratic, and personal demands on chairs are becoming so great that scholars will no longer be capable of filling that function if they are to remain scholars. Although I respect the Waterloo model of rotating administrative positions among scholars, I think the system is burning a lot of us up. It may be time to consider hiring full-time managers as chairs and deans with no pretension that they are faculty. They could be given a contract for 10 years or so with options for renewal.

Les: That doesn't sound terribly attractive. I'm not certain how well a nonacademic person could manage a department.

Steve: I probably have the same concerns you do, but a lot of what chairs deal with is just generic management. Remember, I believe the best departments are really run by the faculty and staff themselves. You simply need a manager who can promote and facilitate a team spirit. It doesn't take a scholar to do that. In fact, scholars are probably the last people you would expect to do it. We're too independent and strong willed.

Les: Well, you still haven't given me a clear answer to my question. Should I aspire to be chair?

Steve: I can't give you a clear answer. I believe you'd be good, but I don't know if you'd be happy.

Les: Then answer this. Would you serve as chair again? Or as dean?

Steve: Hmmm. You have a talent for cutting through the bull, and that's a good sign. Yes, I'd serve again given the right circumstances. But I can also be quite content letting you or someone else do the honors. Let me share a little story with you before we go. When David completed his second term as chair, he gave me three sealed envelopes. He told me, "Steve, you will face a major challenge each year of your tenure as chair. In these three envelopes are the solutions to each challenge. Open each envelope at the proper time and you will be okay." So during my first year, after an initial honeymoon, I was hit with my first big problem. I opened the first envelope. It said, "Blame your predecessor." I blamed David, and I got through the crisis. The second year another problem hit. I opened the second envelope. It said, "Blame the dean." I did, and that crisis, too, passed. The third year I was presented with yet another problem. I ripped open the final envelope and it said, "Prepare three envelopes."

Part III
Making a Difference

These concluding essays stem from a conversation with Alan Watson, a research scientist with the Aldo Leopold Wilderness Institute in Missoula, Montana. Alan mentioned in passing that several of his colleagues were approaching retirement on a sour note, having had second thoughts about their career choices. They questioned whether they had made a difference with their work, and wondered if they might have been better off doing something else. Alan contrasted those individuals with others he knew who, in the twilight of their careers, remained as enthusiastic as ever about the work they were doing.

The purpose of this final section is to explore a variety of questions flowing out of that conversation with Alan. The writing is organized around the general theme of making a difference in academic life. To be sure, the section's contributors have all made a significant difference through the work they do. What we asked of them, however, was not to dwell on their successes, but rather to talk about any misgivings, self-doubts, or insecurities they may have had about their ability to do the job, as well as any other external obstacles they may have encountered along the way that inhibited their ability to make a difference. What we wanted to know, in particular, was how they got beyond those misgivings, self-doubts, insecurities, and external obstacles. How did they manage to stay the course? What was the source of their inspiration? What strategies did they employ? What were their tactics? How did they make academic life work for them?

We ended up with a highly diverse collection of testimonials to the rewards and frustrations of a life spent in higher education as well as some practical tips for making one's way in it. Although most of the contributors are known for their scholarship, many of them chose to focus on teaching-related concerns—the joy of working with graduate students and the challenge of reaching undergraduate students. Others focused on the importance of making connections on and off campus to "make things happen." Still others chose to write about the costs and benefits of choices made and the serendipitous nature of opportunities for professional growth and development.

These essays reveal the genuine satisfaction of working in higher education, the deeply rewarding nature of a career devoted to the "life of the mind," and the hope that springs eternal from working with students. The essays provide strong anecdotal evidence in support of the proposition that a life spent in higher education is anything but academic. We trust this concluding section will serve as a pep talk for professors who are wondering if they are making a difference, as well as a source of inspiration for students who are considering a life in higher education.

19 A Very Privileged Form of Service
Geof Godbey

All events have meaning because they affect everything else.

> The flapping of a single butterfly's wings today produces
> a tiny change in the state of the atmosphere. Over a period
> of time, the atmosphere actually does diverge from what
> it would have done. So, in a month's time, a tornado that
> would have devastated the Indonesian coast doesn't hap-
> pen. Or maybe one that wasn't going to happen, does.[1]

As professors, we are very much like the butterfly whose flapping
wings bring undreamt of change. There is a lot of pretending when it comes
to understanding the impacts one makes in academic life. Part of this pretending is to label teaching or research or service as separate, fairly uni-
form commodities that can be ranked in terms of accomplishment. There
is, however, much mystery in these processes. So much of learning, for example, is unplanned serendipity that I have always been suspect of highly
regimented curriculums based on professors' assumptions that, without a
given course, one's education is incomplete. Similarly, grades are a very
uncertain indicator of learning, acceptance of articles by refereed journals
is an abysmally poor indicator of importance, and the publishing of books
is a very imprecise predictor of the advancement of knowledge. This is
not to argue the system of education we have been a part of is meaning-
less, only that it is so hideously complex we feel forced to reduce its
meaning to what is manageable. One must therefore be cautious not only
of assessing a career in absolute terms, but also in trying to guess about
each of the questions a journalist would ask about the influence one may
or may not have had as a professor: who, what, when, where, why, and
how?

The environment in which young professors work today has become
much more corporate and guided by desire for short-term profit, efficiency,

and good public relations. There are compelling reasons why this has happened. The state, increasingly, is not interested or, in some cases, able to be the primary financer of higher education. Simultaneously, academics have come to expect to live middle- or upper-middle-class lives, and students have come to expect campus infrastructures to resemble Disney World. Massive cost increases and funding decreases mean students whose parents can pay high tuition become "customers" of the university. Alumni who have lots of money can shape a university's mission through donations and must be courted and pleased. Government and corporate funders of research shape tenure and promotion decisions by the grants they give—or don't. In such an environment, there is a great effort to objectify in the name of efficiency. Since I don't accept that much of this process can be accurately measured, judging the impact of one's own career seems improbable.

There is a saying I like that, academically, we can become specialists, learning more and more about less and less until we know everything about nothing, or we can become generalists, learning less and less about more and more until we know nothing about everything. It seems that most professors in our field have opted for specialization. My own program, for instance, assigns people to options in specialties such as outdoor recreation or therapeutic recreation. I have not been assigned an option. Perhaps this is because I wanted to work at a different level of specificity than some others did, wanted to work with people in other academic departments, other universities, other countries, other occupations, and with other worldviews. I managed to do so.

About Teaching

The first teaching I did was to inner city students enrolled in an associate degree program at a Penn State branch campus outside Philadelphia. Then, at the University of Waterloo, in Ontario, Canada, I worked with undergraduates. Most of my career, I have worked at Penn State with a mix of undergraduate and graduate students. I have always done undergraduate teaching and did not buy out of it when I could have—not sure why.

In terms of a teaching "philosophy," most professors don't merely give in to situational ethics in terms of what they think is worthwhile. Here is what I wrote in 2005 when I was nominated for Penn State's Graduate School Teaching Award (didn't get it):

I believe that good teaching involves finding ways to make the subject matter taught relevant to the life of the individual learner. While it is imperative that the learners extend their concern and understanding past their own individual lives, personal relevance is often the starting point. Sometimes students have a limited sense of what is "relevant," so a case must be made that what is being taught is or can be relevant to them. This means, whenever possible, using concrete examples and projects that illustrate the application of theories and major research findings to their everyday lives. The learner may start off with such concern for his or her own life but must gradually develop concern for the life of every other person with regard to the subject matter in question.

Successful teaching requires continuous learning on the part of the teacher, both in terms of the subject matter taught as well as instructional techniques. Thus, successful teaching involves a life of learning on the part of the instructor. For example, major shifts have occurred during the last decade in the very meaning of "literacy." Such shifts must be recognized and incorporated into teaching techniques.

Finally, the cognitive and affective are highly interrelated in regard to most successful teaching. Students learn better when they recognize that the teacher cares about them personally and, in turn, they care about the teacher. This means successful teaching is an inherently passionate endeavor.

Teaching is serving, albeit a very privileged form of service.

Such a philosophy doesn't mean that students become the professor's equal. In the classroom, you know more than they do and need to be the final judge. To the extent a student wants to learn and is intelligent and willing to work, the judging process gradually declines in importance. To the extent that a student's motivation and willingness to work is suspect, things are different. These students learn very quickly that writing counts, specific and detailed knowledge trumps generalities, grades assigned are more likely generous than not, and a professor's time and patience are not unlimited.

As tenure becomes more difficult to obtain, as students (and their parents) pay a larger share of the financial costs of their education, the undergraduate student has also become a "customer." The problem with this, of course, is that "the customer is always right." Unfortunately, students aren't. It is stunning to talk with undergraduate students in China and try and get them to voice an opinion; regardless of how much they know about the subject in question. Undergraduates in the United States are quick to venture opinions on subjects they know virtually nothing about. Somewhere in the middle is a happy medium.

Students do respond better when they get to know you and you them. Over the years, I have taught more than 20 courses at my home. It is amazing to me what a difference this makes.

Research

I was never a very good researcher, although I have done lots of it and won awards for it. I'm simply too impatient. I'm pretty good at the front end when it comes to conceptualizing and relating ideas to strategies for gathering data. I'm also pretty good at the back end when it comes to the "so what" issue. But the data gathering itself is a kind of indeterminate tedium, however critical to the process. It was, therefore, always necessary for me to work with someone else who had the patience and insight to guide the collection of data and management of the grant. Recreation and parks is a field of study, like many others, that invites researchers to basically document what everyone in the field already believes: outdoor recreation is good for you; mainstreaming is functional; eco-tourism is good for the environment; parks serve the public and are supported by the public; leisure is good and important; women are always the victim; ethnic minorities are always the victim; old people are always the victim; people with disabilities are always the victim; corporate sponsored leisure is usually bad; playgrounds are good; entertainment is bad; outdoor education is good; and camping in tents is superior to camping in cabins.

The researcher faces the problem that most research doesn't produce the kind of unequivocal results that the rhetoric of the field implies. Most findings are complex, contradictory, and rarely provide the kind of hoped-for guidelines for practice in an applied field like our own. Research in recreation and leisure rarely involves triangulation, rarely is longitudinal, and rarely has sufficient funding. I was involved in only one or two studies that provided a very clear answer. Dave Chase and I studied members of a swim club and members of a tennis club in terms of how accurately they could estimate their participation. Since both clubs had sign-in systems for participants that were relatively secure, we could determine attendance records accurately. When we asked hundreds of club members to estimate how many times they used these clubs in the last 12 months, their average error of estimation (overestimation) was more than 100 percent.

Since the market sector influences leisure much more than the public sector, working with companies that provide leisure and tourism services has been an interest. It is instructive to see how their approach to research varies and to understand the different constraints under which they work. Being impatient, I love the immediacy of market-sector research. There is rapid application as a product, service, or ad campaign is rushed to market. At this late stage in my career, it seems one of the biggest failings of our field has been to ignore the market sector. Leisure is controlled largely by corporations in the United States, and our academic work needs to play a role in their services.

Scholarly Writing

This has always been my love. Writing is a form of teaching, although one rarely knows who is taught or what they are taught. Early in my life, I had romantic ideas about making a living as a poet. I was also attracted to journalism and wrote for school newspapers, wrote an unpublished novel, and read very widely. I was always interested in philosophical questions as well.

Much has changed in terms of academic writing. A few decades ago, writing a scholarly book or a textbook was a seminal event. Now, assistant professors are admonished to crank out three journal articles a year but not to even think about a book until one is a full professor. One is also advised that the nonrefereed periodicals, such as *Parks and Recreation*—the only thing most practitioners in our field might read—don't count for much. I have written widely—many books, articles, papers, chapters—usually based on what interested me. I have also written for a broad variety of periodicals: *Social Research, Public Opinion, The World and I, American Journal of Preventive Medicine, American Demographics, The Nation, The Futurist, Dialectics in Nature* (A Chinese philosophy journal), and lots of others. Most of the time in universities, I have taught the courses I was assigned (usually without input) but have written just what I wanted.

When I was a new assistant professor, I met Dr. Richard Kraus at a conference. Dick was a leading textbook author and a shrewd observer of academic life. He motioned for me to come over to him. "Godbey," he said without preliminary niceties, "you're an idiot." This was not what I wanted to hear. "Why?" I inquired. "You write twenty articles about different subjects and think people read what you wrote. You have to write one thing twenty times, polish it, improve it, and keep it going until people get the message." Looking back, he was absolutely right.

Part of "getting out the message" involves working with the media. Over the years, I've done perhaps 300 interviews with journalists and writers. This seems partly a service function, but it also helps get the message out—sometimes to millions of people. There are dangers in this. The message has to be simplified; sometimes too simplified. Journalists get things wrong. Most journalists don't know if you are competent or truthful. Nevertheless, it has been pleasing to have done many interviews where leisure studies has been taken seriously.

The important ideas that one writes about are usually repackaged versions of ancient ideas. Ideas such as "flow," or "play," or "leisure," or "specialization in recreation," or "constraints," or "mainstreaming," or "place attachment" are all ancient ideas. The talented writer makes such ideas relevant; sees new possibilities in them. Hence, the statement "Immature professors imitate; mature professors steal." The thief, however, must add, interpret, and look at what is stolen through a different light. Imitation, of course, is also stealing; only it is petty theft.

Lots of my writing has found its way into other languages. This has been a source of joy for me. As the world's economy center shifts toward the Asian perimeter, leisure and tourism have become important topics there. In some ways, "leisure" is a new idea in these ancient cultures. How "leisure" is prepared for in China, or in India, is of critical importance in terms of world stability. China has interested me for two decades. The more I study it, the less I know. Reading Confucius helped a bit. As Dan Dustin made me aware, the Chinese use hospitality as a way of keeping you from understanding much about them. So do people in many of the 20 countries I have visited over the years. Nevertheless, through making friends with people in these countries, I could begin the journey of understanding.

I have written with many other authors during my lifetime—too many to name here. There has never been a serious disagreement with any of them in 35 years. One reason, for this, I think, is that it was agreed upon in advance who would be the "primary" author. That person had the final authority and responsibility for the article, book, etc. Also, I wrote only with people I liked and whose work I respected.

In Sum

Much of whatever difference I made may be attributable to having a somewhat contrarian view of both leisure studies and life in general. While leisure is a hugely important part of life, we rarely know how to study it or don't have the resources when we do. Still, we are getting the subject on the radar screen of higher education. Our curricula are being imitated in countries as diverse as Korea and Australia. Being a part of this has been both frustrating and exhilarating. Some of my frustration is that our field lacks almost any meaningful academic debate. No academic discipline or subject matter can remain important for very long without the hypothesis-antithesis-synthesis process that Hegel and many Greek philosophers espoused. The exhilarating part has been working with faculty who have very high emotional intelligence. By and large, scholars in our field have come closer to perfecting themselves ethically than their colleagues in other departments.

I can't judge what I have contributed, but what has been contributed to me is humbling and marvelous.

"Faith-Based" Teaching
Dan Dustin

In 1990 I published *Beyond Promotion and Tenure: On Being a Professor.*[1]
I dedicated the book to Howard Williams, a professor of education at the
University of Minnesota. In retrospect, it surprises even me that I dedicated
a book to a man from whom I took only one course: a course about which
I remember virtually nothing. What I do remember about Howard Williams
was his gracious demeanor. He was the kind of professor who shut out
the rest of the world when you were in his company. He treated you as
if you were the most important person on earth. He made time for you.
He always had a cup of coffee brewing in his office and a nearby plate of
freshly baked cookies. If the phone rang during your conversation, he let
it ring.

The memory I cherish most about Dr. Williams was his unabashed
enthusiasm for language. He once told me we must be kindred spirits, since
we both loved to roll words around in our mouths and test them out on the
ear before we committed them to paper. He always listened carefully to
what I had to say, and he reinforced my thinking with constructive criticism
and a smile. He made me feel as if we were on equal intellectual footing,
which, of course, we were not, and he appeared to derive genuine joy from
my learning. He made me feel really good about being a student.

There have been other memorable professors as well. I chose geography as an undergraduate major at the University of Michigan not so much
because of the subject matter, but because of John Kolars and George Kish.
Kolars was a bespectacled "Indiana Jones," recounting stories of African-
based cultural geography, and embellishing them with dramatic gestures
and outrageous actions. He once cut his tie in half to make a point, and
another time he threw a pointer across the room like a Zulu warrior. Kish
taught the geography of Europe, affectionately known as "Dining and
Wining Your Way across Europe" by Michigan students. A diminutive,

nattily dressed man in tweed, who placed his pocket watch on the lectern to begin each class, professor Kish exuded culture, refinement, and taste.

A few years later, when I returned to Michigan as a master's student, there was Stephen Kaplan, who began his classes by leaning against the blackboard and waiting patiently for students to ask questions about their reading before he would turn those questions into the day's lecture. The silences were so awkward at first that we soon raised questions aplenty just to avoid the embarrassment of prolonged quiet. It was also during those Michigan years that when the final lecture had been delivered, students showed their gratitude by giving their professors a hearty round of applause.

The academic world I now inhabit is a far cry from the University of Michigan and the University of Minnesota "way back" in the 20th century. Part of the difference, I suppose, is due to the fact that I've spent most of my career at San Diego State University and Florida International University, two institutions that are mainly undergraduate teaching-oriented. They are also, for the most part, commuter schools. They lack the residential atmosphere that made university life so stimulating at Michigan and Minnesota.

My students have also tended to be cut from a different cloth than those with whom I shared a classroom when I was a student. This has been both good and bad for my professional psyche. The good rests in my direct involvement in the democratization of higher education. No longer is a college diploma reserved for a few well-positioned sons and daughters of America's upper classes. All high school graduates now have access to a higher education via community colleges and state-supported universities like San Diego State and Florida International. The rising tide of affordable and accessible schooling has lifted the formal educational prospects for all citizens.

The bad rests in the fact that since we now let "everybody" in, I must deal with annoyances, the likes of which professors Williams, Kolars, Kish, and Kaplan never had to contend; cell phones disrupting class; students exhibiting little or no interest in pursuing ideas; students trying to pass off first drafts of papers as finished products; students becoming upset with me when I critique those drafts, as though I should be able to see the beauty of their well-reasoned thinking inside their invisible interiors even though they have not expressed those thoughts clearly or coherently on paper; students then becoming even more upset with me when I do not reward them for their effort—as if I should be able to see and evaluate, for grading purposes, all the blood, sweat, and tears they assure me they put into their work. Finally, and perhaps most discouraging, most of my students view a college degree as but a ticket into the workforce, a ticket they would gladly purchase outright for most any sum if it would mean dispensing with the hassle of a higher education altogether.

Why, then, you might ask, do I continue in this line of work? The answer, as I have grown to understand it, is rooted in my faith. Not a religious faith, mind you, but in my fundamental belief that somewhere in that vast sea of undergraduate faces is an unpolished "gem," a student who will begin my class by taking my admonition to turn off his cell phone seriously; a student who will be receptive to discussing ideas; a student who will want to read; a student who will want to write and rewrite until his or her paper says exactly what was intended; a student who will take my criticism of that paper to heart and then work even harder to improve upon it; a student who will understand that the real purpose of a college education is not to prepare for a career, but to prepare for enlightened citizenship in a representative democracy; and, finally, a student who will never want the learning to stop. In my 30 years in higher education, I have run across but a handful of such students. That handful has sustained me.

I recall one undergraduate, in particular, who enrolled in my Wilderness and the Leisure Experience course at San Diego State University more than 20 years ago. She wrote a paper on feminist thinking as it relates to our culture's view of nature, a paper I found so intriguing that I spent several years acquainting myself with the feminist literature and thinking about its implications for nature-based issues. Eventually, I gathered my thoughts and placed them in the *Journal of Leisure Research* in "The dance of the dispossessed: On patriarchy, feminism, and the practice of leisure science."[2] To this day, it is one of the articles I feel best about. It came about because of what one undergraduate student taught me. Oh how I wish there had been more like her.

I know I sound elitist. I also know there are students at San Diego State and Florida International who are just as bright as any Ivy Leaguer. There just aren't nearly as many of them. Ensuring that everyone has access to a college education means classrooms are filled with a lot of "students" who aren't really students, and who shouldn't really be there. They reveal themselves in a variety of ways, but it is through their use, or perhaps I should say misuse, of language that many of them let me know who they are. "We take our world for granite," they write. These are individuals who attend college because it is fashionable, or because it seems as good a place as any to come of age. It was no great mystery to me why students frequently took six, eight, or even ten years to get through San Diego State. Why would anyone be in a rush to leave that beautiful city by the sea?

The challenge for me has always been how best to mine the classroom for those rare "gems"? The magnitude of that challenge has been enlarged by the fact that the universities within which I've worked have had less promising "ore" than elsewhere. But when I do find students of promise, I do all I can for them. I do not spend a lot of time, however, trying to create students from scratch. I confess further that I no longer work very hard at trying to bring all my students into the fold. I did at one time. I used to think that if I didn't reach all my students, I was failing somehow. Somewhere along the line my thinking changed. Perhaps I merely learned to rationalize my own inadequacies as a professor, but I have come to believe that all I am really obliged to do for students is share my own enthusiasm for learning. The content of what I teach changes all the time, and typically I focus on half-baked ideas. But, what hasn't changed over the years, what has proved enduring, and what I can teach by example, is my own passion for learning. To the extent that passion rubs off on my students, I count myself a success. My job, I have come to believe, is modeling what being a good student is like.

This perspective frequently puts me at odds with commonly accepted measures of teaching effectiveness. I don't find passing out student evaluations at the end of the semester to be a particularly meaningful exercise. As I touched on in chapter 1 of this book, students might be in a good position to tell me how much they enjoyed my course, but they are in no position to tell me if my teaching is based on the best available knowledge. That kind of determination is best left up to other professors. As it turns out, I don't get that kind of feedback from colleagues visiting my classroom either. I get it from other professors blindly, and sometimes not so blindly, reviewing my written and spoken words.

I also find it unrealistic to expect that any germs of thought that actually take root in my students' heads will bear fruit by the end of a 15-week semester. The seeds of ideas we discuss might take years to germinate, if ever. In this regard, I am still thinking about, and publishing, ideas that were presented to me in rudimentary form when I was a student at Michigan and Minnesota more than 30 years ago. Under the circumstances, trying to measure teaching effectiveness in the context of a semester's passing appears silly to me.

I have also found that my sense of humor helps sustain me. My favorite story in this regard stems from a series of encounters I had with a beautiful coed at San Diego State University. She was particularly attentive throughout the semester. Too much so, I thought. She would linger after class and engage me in chitchat, talking about this and that. I was in my mid-40s at the time, and I couldn't quite bring myself to believe she might have a romantic interest in me. I was flattered, of course, and single to boot. Finally, at the end of the semester, after all her work had been turned in and graded, she stayed after class one last time and waited for everyone else to leave the room. Then she came up to me, smiled, and said sweetly, "Dr. Dustin, I know I've been staying after class a lot, and I know you must have wondered what I was thinking. Well, to tell you the truth, I was thinking that you're really neat, and I really like you a lot, and... well... I was just wondering if you'd be interested in going out with my mother?"

How, then, do I know if I'm doing a good job in the classroom? The answer is once again rooted in my faith. If I remain engaged in my own learning, and if I work hard to share what I learn publicly, whether it is through writing, speaking, or classroom teaching, I can proceed on the faith that I'm doing what is expected of me as a college professor. Evidence of my teaching effectiveness may surface only infrequently, perhaps when a student tells me years later about the educational role I played in his or her life, or when someone tells me how much an article or book I wrote influenced her or his thinking. Those occurrences were few and far between earlier in my career, but they are happening more frequently now. Perhaps it just requires a long time for some things to take.

As Geof Godbey suggests in his essay, I think Chaos Theory may have something to teach us here. As professors, we may do some little thing, or say some little thing, or teach some little thing that someday down the road results in a big effect after all. We can't predict that effect, or when it will happen, or to whom it will happen, but we can be buoyed by the optimism Chaos Theory provides when it postulates that such effects are bound to happen. In the meantime, our faith, reinforced with a good sense of humor, must sustain us.

Think back for a moment on this chapter's beginning. What do I remember of Howard Williams, John Kolars, George Kish, or Stephen Kaplan? Is it what they taught me, or is it who they were? I spoke of Howard Williams' gracious demeanor. I spoke of John Kolars' energy and enthusiasm for his subject matter. I spoke of George Kish's dignity, refinement, and taste. I spoke of Stephen Kaplan's patience and willingness to endure awkward silences, and then to draw the learning out of the students themselves.

Did any one of these professors actually know what effect they were having on me? I doubt it. I was quiet and nondescript. I was but one face in a vast sea of faces. I was but one student among hundreds, if not thousands, they taught over the course of their careers. They, too, I have come to believe, were most certainly engaged in "faith-based" teaching.

Things That We Believe In

Karla Henderson

Cheesy as it may sound to some people, I have always been a big John Denver fan. His music and words spoke to me in 1970 and continue to speak to me today. Some of my favorite lyrics come from "Poems, Prayers, and Promises":

> I've been lately thinking
> About my life's time
> All the things I've done
> And how it's been...
> And I have to say it now
> It's been good life all in all
> It's really fine
> To have a chance to hang around
> And lie there by the fire
> And watch the evening tire...
> And talk of poems and prayers and promises
> And things that we believe in
> How sweet it is to love someone
> How right it is to care...

I began the journey into parks and recreation almost 30 years ago. Before that, I had been "doing" parks and recreation, but didn't know it. What keeps me going is that I believe in the value of leisure, and in parks and recreation as a profession. I look forward to sharing a little about my path and *how right it is to care.*

I believe that I have made a difference in the lives of students, colleagues, and friends. I have to believe that my life matters or it would not be possible to get up every day. *For tho' my life's been good to me there's still so much to do.* In this essay, I describe the trajectory of my academic life and my ability to make a difference during academic turning points. Everyone has turning points, including moments of insight as well as stumbling blocks. As I look back, I see how those turning points provided new opportunities to make a difference and to *talk of poems and prayers and promises and things that we believe in.*

Trains, Leisure, Friends, and Mediocrity

The things that have been omnipresent in my life and that have facilitated my academic work are trains, leisure, friends, and mediocrity. This combination of ideas may seem a bit strange, but I will try to explain them. Ever since I was a child, "The Little Engine that Could" has provided me my mantra: "I think I can, I think I can, I think I can…" It was the original self-help book on the power of positive thinking, and my mother reminded me frequently of the story when I was young. Whether running a marathon or overcoming a writing block, the train metaphor is always foremost in my mind.

I won't say much about leisure, because I have spent most of my life talking about it. A belief in leisure and in our profession is the tie that binds my academic life. Although our field is often misunderstood and underappreciated, I believe in its importance and how much more research and evaluation we need to demonstrate its value.

My friends have always been important to me as they are to most people. Although I have many friends who are not in my academic field, my closest friends are the colleagues whom I have been privileged to know over the years. The older I get, the more important my personal and collegial friendships become (and often those two are inseparable), and the more I realize how much I continue to rely on those individuals who represent mentors, role models, confidants, and buddies all at once. *How sweet it is to love someone… and what about our dreams and all the memories we share.*

Mediocrity probably sounds like a strange element to talk about, and yet that idea has defined my professional career. A turning point for me occurred during my first job in higher education when I saw the movie *Amadeus.* The movie focuses on Antonio Salieri who believed Amadeus Mozart's music was divine. He wished he were as good as Mozart so he could praise the Lord through composing. Salieri's quote in the movie shook me. "I speak for all mediocrities in the world. I am their champion.

I am their patron saint." In my first job as a professor I confronted my mediocrity. I recalled someone once telling me that the more education you get, the more you realize what you don't know. In living the life of a professor at a major university, I realized how much smarter many of my colleagues were than me. They didn't seem to have doubts about themselves and I saw people around me doing "divine" work. Being the "Little Engine that Could" always served me well, but I realized that in the academic world, no matter how hard I tried, I was average. I questioned whether I belonged in higher education, but eventually decided that not everyone could be brilliant, and my hard work and dedication to the field of recreation was the gift I had to offer.

Getting Started

Thus, buoyed by trains, leisure, friends, and the threat of mediocrity, I have enjoyed my academic life and the differences I did and didn't make. My first job at the University of Wisconsin-Madison (UW-M) gave me a plethora of opportunities. Holding a split appointment as an assistant professor and an extension recreation specialist gave me the best of both the academic and practitioner life. I loved traveling around the state consulting with recreation directors and commissions/boards about enhancing recreation opportunities in their communities. Growing up in a land grant university culture (Iowa State University/Go Cyclones!), I believed the boundaries of campus were the boundaries of the state. I loved having the world of research open to me and trying to figure out its practical applications. I loved being a professor.

One experience that made a profound difference in my life was a graduate seminar on "women and leisure" that I taught in 1981. Interestingly, this course was not my idea. A group of progressive female graduate students came to me one day and said they were concerned that everything about recreation, leisure, and continuing education was male biased. Wasn't there anything written about women and leisure? Their question was a turning point for me. I had no answer for them. Although I considered myself a feminist, it had not occurred to me that something was missing in our field. I designed the course with huge input from those students. We read articles about recreation/leisure and women's studies, and then put it all together. Little did I know in 1981 that this line of research would sustain me for the next 20 years.

UW-M also provided the most difficult professional turning point in my career and forced me to confront my mediocrity and commitment to the field of recreation. I was denied tenure and promotion. I was devastated and really did not know what I wanted to do next. Fortunately, I received dozens of letters from colleagues and former students who protested my situation and boosted my ego. I also will never forget the words of my Department Chair, Jerry Apps, who said, "Do your work with professionalism and integrity, and the rest will follow." I had worked as hard as I could, and I had not sold my soul to the tenure process. Some politics in my Department contributed to the negative tenure and promotion decision, but I also knew that I had tried to do too much. My research was not focused and, in retrospect, not of the highest quality. I loved Madison and the wacky liberal ambience of the city, but I knew I had to leave if I was going to continue with the research I had only begun on women and leisure. I also wanted to continue to proselytize about the value of recreation for individuals and communities.

I accepted my next job mainly to save face. I thought being Department Chair was what I wanted, but I soon learned that the fit was not right for me. I quickly became uninterested in an administrative fast track. I was planning to leave academe until Chris Howe changed everything for me with a phone call. She invited me to co-chair the 1986 National Recreation and Park Association Leisure Research Symposium. Since it was a two-year commitment, I could hardly leave higher education. More importantly, however, I considered Chris' research and thinking to be divine and she saw me as a worthy person.

The two years I spent at Texas Woman's University were not easy. Nevertheless, I brought a broader progressive feminist view to my students and the university. I developed really important friendships with what I thought were the only four feminist colleagues on campus. And finally, after many rejections, some of my research on women and leisure was published.

Opportunities to Make a Difference

Doug Sessoms, whom I will always consider my most cherished colleague, "saved me from Texas" (his words, not mine). He invited me to come to the University of North Carolina-Chapel Hill (UNC-Chapel Hill) for a one-year visiting associate professor position, which became a tenure-track position the following year. UNC-Chapel Hill offered an opportunity to return to a more liberal environment where I could nurture my research and teaching about women and leisure as well as explore new ways of doing research.

My 17 years at UNC-Chapel Hill offered many opportunities for creative teaching, innovative and social change-oriented research, and enthusiastic service. "I think I can, I think I can," provided my passion for the work. I had the opportunity to write about my research as well as my view of our profession. I got the opportunity to serve professionally in the Society of Park and Recreation Educators, the American Alliance for Health, Physical Education, Recreation and Dance Research Consortium, and in journal editing, and to meet many colleagues and develop significant friendships. Colleagues inside and outside the university rewarded my efforts with recognition. Promotion to Full Professor with tenure was a fairly seamless process. Five years after arriving at UNC-Chapel Hill, and I had already established a reputation with my focus on women and the use of the interpretive research paradigm. I was given the opportunity to be Department Chair again and served reluctantly, and mostly with mediocrity, for eight years. I tried, however, to always do my academic work with professionalism, care, and integrity. I believed in our field, and I felt that the recreation faculty at UNC-Chapel Hill was contributing to the liberal education of students as well as providing a solid general education in recreation for our majors at the undergraduate and master's levels. The UNC-Chapel Hill recreation program was small, but per capita we were every bit as productive as any other unit on campus in terms of credit production and scholarly output. Looking back, three turning points are evident from my UNC-Chapel Hill days.

First, I received many comments about my scholarly publications. One person commented on how "accessible" my writing was. I was perplexed by that. What did this person mean? Was the writing anti-intellectual? I pondered the comment and other similar remarks for some time. I thought my mediocrity was being reflected once again. Today, however, I take those comments as a compliment. If my writing isn't accessible to most people, then it probably doesn't matter because it won't be read. I am glad that perhaps my mediocrity makes me better able to communicate some of the ideas that are most important to me. As I have the opportunity to edit my own work as well as the work of others, I want to make sure the research in our field is accessible and user-friendly.

A second turning point for me was the day I learned of Chris Howe's untimely and tragic death. We were friends and she was Mozart to my Salieri. Unfortunately, Chris was not always what she appeared to be. She had self-doubts and remarked to me on several occasions that she wondered if anyone in our field knew what they were doing and whether or not any of it mattered. I sometimes shared those doubts, but the shock and sadness of Chris's death gave me a renewed goal to erase those reservations and work harder to show the difference that our profession makes in the world.

Three years ago I had to confront a third turning point that was a huge disappointment in the waning years of my professional career. Because I was Department Chair, I will always feel a great deal of responsibility for what happened at UNC-Chapel Hill when our Department was dismantled. Although I did not agree with the way the situation was handled, I did agree that a small unit like ours was administratively inefficient in a large university. I believed, however, that our recreation program should have curricular autonomy. I was devastated when I realized the administration thought recreation was the same as exercise science, and that the title of the major didn't make any difference. Leisure and recreation were *things that we believe in* and I wasn't sure I wanted to remain in a university that did not value my work and field of study. I was deeply saddened that UNC-Chapel Hill had just stepped back in time 40 years. *What about tomorrow and what about our dreams...*

The old saying goes that when a door closes a window opens. I believe in karma. My friends and colleagues, Beth Wilson and Doug Wellman, from North Carolina State University (NC State) "saved me from UNC-Chapel Hill" (my words, not theirs). They had plans for me at NC State and helped reinforce for me the idea that *there's still so much to do*. My commute is now 22 miles instead of seven, and I have never been more satisfied professionally. I have new areas of research to explore and new opportunities to mentor Ph.D. students. I am ready once more to make a difference. "I think I can, I think I can, I think I can..."

It's Been a Good Life All in All

I am proud of several aspects of my academic career. I am thankful that I never gave up, even though I wanted to several times. I am satisfied that I worked hard with professionalism and integrity and still found time to pursue my own leisure interests in running, music, hiking, writing, and spending time with friends. I appreciate the privilege and the platform I have had in teaching to provide some "cognitive dissonance" and some new ways of thinking for my students. I know from course evaluations and periodic notes that my efforts have not been in vain. I do not regret venturing into new areas of research even though they weren't conventional at the time. My recognition of the demon of mediocrity has challenged me to work harder and write better. I have made a contribution to the body of knowledge and the way people in our field think about gender, diversity, and qualitative data.

My life has been enriched by many people. I have mentioned some of them in this essay, but dozens more influence me and have become friends. I am not going to make a list because I will miss someone, but I hope each of them knows who they are. I hold each of my friends in great esteem whether they are colleagues, students, mentors, role models, or some combination thereof. Although "thinking I can," mediocrity, and my commitment to recreation and leisure shaped the foundation of my academic career, I couldn't do anything without my friends. Together we have made, and continue to make, a difference.

> And I have to say it now
> It's been a good life all in all
> It's really fine
> To have a chance to hang around
> And lie there by the fire
> And watch the evening tire
> And talk of poems and prayers and promises
> And things that we believe in.

22

A Gleam in the Eye
Leo McAvoy

A bit of reflection on how I reached retirement should help put the past 33 years of teaching and research into perspective. I confess, I do have some apprehension about retirement. Will I find other engagements that will bring me as much satisfaction and fulfillment as being a full-time professor? I think so, but I am still a bit uncertain about how I will make the transition to my next life adventure. Reflection now is a good thing.

I'll focus on my personality and how it influenced my approach to my work and on three elements of being a professor that have made this such a wonderful career for me: (a) the opportunity to work with students; (b) the opportunity to direct my research and teaching towards my own interests; and (c) the freedom-flexibility-variety elements of being a professor.

Personality

I am the eldest of four children, thus one who would feel obligated to lead, do well, set an example, and succeed. I'm also a "Leo" (August 16th birthday) with the name of "Leo," so you can see the possibilities for being a first-class jerk in an academic gown. I don't think I turned out that way, but who is to say? When I ask myself the question, "What has kept you involved as a professor even though you are in the twilight of your career and could retire in place as have so many others?" I think the primary answer is pride. I can go on here about how my work is important and how I am making a difference in people's lives, but I think the reality is that my pride will not allow me to do a half-baked job on anything. I just could not face students or colleagues if I had not done my very best in teaching, advising, research, and writing. Maybe that is fear of failure, or fear of embarrassment for a job not done well, but I think it is just plain pride.

This drive to do a good job was shaped by my family and by my early experiences. I believe I learned all I ever needed to know about being a successful professor from my parents. My dad was a farmer with an eighth-grade education, and my stay-at-home mom completed one year of college. I grew up in an idyllic situation on a small dairy farm in central Michigan. I attended a one-room country school for eight years of elementary school, where my teacher for the first four years was my father's cousin. She had been my father's teacher in that same school when she was 18 years old and just a year out of teacher training back in the 1920s.

My dad was the nicest, most respectful man I have ever known. He was physically the strongest man I knew, and the most gentle. He always stressed that we should do good work and do our best. We all worked together on the farm milking and caring for cows, planting and harvesting crops, and all the other seemingly endless jobs that needed to be done on a small farm. He always stressed to his children, "Do the job well today and don't put things off until tomorrow—it might rain." My mom was a strong woman with a loving yet forceful personality. She urged all of her children to "plan ahead, make good decisions, and then go for it. You can do anything." My parents both emphasized that education was the key to success. All four McAvoy children graduated from college, which was quite unusual for families in that area.

The other source of my motivation to stay active and productive is the package of elements that makes university work so rewarding and fun for me; the students, the opportunity to direct my research and teaching towards my own interests, and the freedom and variety academic work has provided me. I will address each of these elements and try and show how they have influenced my work, what the major challenges have been in those areas, and how I think I was able to carry on in the face of some challenges.

Students

The opportunity to work with capable and caring students has sustained my enthusiasm for the life of a professor. If I have made a difference it probably has been with, and because of, students. *A Gleam in the Eye* refers to the spark I see when a student understands a concept, acquires a skill, or gets turned on to a topic. The title also refers to a spark I see when students, or former students, realize they have made a rewarding career choice serving people and the environment. That spark keeps me going.

My teaching has three components: in the classroom, in the wilderness, and advising graduate students. In the classroom, a "gleam in the eye" usually comes from some form of experiential learning. I am not a spellbinding lecturer so I tend to use case studies, simulations, and group project methods of teaching. For example, I now teach a class called "Recreation Land Policy." To help students understand the process of decision making that goes into planning and managing parks, and the interest groups and actors involved in these decisions, I use a simulation game centered on a series of public hearings. The game was developed by Dan Dustin when he was a doctoral student at Minnesota. Students are given roles, determine how people in that role would act at a public hearing, collect data to support that position, and then interact to make planning and management decisions about a new national park. Students are often skeptical at first, but after studying the issues and the interest groups involved, they soon play their roles with gusto. I often find myself having to tone down the discussions to keep from disturbing adjacent classes.

My mentor for classroom learning was Father Warren Nye, a wonderful anatomy professor at Loras College in Dubuque, Iowa. Dignified and respectful of students, he really knew his stuff. In those days dissections were the main form of teaching anatomy, an early form of experiential education. Father Nye had a masterful way of guiding us through those complicated procedures. Though my teaching style is different than his, I try to reproduce his gentle yet demanding approach to learning.

Teaching in the outdoors, especially in the wilderness, keeps me enthused and involved. I am at my best teaching in and about the wilderness. I taught courses in outdoor education and wilderness adventure programming all my 33 years as a professor. Each semester I taught a course that included a 4-day optional wilderness field trip; in the fall a canoe trip on the St. Croix River; in the spring a winter camping trip to the Boundary Waters Canoe Area Wilderness. On these trips I saw the most intense "gleam in the eye" of my students. Seeing that spark as a student mastered the "J" stroke so she could paddle a canoe straight down a river was a wonderful experience as a teacher. Seeing a student, certain he would freeze to death sleeping overnight in a snow house, emerge the next morning warm with a "gleam in his eye" was reward enough for me.

I admit that one of my reasons for taking students to the wilderness was to try to convert them into "tree huggers." I was trying to help create a cadre of people who would champion the importance of untrammeled nature. I hoped to counter the barrage of messages promoting unrestrained consumption by helping students realize the value of wilderness, especially its spiritual value. I don't feel guilty proselytizing about nature. In *Last Child in the Woods: Saving our Children from Nature-Deficit Disorder*,[1]

Richard Louv makes a case for nature being an integral part of growing up. Modern society virtually deprives children of experiences in nature. Louv describes the human costs of alienation from nature as diminished use of the senses, attention difficulties, and a higher rate of physical and emotional illnesses. He says the most important gift a parent, teacher, or youth worker can give a child is an infectious enthusiasm for the outdoors. I have been trying for years to do just that with my recreation students.

A mentor who served as a role model for my wilderness teaching was Paul Petzoldt, a larger-than-life mountaineer and founder of the National Outdoor Leadership School (NOLS). In 1970 I attended a NOLS course consisting of 35 days in the wilderness of the Wyoming Rockies. Petzoldt was the lead instructor for the first five days of that course. He instilled a great respect for wilderness in us, stressed the necessity of learning wilderness skills to stay safe, and emphasized the need for training highly skilled outdoor leaders. That course was a major turning point for me, and I patterned much of my wilderness teaching after his approach. From 1977 to 1988 I taught a 2-week wilderness course in the Absaroka-Beartooth Wilderness Area of Montana. It was as much of a 35-day NOLS course as I could cram into 10 days in the mountains. I loved every minute of it, and I feel it was the highlight of my teaching career.

The third component of teaching for me has been advising graduate students. I think I made a difference in this area as well. I have advised 34 Ph.D.s to completion, and about 80 master's degree students. Most of the Ph.D. graduates are now professors in recreation, park or outdoor education programs around the country and the world. ·

The "gleam in the eye" of my graduate students tends to come at three different junctures. The first time I see it is when they find a direction for their dissertation and when they settle on research methods that will work. The second time is when they successfully defend their thesis. And the third time is when doctoral students realize they can succeed as professors. With the exception of a few friends and colleagues my age, most of my friends are former graduate students. They are a constant source of encouragement, enthusiasm, and just plain fun.

Opportunity to Work in My Area of Interest

One of the reasons I stayed at the University of Minnesota my entire career is that no one ever told me what I should be studying. I was able to pursue my own interests. Of course, some of those pursuits were influenced by the availability of funding, the interests of graduate students, and the realities of keeping a program together, but all in all I have had complete freedom to select my research areas.

I am interested in nature and how humans relate to nature. More specifically, I am interested in how recreation can serve as a way for people to connect with nature. I feel privileged to have been able to devote my entire career to studying this nature/human connection, to teach about it, and to write about it.

Research has always been a real challenge for me, and that challenge has often had me wondering if I actually was making a difference, or if I was even in the right line of work. I'm not sufficiently analytical, statistics are a blur to me, and even qualitative analysis leaves me confused part of the time. Further, writing is difficult for me. I have gotten by on doggedness and by being willing to put in the time to get stuff done. I have also been blessed with wonderful graduate students who have made up for my weaknesses in research and writing.

Despite my shortcomings, I have succeeded in conducting research and publishing results. I have been recognized for excellence in research and writing by the National Recreation and Park Association, but it took me a long time as a researcher and scholar to feel I was making a difference. Early in my career I was fortunate to team up with Dan Dustin on a number of publications that were more thought pieces than research reports, but they were well-written and appeared in good journals. I also collaborated with Rabel Burdge on a large research project. That experience helped me better understand how such projects were managed, how data could be generated and analyzed, and how teams could produce articles. Another turning point was when I started working with Stuart Schleien in my department and with Wilderness Inquiry, Inc. to do a series of research projects focused on persons with disabilities participating in outdoor education programs. Collaboration with other researchers and scholars helped me find the "gleam in the eye" of students who eventually read my research, of practitioners who attended my research presentations or read my research reports, and of other scholars who used and cited my research.

University Work: Freedom, Flexibility, and Variety

I remained a professor because I was free to pursue topics of interest to me. I was also free to select the classes I taught and the subjects I studied in my research. No other profession offered as much freedom, and that freedom also provided some security. People argue against tenure, and I know there are problems with it, but tenure afforded the level of freedom and security I enjoyed at the University of Minnesota.

Still, the tenure system and the quasi-civil service system of the university setting can also protect people who are, at best, unpleasant. This is a part of university life I've found distasteful since my time as a graduate student. Another challenge arises from being in a small program in a very large university. Our program has often been on the edge of elimination in the periodic "pogroms" university administrators launch about every eight years. Small programs like ours are continually forced to justify their existence.

Some excellent small programs in our field have been eliminated. That is often the result of some form of campus politics and in-fighting. Although I was program head at Minnesota for 13 years, I never sought the position. It just seemed there was no one else available to take over the duties. Because of campus politics, I never liked being program head. I always yearned to just be a professor and do what professors do.

I did not seek higher administrative positions, because I was not interested in, nor was I very good at, politics. As program head, my way of dealing with politics was to try to protect faculty from it, to keep the overall productivity level of our program high, and to keep our program off the radar screens when those aforementioned "pogroms" came around.

The Nature of a Professor's Life

I want to end with a word of encouragement for future professors in recreation, parks, and leisure studies. Being a professor in our field is a wonderful privilege. There are tough times, it is hard work, the politics can be brutal, and no one knows how long your job may last, but that is common in most professions. What is uncommon is the freedom and opportunity for variety this profession offers. So there are many different ways your work can produce the "gleam in the eye" of your students and others with whom you work.

In a typical week I prepare for classes on topics that really interest me. I read books, journal articles, and websites that bolster my teaching. I meet with graduate students working on interesting research projects. I may prepare a funding application for a project that is exciting and interesting. I may be directing a research project with graduate students where we work with practitioners to solve problems and evaluate services. I may meet with undergraduate students to help them plan their course of study, or a group of students working on a class project. I may plan a wilderness trip. I may teach a number of classes with capable students who want to learn. I may chair a graduate student committee when the student completes her or his oral examination. I may collaborate with a faculty member in another department or team-teach a course. I may work on some aspect of writing or rewriting a journal article or preparing a presentation for a conference. I may have some administrative tasks to accomplish. I may work with a local practitioner in a training role or in evaluating the effectiveness of a program. During a subsequent week I may go to a conference where I interact with practitioners or with other academics who share my passion for parks, outdoor education, and research. During yet another week I may take a group of students into a wilderness area for four days of camping or canoeing where my teaching is very outdoor skill-oriented, and very much hands-on. While in the field, we may have discussions on park management, the role of wilderness in our culture, or leadership styles. I may go on a wilderness trip that includes persons with disabilities or collect data for a research project I am coordinating. And so it goes.

Clearly, being a professor has given me all kinds of opportunities to see the "gleam in the eye." I know of no other profession that provides so many and such varied opportunities.

23 My Parents Led the Way
Deb Kerstetter

In October 1961 my parents left a comfortable life in Chester County, Pennsylvania to work as educators on Pohnpei, Micronesia, a small island in the Caroline Islands. They left behind parents and siblings who had never traveled west of the Mississippi and generally did not understand why one would. They left behind opportunities for regular family get-togethers, chances for their children to grow up in a "neighborhood," and something they could not have anticipated—a period in American history (the 1960s) that would transform the world they knew. Their decision not only changed the course of their lives, but mine as well.

I was three years old, going on four, when my parents traveled west, away from a world I knew to an environment that would have a profound impact on who I am as an individual and educator.

Island Life and Its Influence

My family lived on Pohnpei for nearly two years and spent an additional seven years on the island of Saipan in the Marianas Islands, Micronesia. During this time other families came and went. Most were American and the vast majority was involved in education or the Peace Corps. Because most did not stay in Micronesia for an extended period of time, I have some recollection of individuals, but my strongest memories are of experiences. I remember building forts and exploring caves; spending countless hours in and along the ocean; meeting new friends every year; playing with children whose hair, eye, and skin color were much different from mine; and attending local festivities that involved unique foods, lots of sound, and the warmth associated with big, welcoming smiles. I also remember having to create and organize my own fun. We did not have television, radio, or other passive forms of entertainment. I made my own troll dolls from coral and seaweed, baked cookies with my younger brother who could read but not yet master the art of mixing, and spent days making "art" that probably should not have seen the light of day.

Why are these memories important? They are important because they help me understand why I have little difficulty adapting to new circumstances or people, why I have empathy for others, and why I am very organized and able to work independently. My memories also help me understand why I continue to question whether State College, Pennsylvania is really home, if my need to be alone at various times is okay, if the contributions I've made thus far really matter, and more. My traits, developed as a child and partially due to the environment in which I spent my formative years, have affected my ability to make a difference. In the remainder of this chapter I use excerpts from letters my parents wrote to my grandparents during the first six weeks of their journey, as well as my own thoughts, to help you understand how and why I believe I've made, and hopefully will continue to make, a difference in academic life.

The Ability to Adapt

In a letter written at the end of October my mother indicated:

> *Food is expensive and not always available. We are sending an order to Guam and hope it gets here on the December boat. We use all canned or dry milk, can't buy eggs, cookies—many other things. ...I think I'll bake some things now while I have eggs and freeze them. We may not get any more when these [eggs] are gone.*

My mother had to adapt to an environment in which change and adversity were constants. I've had to do the same. I've been teaching at Penn State since 1983. During that time, the College of Health, Physical Education, and Recreation, which housed the Recreation and Parks Department, was merged with the College of Human Development. The Dean of our new College of Health and Human Development attempted to eliminate our department. Our department was then merged with Hospitality and Institutional Management, and both became programs in the School of Hospitality, Recreation, and Institutional Management. Two years ago we became an independent department again. I've worked for seven department heads and five deans, a few of whom graciously served as "interim" heads or deans. Further, during this time I was an instructor working on my Ph.D., completed my Ph.D., obtained a tenure-track position, and finally secured tenure in 1999. I have no doubt that my ability to adapt has helped me navigate the tenure process, maintain my research agenda, and continue to be positive about our program, especially when talking to alumni and students. In addition, I am quite sure that I could not have adapted to the changes at Penn State without the support of my colleagues, all of whom recognized that adaptation was the key to survival.

Being Responsive to Others

In describing the boat trip from Guam to Pohnpei, my father wrote:

> *The islanders, on the islands we were able to visit, welcomed us warmly, especially the children. The people are sincerely friendly. They are a simple, happy folk—with no modern sophistication.*

I love the warmth that emanates from a group of individuals who are comfortable sharing and who truly care about each other. Perhaps my years in Micronesia with "simple, happy folk" have influenced me in this regard. I believe caring and sharing are vital to maintaining the "family" that exists within a department. Unfortunately, many new faculty and graduate students have to be mentored into this culture of "caring and sharing." They tend to believe that it is all about them and their only responsibility is to do what it takes to get tenure or their degree. I disagree.

I've responded to my concern by mentoring junior faculty and graduate students. I take time to talk to them. I make sure they understand the politics of a university. I tell them that much of what I've learned and am sharing with them has come from many years of experience; years that are filled with successes and failures. In essence, I share that I am human and have as many insecurities and concerns as they do. For example, I let them know that I still get butterflies in my stomach on the first day of class, I continue to have lectures that bomb despite the many hours I've spent preparing for them, and I too get remarks from reviewers that are hurtful. I also let them know that without the support and care I've received from others I would not be able to do my job and contribute in the way I do to the department, the university, or the profession.

Organization, Organization, Organization

The attire here seems to be shirts, pants, shorts for men, cottons or mu-mus for women. If you see any pretty mu-mus (short, not too full), I'd like to have some. They say our things may not arrive for six months, so I won't be able to sew. Also… please send… any recipes for freezer cookery, especially cakes, cookies and baked goods, which aren't available. …[Further,] we can order from Sears or Montgomery Ward in Los Angeles, so when the new catalogues arrive, please send the pages of children's things.

Clearly, to maintain the life they'd known, my parents had to plan ahead. Toys for children had to be ordered six months in advance, baked goods had to be prepared and frozen when ingredients were available, and clothing for three young children, not to mention two adults, had to be obtained. Life was not as simple as it had been, and organization, including pre-planning, was the key to survival in the islands. Organization is also the key to survival for tenure-track faculty, many of whom feel they live on an "island of their own."

When I started teaching at Penn State, faculty had to be adequate teachers. Today they have to be good to very good. When I began in my tenure-track position, two articles per year were good enough. Today faculty need more, and they had better publish in top-tier journals in their area of expertise. Further, service was important, but today doing too much is frowned upon, especially if it is impacting one's ability to obtain a sizeable amount of external funding. Bottom line? Faculty in research-based universities must be skilled, organized, and able to multi task.

Luckily, I have some skills, am organized, and multitasking is second-nature. But, there is a downside. Because I am efficient, organized, and able to handle multiple tasks at one time, I am constantly asked to do more. People know that if they give me a task it will get done on time and well. As you may well know, this is a blessing and a curse. It is a blessing, because I feel I am contributing to my students, department, and profession. It is a curse, because I often feel like my goodwill is being abused and that I'm being taken for granted. I am just now learning to say, "No." It has taken me 23 years. Interestingly, I have no difficulty counseling my students to say, "No." I realize it is in their best interest to protect their time and energy. New faculty must do the same.

Having Empathy

Getting to Pohnpei was quite an adventure. The trip which usually takes four days took eight. We were on a cargo ship that had few cabins so our quarters were "in a tent-like structure at the stern of the ship." My father wrote:

> *Captain Davis gave us free run of the boat and even asked the women to use his shower and toilet. …Thanks to the Micronesian love of children, many of the sailors played with [the children], and often.*

The empathy Captain Davis and his crew had for my family and others aboard the ship made the experience bearable. We must respond similarly in an academic environment. In the last few years the problems experienced by students have escalated. Many are working full-time jobs to pay for school. Others find themselves stepping gingerly through their parents' divorce proceedings. Still others experience devastating health problems. They need someone to care about them and listen. While I recognize I am not a trained professional, and at times I'm frightened by the information students share with me, I know that the time I've given to students and the limited amount of help I've been able to offer them has meant more than most, if not all, of my lectures.

Accepting What Is and Moving Forward

> *"The last night aboard the sea became rough. Power-ful waves broke over the bow, sending salt spray to the cautious faces on the bridge. About midnight the storm broke loose, showering—with thunder and winds up to 40 MPH. Our canvas [cover]… flipped and flapped… A sec-tion above Derek [the 1 ½ year old] split open and he got soaked. He woke—I jumped out of bed—Peg picked him up from the sea in the sack—he looked at me and said, pointing, 'Daddy, stop that.' [referring to the storm.] …As the storm subsided, we were 15 miles from Pohnpei, but couldn't see it for the fog. After an hour or so of searching along the reef, we finally found the entrance. Once inside the reef, the seas calmed and the land was visible…*

I've found the opening, but the seas aren't always calm, and a fog often obscures my goals. Yes, I've successfully navigated the tenure-track process, and I've been recognized for my work, but I still wonder whether I'm "good enough." In terms of teaching, I've always received high scores, but I know that traditional course evaluations are a poor measure of my effectiveness; hence, I enroll in courses and workshops in an effort to find the new "magic bullet" that will make me the greatest teacher on earth. Has this helped? A little.

I also question my abilities as a researcher. I love to do research. I believe it informs my teaching and helps me to do a better job of advising my students through their own research. But I know that I'm no genius. So I've begun to work more collaboratively both with colleagues and teams of students. Doing so allows me to build on the strengths I do have, including adaptability, empathy, and organization. It also forces me to depend on others and recognize that I don't have to do everything by myself.

Finally, I am drawn to service. For some reason I feel that it is my responsibility to "step up to the plate" and "make things better." I don't know why and I'm not sure I will ever change. What I do know is that I can't get angry at those who don't choose to do the same. I must live with the choices I've made and the repercussions they have had and may continue to have on my career. Consider the time it took me to run the Leisure Research Symposium for the Society of Park and Recreation Educators/National Recreation and Park Association. I could have written multiple proposals and manuscripts during that time, all of which would have meant much more to my career. But, would I have had the same "warm and fuzzy" feeling? Would I have met as many interesting people, many of whom have become friends? I don't think so. My choice was a good one for me, which ultimately is most important.

My parents led the way. They taught me to experience life and to accept the consequences of doing so. I suspect you can also reflect upon experiences you've had in your lifetime, experiences that have shaped who you are. I encourage you to consider how you've come to this juncture in life and to build upon the strengths you've developed along the way.

24

Deb's Feel Good Folder

Deb Bialeschki

I doubt that many of us think about why we are professors; you know, really think critically and examine why we go to our offices every day. For me, I got caught up in the day-to-day professor stuff, the "being busy" with class preparations, writing articles, being on committees, and just trying to keep up. All that changed, however, when our recreation department was merged with another department. The result of the merger was not only the loss of our autonomy, but the indefinite suspension of our undergraduate major, questions about our graduate program, and few resources to support any of our efforts. Like it or not, I had some soul-searching to do.

With all these perceptions of loss, what was the essential core of being a professor to me? Where had I made a difference? I knew that I enjoyed my research efforts, especially the work focused on gender as it related to leisure, and more recently research on youth development opportunities offered through the camp experience. I felt that the gender research done with Karla Henderson was some of my best work, and it surely had impacted our body of knowledge and the development of new research efforts by other scholars interested in gender. These initiatives had allowed me to share my learning through publications and presentations, and they seemed to attract some very good graduate students to our program. At the end of the day, though, I often wondered if the initiatives really mattered.

What about the students? As I thought of them, I felt my "waver-meter" swing, and I decided to stay for my 20th year at the University of North Carolina-Chapel Hill despite knowing it would be difficult. That decision to stay for the students became the context for this chapter. I have always thought I could make the most difference working with students. I'm not sure I purposely tried to "make a difference" with them, but I sure wanted them to have a solid academic background with a good set of practical skills, an appreciation for the world in which they live, respect for the folks they would encounter in their lives, and a passion for the recreation profession—even if they were not majors. But how could I know if I had made a difference? What evidence did I have? Then I remembered a special folder I kept tucked away in my files over the years—"Deb's Feel Good Folder." I had collected special mementos and saved them in this folder. There were graduation notes, a variety of cards, emails, wedding announcements, and even a couple of funeral programs. (I know, funerals don't sound like "Feel Good Folder" material, but one student in particular had meant a lot to me, so in a small way that program with her picture was a comfort.)

As I looked back over these notes and letters, I began to see where I had really made a difference; at least to these students. I began to read as if I was analyzing qualitative data, and as I went through each item, some patterns began to emerge. After about an hour of reading and thinking, I had found eight "differences" that these students had attributed to me. I took each of these differences, tried to describe what I thought might be behind them, and now share them with you.

Learning Can Be Fun

My belief is that learning should be fun and exciting. Every single day you should feel challenged and learn something new. I always tried to approach every class with this thought in mind, and I tried to share this idea with my students and involve them in the process as much as I could. If we could learn a concept through a game—great! If I needed to don a white lab coat, put on thick black-rimmed glasses, wear a pocket protector, and carry a clipboard and stop watch in order to portray "Dr. Positivist" when we talked about paradigm differences, then I'd do it! I figured I needed to be okay with stepping outside of the box of normal teaching techniques and take risks that sometimes were going to fall flat. But when a new idea worked, it was worth every ounce of risk. I often encouraged students to be creative in their assignments and have fun with them. So when an instructor of another class down the hall asked us to "pipe down" the day the programming class presented their final projects in some very hilarious ways, I really was not too upset. I know from some of the letters I read from my folder that those funny experiences were often the very classes and content the students remembered most.

Students Come to Know Themselves

In some of the letters, students commented on how much they learned about themselves in my classes: about their fears, biases, and unquestioned values. Several of them talked about the contract grading system I often used. This system was designed to maximize their learning strengths by choosing from a menu of learning opportunities and then designating the weights they wanted attached to their selected assignments. Some stressful times occurred for them when given the responsibility to determine their contract parameters and then sign it, knowing they had to live with their decisions. They frequently had no idea of how they learned best, what styles suited them, or even how to effectively manage their time.

I also asked them to examine their values around different content areas—not what they "had always done" or what someone had told them to do, but what *they* believed about issues. Whether it was in a majors class like programming or a social sciences perspectives class like "Women, Work, and Leisure," I wanted students to confront their biases around societal issues such as gender, race, sexuality, class, and ability. I remember running into a student years after teaching an environmental course where I had presented students with ethical situations to discuss. As we chatted, Laura mentioned thinking about that class and encountering one of the specific situations we had discussed and she shared how she responded to it. She noticed I was a bit surprised that she remembered that class and the situation. I will never forget her response as she turned to me and said, "Deb, we always talked about your class after we walked out the door, because you made us think about ourselves and what we would do. You didn't give us 'the' answer. You challenged us to find our own."

Students Get to Know Me

Many professors believe faculty should maintain a "distance" from their students. They demand to be called "Dr." or "Professor" as a sign of respect. They believe students should know little to nothing about their personal lives. That way of interacting with students just never suited me. While I never wanted to be "one of them," I wanted them to know me as a person and not just as someone they saw two or three times a week for 50-75 minutes. I always felt that being real with them would allow me to reach them in ways unavailable to professors who remained aloof. I used to have a "Dinner with Deb" night where I'd pick a place to eat and whoever wanted to come would show up, some even with friends. The students loved it and so did I. We'd talk about families, things we liked to do, and social issues. We got to know each other a little better on those nights, and the atmosphere in class was always a bit "warmer" after those dinners. Whenever appropriate, I tried to let them know about my background, family, and interests. Contrary to what some may think, this sharing seemed to increase their respect for me and the openness of our interactions in and out of the classroom. The students always commented on how nice it was to feel like their professor was "just a normal person" who they got to know better than most of their other professors. For some of my students, this sharing made a big difference to them. They were more than a number, and I was more than a grader.

Feelings of Rapport

I was raised to respect people. I think all of us who teach probably hold respect at a premium. Yet, I was surprised to see how often students acknowledged the respect they felt from me. I tried to show respect for their experiences, their knowledge, and the perspectives they brought to class because of the lives they had led and the challenges they had faced. Some of the students commented on how they felt respected, because I "set the bar high" for them, and I expected no less than their best. One of the most challenging events for graduate students was their presentation at our Department's Graduate Research Symposium. After all these years, I know that many of them still savor the memories of that day. They worked hard, were proud of their accomplishments, and often raised the expectations bar for subsequent classes. They experienced the respect of their classmates, the faculty, and themselves. I know from their letters that this specific experience and the pride and confidence that resulted from our respect for them have endured.

Passion for the Profession

I strongly believe in the good that comes from recreation, and I wanted every recreation major to be proud of their chosen profession. I also wanted non majors to appreciate the benefits of recreation and to become strong advocates for the field. I believe my passion motivated me to approach each class with enthusiasm and commitment. I learned from many comments on my teaching evaluations, as well as from personal conversations with students, that professors do make a difference in the development of their students' passion for the field when they make their own passion apparent as well.

Being a Role Model

I had no idea that I had been a role model until I received several notes and emails as I approached my retirement from UNC-Chapel Hill. Former students said they had been inspired to take up running, go to graduate school, and volunteer in their communities. I always tried to "walk my talk" in and out of the classroom. That meant I came to class prepared, was timely with my grading, and kept my office hours. I tried to be a good professional, and I tried to do things with students to create social change. Among many such efforts, we worked together to set up student-organized volunteer efforts to establish a recreation program for children at a homeless shelter and Sunday evening youth recreation programs at a public-housing project. Not only do I think I made a difference with my students, I know they made a difference in the lives of the citizens of our community. Together we did some very good things.

Someone Who Cares

I have come to believe that many professors make a difference in the lives of their students through an ethic of care. I tried to really get to know my students. I treated them like the individuals they were. I cared about how they did in my classes, how things were going for them outside of class, and how they were developing personally and professionally. As a consequence of letting students know I cared, they often included me in things important to them. I've attended birthday parties, baby showers, karaoke nights, and weddings. I've even spoken at their memorial services. They have seen me laugh, cry, be frustrated, be emotionally down, and be incredibly happy: all because I truly cared about them. And I know my caring has made a difference to them.

One experience from my very first year teaching at UNC-Chapel Hill dramatically shaped my perspective. I was teaching a large introductory class. About half way through the semester a young man from class came to see me on a Friday afternoon. He was not one of our majors and he had rarely attended class. So I was glad to finally have him initiate a conversation. He did not go into detail, but he said he had been struggling with some personal issues that he thought he now had under control. We discussed what it would take to get him back on track in class, came up with a plan that he seemed acceptable to him, and just chatted. From that brief visit, I found that I really did care about him and wanted him to succeed. It was a very enjoyable conversation, and I remember noticing him relax as we talked. He left with a written plan of action in his hand, and he flashed a cute shy grin as he left. "See you in class on Tuesday," he said.

On Monday morning I received a phone call from Student Affairs. The young man had taken his life over the weekend. I have no idea what led him to that action. I replayed our Friday afternoon conversation over and over again in my head. Had I missed something, some sign of trouble? Should I have asked for more details about his situation? I finally accepted his fate and took solace in the thought that I had spent quality time with him and that he knew that I cared about him. I had, at least, been there to listen. I have never forgotten that encounter, and I have reminded myself repeatedly to let my students know I care.

An Open Door

I never really thought much about my office door, but my students did. Many of my "Feel Good" notes from students mentioned that they felt comfortable coming to talk in my office. They often just liked to stop in to say "Hi," and they appreciated the time I gave them. However, some of these conversations took serious directions with talk about job possibilities, graduate school, recommendations, life goals, and other personal challenges. I think the students just needed a chance to talk with some trusted adult who could help them identify and consider options. They said it mattered to them that I was available, and that I made time for them. They felt that if it was important to talk, they knew they would not find my door closed. For some of them, my open door was symbolic. It meant I was open-minded. I hope I lived up to that expectation.

I do not for a minute believe that my story is unique, much less compelling. It is just one professor's thoughts on making a difference in academic life. Over the course of my 20th year as a recreation professor at UNC-Chapel Hill, I had to make some hard decisions about my career. Without our undergraduate major and our graduate program, my opportunities to make a difference all but disappeared. So I packed my bags and moved on to a new challenge outside of academe. But there are days when I walk over to my file drawer, pull out "Deb's Feel Good Folder," and select a few notes or cards to read. They always make me smile, and in my heart of hearts I trust that any difference I might have made is still part of those students' lives. I know the difference they made in my life is, and always will be, an essential part of me.

On Undergraduate "Benevolent Coercion" and Graduate Collegiality

25

John Crompton

After eight years at Waterloo Grammar School (from ages 11-18), I was admitted to Loughborough College, which was reputed to be one of England's best teacher-training institutions. My career intent was to teach physical education and geography at the middle or high school level. The premise that undergirded most of the theory, conceptualization and pedagogical instruction during the three years at Loughborough was that the children whom I would be teaching were naturally curious and that they delighted in learning. We were informed that education was the process of nourishing, since its root is derived from the Latin, *educare,* meaning to nourish (others have suggested its Latin root is from *duco, ducere* meaning to lead). A popular analogy among our instructors was that teaching is like lighting a fire—teachers provide the initial spark to the fertile kindling that then blossoms into a mighty fire.

During my four blocks of teaching practice in various schools while at Loughborough, I seemed unable to light mighty fires. I assumed this was a reflection of my status as a neophyte and that over time, experience, on-the-job experimentation, alternate approaches, and added self-confidence would cause my obvious ineptitude to dissipate. However, after a couple of subsequent years of experience and growth in self-confidence, nothing changed. The only conclusion my ego could handle was that the undergirding premise was wrong; in other words, that most young people were not naturally curious and/or they didn't delight in learning—perhaps because the educational system had defused this natural curiosity and it had been replaced by cynicism that had become habitual and ingrained.

This counter-premise has been the beacon that has guided my interactions with undergraduates at Texas A&M University. It differs from my approach to working with graduate students, which is discussed later in the chapter. The articles of the counter premise are: (i) most undergraduates are not intellectually curious and have no intrinsic love for learning;

(ii) like most of us, they have a propensity for procrastination; (iii) they will take the line of least resistance and do the minimum amount of work needed either to graduate or to meet the expectations of their parents. In short, they resemble my own *modus operandi* at Waterloo Grammar School and Loughborough College 40 or 50 years ago! These counter premises have guided my pedagogical approach to undergraduate education, which may be described as "benevolent coercion."

Evidence supporting the counter-premise is easily obtained: announce either that a class or an assignment has been cancelled, or finish a class early. The predominant response is likely to be delight rather than disappointment. Not many student protest letters will be written to the department head declaring that they have been cheated by not receiving some of the educational experience for which they paid.

In every undergraduate class, there are some stellar students who validate the traditional educational premise of intrinsic motivation, but invariably they are a relatively small minority. Another aphorism absorbed in my Loughborough days was that the role of teachers was not to get the eagles to soar; rather it was to get the turkeys to fly. Intrinsically motivated students will learn either because of, or in spite of, us. We simply have to avoid screwing them up. However, 30 years of teaching undergraduates at Texas A&M has revealed that such students, too often, are a relatively small minority.

Challenge: The Key to Effective Undergraduate Education

In my view, the real challenge confronting undergraduate teachers is to stimulate growth among the disinterested majority. My intent is to jolt them out of their tendency to pass through college in a state of what I characterize as "permanently superficial," never experiencing anything in depth, just passing through and getting the boxes checked. From this comes only mediocrity and tedium. I admire people who immerse themselves in a project or cause. I believe this is the key to a happy, fulfilling, satisfying life. I feel no affinity for those who merely dabble, who go through the motions without any emotion. They don't feel good about themselves and they demoralize those around them.

The advisor to our varsity track team at Loughborough (we didn't have paid coaches) was fond of saying, "training isn't fun, it's darned hard work." He was a firm advocate of the "no pain, no gain" school of training. Sure, many of the ancillary benefits of being part of the track team were fun: socialization and camaraderie with like others; the respect of peers; the kinetic exuberance emanating from fast and fluid running; the exhilaration that accompanies complete physical exhaustion; and the ego satisfaction of accomplishment. But none of these outcomes occur without the "darned hard work" of training. Similarly, the notion that learning is "fun" does not resonate with me. It is hard work, requires much self-discipline, is sometimes frustrating, and on other occasions is tedious and boring. Becoming an educated person is a difficult, demanding endeavor.

Joy in learning, like joy in sport, comes from overcoming genuine challenges and cannot be experienced without effort. William James was right when he observed that a full "life shall [be built in] doing and suffering and creating."[1] The real satisfaction in life comes from total creative absorption in a task, and not in the extrinsic rewards associated with it. You get the most out of life by being immersed in some facets of it. The deeper we dig into the reservoir of our potential, the happier we become. I subscribe to the idea that "the nectar is in the journey." The reaching and striving are more important than the result. If you don't hike to the top of a mountain, then you don't see the optimum view. The view when you ride up in an aerial tram or automobile is never as good.

Physical challenges are one medium for finding out who you are, but they are elective and so most opt not to explore their potential. The undergraduate academic experience can be conceptualized as being in the same genre as physical challenges, in that it offers a medium for young people in the most formative years of their life to figure out who they are. It has the meritorious attribute of being unavoidable for many.

To excel means to be better than, or to outdo, others. By definition it is limited to the few. Excellence is not achieved without extraordinary effort. If an A or B grade is the class norm and it is achievable with minimum effort, then the incentive for those with high ability to invest extraordinary effort, and the opportunity for them to experience the extraordinary satisfaction that accompanies genuine excellence, is foregone. Further, it deceives ordinary students into believing that their ordinary efforts will be sufficient for them to be professionally successful in society, and discourages them from seeking to enhance their skills and thought processes. Hence, the class syllabus always states, "10 percent of students will receive an A grade, 20 percent a B, 40 percent a C, and 30 percent a D or F."

College is about the process of young people growing into being themselves, about gaining wisdom, and the formation of character. It is about them finding out who they are. So, I declare on the first day of class, "You are a hunter, and the prey is yourself." The failure to live up to one's potential is the supreme tragedy in a human life. Satisfaction in learning comes from overcoming genuine challenges and cannot be experienced without toil. It is only through commitment to a goal, sweat, endeavor, and honesty with oneself that we discover who we are and become who we can be. My obligation is to engage in "choreographed histrionics" designed to harangue, coerce, intimidate, persuade, and encourage those who are not intrinsically driven to narrow the gap between their accomplishment and their potential, so they leave the class changed, believing they can accomplish more than they had ever before imagined.

One of the advantages of being at the same institution for a long period of time is that a reputation is established and it substantially reinforces the immediate actions. "Survivors" of the class exaggerate its challenge with hyperbole designed to positively emphasize their strengths in surmounting it, and a mythical aura envelopes it. The fortuitous consequence is that intimidation is present from day one without me having to be intimidating, which enables me to subtly loosen the apprehension rather than reinforce it.

The approach is deliberately confrontational and intimidating, and its justification is based on the three articles of the counter-premise described in the opening section of this chapter. It is intended to facilitate Thomas Huxley's admonition:

> Perhaps the most valuable result of all education is the ability to make yourself do the thing you have to do, when it ought to be done, whether you like it or not; it is the first lesson that ought to be learned; and however early a man's training begins, it is probably the last lesson he learns thoroughly.[2]

The "benevolent" qualifier in my "benevolent coercion" approach is central to its effectiveness. Naked coercion would merely induce fear, intense dislike, resentment, and distrust. It likely would exacerbate the disinterest in stretching and growth. The haranguing will often be accompanied by a wry smile—the phrase "smiling assassin" was coined by one wit—and will be done in private; by a genuine concern to help students grow; by empathy that students recognize as being sincere; and by an investment in time and energy that close monitoring of each student's progress requires. (This includes individual 15-minute interviews with all 60 students.)

I believe that no human motivation is stronger than the desire to validate the confidence of those who believe in you. My experience has been that most students are responsive when they are told up-front that they have the aptitude to do well in the class, but that they will be pushed; that occasionally ostensibly outlandishly taxing demands will be made upon them, as periodically happens in the "real world"; that standards will not be compromised; that their work will be criticized bluntly without euphemisms; and that if their performance does not reflect their potential or the expected standards, they will be subjected to ongoing, unrelenting haranguing.

For some, the pressure is too great, and they wilt and fold. If their effort is high, then the standards are not shifted, but empathy and encouragement are offered and contingency plans developed (which remain out of sight of the rest of the class). This has to occur since the goal is for all students to finish the class proud of the effort they have invested and the growth they have experienced. If the effort is low, then they will have the opportunity to surmount the challenge in the following semester.

In the 1970s, I shared a platform with Kevin White who was mayor of Boston for 16 years. He said something that resonated, "I hate these constant crises; but without them would we ever get anything done?" A few years later I was discussing this notion in my graduate class, when a Chinese student stood up and drew the Chinese symbol for crisis on the blackboard. It consists of two characters, one meaning danger, and the other meaning opportunity. A crisis is *dangerous*—it creates a level of uncertainty, an element of risk, a margin for failure—but it raises our energy level, gets us agitated, forces us to do things in a different way, to look for better solutions; so it is also an *opportunity* for us to grow and develop.

Thus, on the first day of a new semester, I lay out my goal for the class: "My job is to create a series of crises for you and to help you grow through resolving those crises. Growth requires that we redefine the perceived limits of what we believe can be achieved. Hence, the objective is to back you into a corner and make the standards higher than you feel are reasonable." As John Stuart Mill noted, "A pupil from whom nothing is ever demanded which he cannot do, never does all he can."[3]

Students as Producers of Education

I have always had problems with some of the nomenclature associated with education. The term "teacher" has been particularly bothersome.

When I left Loughborough College, my first job was in a comprehensive school (high school) with 1,500 students in Kirby, just outside Liverpool in England. Kirby was one of Britain's post-war new town disasters. The planners transplanted 50,000 people out of the central city slum areas of Liverpool, into a green field's public housing project, which constituted the new town, ten miles out of the city. There were no public amenities, few social institutions, and no social networks. Not surprisingly, when I arrived in Kirby it boasted the highest per capita juvenile crime rate in the United Kingdom.

It took all of two days of standing in front of classes in that comprehensive school for me to realize that I wasn't going to teach anybody anything. Rather, the children elected whether or not they were going to learn. Tragically, the great majority opted not to learn and helped formulate my counter-premise of education. This experience led to the revelation that students are not consumers of education, they are producers of it. This is the essence of the Chinese proverb, "A teacher can open the door. You must enter by yourself."

The term "teacher" did not describe what I did in Kirby. I came to realize that my role was that of facilitator. It involved creating an environment that would encourage, cajole, or intimidate children to invest effort in learning. A corollary of this role recognition is that education only occurs if a student is encouraged, or can be persuaded, to exercise the self-discipline needed for learning to occur. Education is one of the few remaining facets of life about which one can say, "You get out of it about what you invest into it." Through being intellectually challenged, students find out who they are.

In my first week at Loughborough College, I met with my education tutor. He asked, "Mr. Crompton, what are you going to teach?"

"Physical education and geography, sir," I responded. "No lad," came the reply. "You are going to teach children."

That wonderful, fundamental insight passed along on day one of my formative teacher-training period has stayed with me throughout my career in education. Parks, recreation, and tourism are merely a convenient meeting place that provides a medium through which I can help students find out who they are. After being in classes, if students pick up an idea or two which is of some use to them in a career in parks, recreation, and tourism, then that is pleasing; but it is not really important, and it is certainly not my primary desired outcome of our interaction together. In my view, we have minimal responsibility to impart vocational knowledge on how to perform pragmatic, specialist skills used by practitioners. In the Internet era when knowledge is instantly accessible, it is redundant and useless for students to be required to memorize so-called "facts." The seven points of this or the five stages of that are not meant to be memorized. That is what the Internet and books are for—as references to consult when factual information is required. I certainly do not know all of the so-called facts that are between the covers of the books I have written. If I do not feel it necessary to memorize all that material, then why is it necessary for students to memorize it?

I spent one hour of every school day in my last two years at Waterloo Grammar School studying English history from the end of the Napoleonic Wars in 1815 to the start of World War I in 1914. If you were to ask me now—45 years later—to write an essay on that 100-year period, it would be a challenge to fill five sheets of paper. Is this indicative of wasted time? Of course not! Education is what is left when all the facts are forgotten. The facts of history were not important *per se*. It was a wonderful medium for enhancing understanding of contemporary society; gaining insights into the deterministic role of societal characteristics in molding events; developing critical thinking ability; learning to write, through having to do lengthy weekly essays; gaining confidence in speaking through arguing the relative merits of different interpretations of events, their consequences, and their implications; and learning to conceptualize interrelationships between ostensibly unconnected events.

My responsibility at the undergraduate level is to insist students develop a higher level of competency in literary, numerical, and computing skills; to facilitate their learning how to analyze and solve problems; to develop confidence in their public speaking and presentation abilities; to develop group-process skills; and to build self-confidence and self-esteem. It is not a question only of acquiring factual, technical knowledge; it is a question of students being pushed hard to make mental efforts that are subjected to criticism. My challenge is to move them past "permanent superficiality" to help them form good habits in terms of basic skills, thinking processes and so on, so they gain insight into what constitutes excellence. If students have not experienced being intellectually stretched they remain unaware of the upper boundaries of their capacity, and they will, by definition, lead a suboptimal life.

A few years ago I received a fax from David A. who was a former student. He is my record holder. He took a class six times before finally passing it with an "A" grade. He failed the course twice; he dropped it three times; and finally he immersed himself in it and emerged triumphant. David had graduated ten years prior to my receipt of the fax, and he now had a position as head of quality control for a large retailing chain. He wrote: "Never change the standard or the approach. It was the best thing that ever happened to me." I suspect the philosophy espoused towards undergraduate education in this paper would earn me an "F" and much derisive chastisement in many pedagogical theory and technique classes offered in education curricula. But 30 years of undergraduate teaching at A&M and feedback from those students have convinced me there is merit in the counter-premise and an approach of "benevolent coercion."

Graduate Collegiality [4]

Interactions with graduate students are different from those with undergraduates because the conventional premise of intellectually curious people who are enthusiastic about learning for the most part is validated. As my career has progressed, I have become increasingly conscious of how little I know. There appear to be three reasons for this growing awareness of my inadequacies. First, it is a natural manifestation of the aphorism: The more you know, the better you understand what you don't know. Second, the exponential expansion in the number of those engaged in research in this area and allied fields in the past three decades has made it increasingly difficult to keep abreast of this work as it relates to my research programs. Sixteen years ago it was noted that, "The explosion of publications and electronic information in most fields has made it difficult to feel confident of mastery outside a single theoretical paradigm and methodological attack on a designated problem."[5] Since that time the difficulty has only been accentuated. The third factor is the evolution of computing technology and the more advanced statistical analysis techniques and research designs this has facilitated. The aggregate effect of these factors is a realization that my knowledge base is relatively small, and the only way that I can sustain a viable research program is to partner with others whose skills and talents complement mine.

Early in my career, I wrestled with answers to the fundamental question: What business am I in? Recognizing my limitations, the conclusion I reached was that I am not in the business of doing research; rather I am in the business of getting research done. My primary partners in this endeavor have been graduate students. The term "graduate student" bothers me, but it is a convenient "handle" that I have been unable to replace. Unfortunately, the term connotes a sort of modern day serf who serves his or her apprenticeship at the beck and call of the master, before emerging from the departmental chrysalis as a full-fledged professional or professor. This is demeaning and entirely inappropriate. Many of the individuals pursuing graduate degrees with whom I have worked, have intellects, experience levels, skills, and talents that exceed my own. They are students only in the classic sense that we are all, or all should be, students.

The professor-graduate student relationship is frequently perceived as being one-way, with knowledge flowing from the professor to the student. But that is a myth. Indeed, in my case the antithesis is the case—the unidirectional knowledge flow for the most part is directed from graduate student to professor.

The graduate students with whom I am privileged to work are my primary colleagues. My faculty peers at A&M are supportive of my research endeavors and they are my friends, but their particular professional interests are different from mine. My graduate students and I have sought each other out because we share common professional interests, have a mutual respect for each other's talents, and because the chemistry between us is good.

My primary role is to conceptualize and manage the research program, generate funds to implement it, and recruit good graduate students to do the actual project work. I am captain of the ship, responsible for steering it safely to its destination, and making sure the resources are deployed effectively, but I don't work the engines. This perception of my role emerged early in my career from a conversation with Dr. Albert Cotton, a distinguished professor of chemistry at A&M. He has published over 1,500 refereed papers—his typical output is 50 per year. He told me, "I do not work at the bench with the test-tubes. If I did, my productivity and that of all the people who work with me would plummet. My job is to facilitate the work of my doctoral candidates and post-doctoral associates, ensure they get good training, and ensure goals of the long-term research program are accomplished." He is right. Texas A&M does not pay me a distinguished professor's salary to collect data and work computers. My challenge is to leverage my resources to maximize output, not to do it myself.

Working collaboratively with my graduate student colleagues enables both sides of the partnership to focus on our strengths. We all need to retrain, but we are limited in the extent to which we can do it. I believe that if I invested the time, I could probably learn some of the things I do not know. But I have always believed in concentrating on my strengths and covering my weaknesses by collaborating with others who are strong in those areas. This seems to me to be a much more efficient and productive approach.

My graduate student colleagues are exposed to cutting-edge courses with excellent instructors from across the campus. My cutting-edge courses were done 30 to 35 years ago. The result, of course, is that they know more than I do about research methods, statistical tools, and the current literature. I learn through them, secondhand—they take the courses. All my doctoral candidates who have graduated were technically more knowledgeable than I was. If they were not, then I would have screwed up badly as their advisor and facilitator.

Working collaboratively in this way means that almost all my publications are coauthored. The primary author will usually be a graduate student, reflecting that he or she did the nuts and bolts of the research. I will be second author, reflecting my conceptual and intellectual input, my provision of resources needed to do the work, and my contribution to actually writing the paper. I have been criticized for this—although not to my face. Some people have suggested that my reputation has been made on the backs of my students, and that my approach is exploitive. Of course, they are right. I do exploit the people who work with me by using their talents to complement my own and further my research program. That is the best way I know to provide them with opportunities to learn to do good research, and the best way I know to get the threshold volume of research done that moves a research program forward. If others do not approve of my *modus operandi*, then that is their problem. I am comfortable with the way I operate and to the best of my knowledge so are the 60 people whose graduate committees I have chaired to this point. As far as I am concerned, nobody else's opinion matters.

My motives in working with graduate candidates are entirely selfish. In addition to constituting the engine that moves my research program forward, a partnership with them is the only way I know to institutionalize any impact I may have on the field. My own books, papers, speeches, and workshops can have only a transitory influence at a point in time. However, if I can place in my career 30 well-trained professors in university positions and 50 well-trained practitioners with master's degrees in agencies, I believe it will make a difference. That is what I have been seeking to do.

As my primary colleagues, I view my graduate students as being equal in stature to myself. The easiest part of encouraging them to recognize this equality is to listen and act upon their advice and input. To further reinforce it, I ensure their offices are close to mine and that we interact on most days. If there is no professional reason for them to come to my office, I go to theirs to make a social visit. In a conscious attempt to reverse the inherent power structure in our relationship, they have keys and access at all times to my office and laboratory, and to all the equipment within them, such as phones, photocopying, postage, books, computer accounts, and so on. I quite deliberately do not have access to their offices.

Since they are my primary colleagues, their work takes priority over everything else I do. Momentum and morale are everything. If graduate student colleagues want to visit, it happens immediately. I am not into appointments or office hours. If they want me to review something, it will get a one-day turnaround. My primary professional reason for being is to facilitate their work. Everything else I view as being of secondary importance.

To maximize the synergy among my graduate students, for most of my career I was committed to fostering a research team. This meant encouraging and nurturing professional relationships among them. I believe social engineering is of prime importance in achieving this. They need to be either in offices together or in proximate offices, because they have much to learn from each other. Inter-peer learning develops from working together on joint projects; by toiling together on the same courses; at social events; and in meetings of research project groups. There is no single formula for developing inter-peer learning; it depends on the chemistry of the people, their particular interests, and stage of their degree program.

Because learning from peers is critical, I believe it is imperative that a research team has a threshold number of individuals who frequently interact. Without this, the learning process is likely to be substantially impaired. The power of this bonding, of course, endures long after graduation. The bonds built among people working together in graduate school last forever. Indeed, one of the most exciting aspects of the process for me, is seeing the professional and social bonding continuing to build between the 60 or so people whose graduate committees I have chaired. Observing the respect, trust, and support for each other that they exhibit is enormously gratifying. Of course, the bonding is not only between peers, it is also between them and myself. What a privilege—the opportunity to develop and nurture friendships that last a lifetime and which span national boundaries and political ideologies. These friendships and networks remain supportive long after students have graduated, and they provide reinforcement that contributes to sustaining a research program over the long term.

A Caveat

The careers and lives of each of us constitute an empirical experiment with an "n" of one. The observations made in this paper merely reflect conclusions derived from my personal journey through the academic landscape over the past 30 years at Texas A&M University. Texas A&M is a large (46,000 students) Research 1 (R-1) research university, with a student body that traditionally has been predominantly Anglo, middle-class, and conservative. The extent to which the approaches I've described are appropriate for use in other academic contexts has to be evaluated by the reader. The conclusions from my experiment are willingly shared, but they come with the obvious caveat that they are biased by my personality, and by the institutional, social, and professional milieus in which I have pursued my experiment.

Beyond the Social
26 Science Citation Index
Dennis Howard

In the academic world I inhabit, citations in sources such as the Social Science Citation Index (SSCI) have become an increasingly prominent measure of one's "intellectual impact." Citation analysis determines the extent to which one's published work has been integrated into, and then helped shape, the work of others.

I'm not sure the SSCI even existed when I started my career as an academic in the mid-1970s. Now, and this may be more evident in Colleges of Business, citation counts have become a critical determinant of whether faculty receive tenure and/or promotion. Just as I sat down to write this essay, one of my former doctoral students sent me a citation analysis he recently completed drawn from the SSCI for six primary leisure, tourism, and sport journals (*Journal of Leisure Research, Leisure Sciences, Annals of Tourism Research, Journal of Travel Research, Journal of Sport Management, Sociology of Sport Journal*) over a seven-year period from 1999 to 2005. His analysis is basically an extension of Diane Samdahl's 1999 examination of the impact of the *Journal of Leisure Research* and *Leisure Sciences*.

Frankly, the results are pretty discouraging. Across all six journals, nearly half the papers published between 1999 and 2003 had not been cited. This dismaying pattern was most evident for the sport journals, particularly the *Journal of Sport Management*, where only four papers published in that journal had been cited five or more times (all had been in circulation at least five years).

Basically, it's a relatively small group of folks whose work appears to be making a discernible impact in leisure, tourism, and sport. You can count on one hand the number of people in each of these specialty areas whose work is cited more than ten times. I'm not going to elaborate here on the multitude of explanations for why the impact, at least measured by citation counts, is so inconsequential. I'll leave that for my former doctoral student. Suffice it to say that, for most of us, using citation counts to validate the question of whether we're making a difference in the academic community can be pretty discouraging.

So, if we're not comfortable relying on these electronic/external measures for our validation as academics, where else can we look to see if we're making a difference? Thankfully, there are other places we can go. Perhaps, the most gratifying are those unexpected or out-of-the-blue moments when a former student will tell you that you made a difference in his or her life. When you've been at it as long as I have, you receive the occasional note of thanks from former students. My wife has begun to collect these notes and e-mails of expressed gratitude and has placed them in a file. Someday, after I'm retired, I'll sit down and take a close look at them. I'm sure I'll savor the wonderful memories they invoke. How fortunate we are to be in a profession where it is possible to receive this kind of heartfelt gratitude for something we might have said or done to help a student.

Finding Balance

It's clear that the real joy I draw from my professional life is helping students. Yet, the reward structure I've been part of for so many years at Research 1 (R-1) institutions is predicated largely on research productivity. Serving students effectively is not enough to ensure continued employment. Thus, increasingly, citation counts have become the objective measure of my place and status as an academic. It's no surprise, as the Business School culture I've lived in the last eight years tends to be conservative, and at R-1 level institutions like mine, rewards and sanctions are based on tangible, objective measures. Only certain journals "count" and the number of times cited in the SSCI matters a lot. There is unrelenting pressure to publish in "top tier" journals. A fellow department head recently exclaimed in a personnel meeting, "Why would anyone publish outside of an A-level journal?" Within my college, only four journals now count as "A" outlets in the marketing discipline: the *Journal of Marketing, Journal of Consumer Research, Marketing Science,* and the *Journal of Marketing Research.* Given that acceptance rates are in the single digits for all of these publications, the competition for placement in these top-tier journals is ferocious. Anyone contemplating a career path inside an R-1 business college must consider this daunting reality. Not only must one publish regularly in these hard-to-get-into outlets, the work must be heavily cited to be assured tenure and promotion.

Labor of Necessity

Finding a balance between the "publish or perish" mandate and the personal pleasures of teaching has been a constant struggle, aggravated by the fact that writing is largely a torturous ordeal for me. Given that fact, surprisingly I have written quite a bit over the last several decades—several books and probably 100 articles. I say "surprisingly" because I don't approach writing with any eagerness. It is not a calling. I envy and admire colleagues who bring a passion to their writing. In my case, writing doesn't come easy. I've never experienced anything resembling a "writer's high." Writing is lonely work, and it's hard—hours spent laboring over a single paragraph, never feeling I've got it quite right. Often the only positive emotion I experience related to the activity is the relief I feel when I've completed the task. So why do I write?

Honestly, the first thought that comes to mind is, "Because I have to." The pragmatic reality of academe goes back to "publish or perish." Also, I write out of a sense of obligation, particularly to my doctoral students. It's crucial that I mentor by example. It's the only way they are going to learn the craft and the expectations of their chosen career. Needless to say, since I am trying to inspire them, I don't divulge my true feelings about the process. If I'm honest with myself, another powerful motive for writing is that I am very competitive. I used to scoff at a former colleague who'd run down the hall with every new book to show me how many times he'd been cited. Frankly, I experience the same personal delight or satisfaction, but I'm not quite so public in my expression. So yes, some of the notoriety that comes with being a recognized author does make a difference to me.

Both major book projects I coauthored with John Crompton were products of necessity. In each case, the impetus was to fill a vacuum. There were simply no credible written materials on the subjects we were teaching. Our first book, *Financing, Managing and Marketing Recreation and Park Resources* (1990),[1] was intended to provide students and practitioners with a radically new approach to the delivery of public park and recreation services. Many of the concepts and practices included in our book were adopted from contemporary literature in management, budgeting, and marketing—topic areas that had largely been ignored in existing public parks and recreation administration textbooks. Many innovative practices were introduced, including a range of public-commercial sector joint venture arrangements, new capital financing methods, and consumer-driven marketing concepts related to targeting, pricing, and promoting leisure services. Our book certainly found a market. Not everyone was pleased with the new ideas we were advocating. I don't know about John, but I received a lot of mail, some of it quite angry, about our advocacy of such private sector ideas as charging a fair price—yes, even for seniors—for many traditionally "free" park and recreation services. Today, it's gratifying to see so many of the ideas we introduced in our book now commonly utilized at all levels of government. From my perspective, at least, the impulse to write the book had nothing to do with trying to achieve some kind of transformational impact. The genesis was in part selfish: to create resources we could use with our own students.

While we were colleagues who shared an interest area initially, the serendipitous result of my collaboration with John has been a lifelong friendship. Now, what truly sustains my commitment to each new edition of our most recent book, *Financing Sport*,[2] is the opportunity to sustain the working and personal relationship with John. So again, almost in spite of the writing process itself, I am drawn to writing because of all the byproducts of that effort—the opportunity to help students, sustaining a friendship, and professional recognition.

Labor of Love

While I view writing as largely a necessity of the job, my attitude toward teaching is altogether different. I derive enormous pleasure from almost every aspect of teaching (grading is the glaring exception). It's personal, dynamic, and unlike writing, the rewards are immediate.

I still spend three to four hours on preparation for every hour I spend in front of my students. I don't need to, but that's been my operating style for 30 years. I feel I'm not fully prepared if I don't devote that much time to getting ready for class. In part, the extensive time spent on preparing class materials is a function of the fact that the subjects I teach related to the sports industry are very dynamic. Trying to stay abreast of the changing financial landscape of professional and intercollegiate sports leagues and properties requires constant attention.

I still handwrite all of my lecture notes, but I have grudgingly made concessions to technology. I prepare most of my visuals on PowerPoint slides and post them on our electronic blackboard for students to access. I carry around my PowerPoint presentations on a thumb drive. Thank God for doctoral students with technical expertise.

I have no idea how any of this technology works. I'm trying valiantly to get up to speed. It's important to understand that when I started 30 years ago, the handouts I distributed in class were prepared on hand-cranked mimeograph machines. Remember, this was back in the day when in our leisure philosophy classes the prominent discussion topic was how America could cope with the abundance of leisure that would character-ize life in the new millennium. It wasn't that long ago those "correctable" typewriters were at the forefront of technological innovation. Now I'm not sure I can even find a typewriter on our new Business College "cam-pus." I find I'm increasingly dependent on my graduate students to deal with the rapid adoption of all of this new technology in and outside of the classroom. It's not that I resist these new innovations. It's more a function of the learning curve being too steep. I just don't have the time or incli-nation to learn how to use, or fully exploit, all of the new opportunities provided by these technological advancements. But I also worry that I might become too enamored of all the gadgetry, jazzy PowerPoint slides, streaming video, etc. To me, teaching will always be about the face-to-face interaction I have with my students.

What Difference Has Academe Had on My Life?

I don't know if I'm making a difference every day, or any day for that matter, but I love the fact that I've been given the opportunity to make a difference in my students' lives. It gives my life meaning, and it is this privilege that brings me to my next point. Until now, I've focused on the question I've been asked to address: Have I made a difference? But, after more than 30 years in this profession, it's only fair to address the flip side of that question. What difference has higher education made in my life?

A career in academe was never my goal. In the late 1960s, I gradu-ated with a master's degree in Parks and Recreation from the University of Illinois and returned to California to begin what I hoped would be a lifelong career in municipal parks and recreation. At that point, I aspired to become a Director of a large city parks and recreation department. I was on that path, happy in a new job as a Supervisor of Recreation in Mountain View, California, with a new home and an eight-month old son when I was invited by Paul Brown, a Professor of Parks and Recreation at San Jose State University, to be a guest speaker in his class. Following class, as a courtesy, Paul took me out for a cup of coffee. Making polite conversation, I remarked on how much I had enjoyed talking with his students and that someday I might consider going back for a Ph.D. I also indicated that I would love to get back to Oregon, where I had done my undergraduate work at the University of Oregon.

Within days of speaking to Paul's class, I received a phone call from Ed Heath, head of the Parks and Recreation program at Oregon State University (OSU), asking if I would consider coming to OSU to teach for a year on a full-time basis and go on for my Ph.D. I had never met Ed Heath, so this was quite a surprise. But Ed had just talked to Paul Brown and was clearly desperate to fill a last-minute vacancy. Three weeks later, leaving my wife to finish painting our new home and pack for the move, I arrived in Corvallis, Oregon wondering what on earth I had just done to my family and myself. I can laugh about it now, but the first words out of the Dean's mouth when I was introduced to him were, "Dennis, I hope you haven't sold your home." Apparently, Ed had left out a few details. There was no definite funding yet for the position he promised me. And so I began my career in the world of academe.

The first year was extremely difficult. I had no idea what I was do-ing. I still vividly remember my first hour-long class. I was so nervous that after hours of preparation and with copious notes I finished my first "lecture" in 15 minutes. When I realized I had zipped through all my material I remember saying to the class, "Well, that's it for the first day. Just wanted to give you a quick introduction to the class material. Roll up your sleeves and we'll get after it during our next class period." I walked out of that classroom in a state of shock. Teaching was a lot harder than I ever imagined.

It was an inauspicious beginning to what has been an incredibly re-warding career. The work itself has been a good fit for me, and immensely satisfying in most respects. I'm aware of no other occupation that allows for so much individual freedom. Aside from classroom-related obligations, I have almost complete discretion over how and where I spend my time. That autonomy is a unique and extraordinary privilege. I can't say that I've managed this freedom of choice as well as my family thinks I should have (I tend to over commit.). Freedom is both a blessing and a curse for me; there are always exciting new opportunities and never enough hours to tend to them all. As a result, I spend at least half a day every Sunday, most vacations, and many weeks each summer in the office in a futile attempt to catch up. I find it ironic that one of the initial attractions to teaching was the fact that I would have summers "off" and lots of vaca-tions. However, I really enjoy what I do, so I keep doing more of it. And I understand that it is my choice.

As much as I appreciate the autonomy this profession provides, what I cherish most about my 30 years in higher education are the lifelong friendships I have formed. What have really made a difference for me in my own professional development are the partnerships I have sustained with colleagues like John Crompton, Leo McAvoy, Frank Guadagnolo, Jim Murphy, and Dan Dustin. My best work and any contributions I may have made to the field are the product of working collaboratively. One of the things I most appreciate about this profession is that I always have the choice to work alone or with others. I prefer collaboration. For me, making a difference has always been a shared endeavor.

Finally, one of the things that makes a big difference for me in this profession is the variety of new experiences it offers. What other profession provides, in the same year, the opportunity to testify as an expert witness in a billion-dollar National Football League lawsuit and then, months later, to spend a week in China meeting with members of the Beijing Olympic Organizing Committee? Opportunities to apply my academic knowledge to the sport industry abound in my field. It is stimulating to put on a consulting hat and be allowed to test ideas in applied settings.

I could not have imagined 36 years ago, after making an impetuous decision to step into the unknown (yes, I had sold my house), that the profession I chose, and the life I would end up leading, could have been so rewarding. I would do it again in a heartbeat.

27 A Fair Share for All
Jim Murphy

There has never been anything more important to me than providing a productive learning environment in which students can explore interesting perspectives and insights into the human condition. Further, I have tried to engage students in discourse about concepts and practices that impact and improve the quality of life. I have always felt it was my responsibility to provide provocative ideas that challenge conventional thinking and ultimately "raise the bar" with regard to how organizations provide services.

When I first started work as an instructor in higher education, faculty in recreation and leisure studies programs were largely presenting "lists" of ways to provide programs and services: major functional categories of managing, supervising, and programming; evaluating services and personnel performance; and types of activities that might engage constituents and/or clients. There was little theoretical underpinning to guide the delivery of recreation services.

As a student majoring in recreation, I memorized lists of tasks and methods to be utilized by a leisure service manager. However, I found that my experience as a playground leader, camp counselor and program director, and supervisor of parks and playgrounds for a large municipal agency was unrelated to these lists. The lists, simplified by the use of acronyms such as DDAD (Describe an activity, Demonstrate it, Ask for questions, and then Do it), did little to inspire hope or provide insight into the complexities of the human condition, or inspire participants to achieve a desired goal or remove a constraining barrier to engaging in recreation. Further, these lists provided little or no insight about non-users or those otherwise excluded by the community.

As a child living in a blue-collar family in Oakland, California, I was brought up to appreciate diversity. We routinely went to different churches, synagogues, and temples for various religious celebrations and services. My mother also felt it was particularly important to embrace all races. In the 1940s, 1950s, and 1960s, amidst raised eyebrows from neighbors, we often hosted Blacks, Korean, Chinese, Japanese, and Mexican acquaintances. In high school I belonged to the Kiwanis club chapter. So while my male classmates were chugging beer and looking for the next wild party, I was involved in community service projects for Kiwanis International. Thus, my egalitarian and community outreach roots, nurtured as a child through my parents' openness and acceptance of all religions and races and by my high school service club experiences, moved me to believe, as a young practitioner, and then as an academician, that leisure service agencies were obliged to serve everyone in the community.

Getting Started

While an undergraduate student at San Francisco State University, I worked for both the Parks and the Recreation Divisions in the City of Oakland. Oakland's municipal programs had spawned such nationally and internationally renowned icons as Jay M. VerLee, Jay B. Nash, Alta Sims Bunker, Bob Crawford, and William Penn Mott. I remember my first orientation as a park attendant at age 16. Both Mr. VerLee and Mr. Mott addressed us on being responsive to our participants' needs.

In 1967, I was a National Recreation and Park Association (NRPA) intern with the Baltimore Bureau of Recreation. When I assumed my duties, I found myself thrust into the middle of a steaming racial and political cauldron, fanned by flames of anger expressed by African Americans toward a bigoted White establishment and years of discrimination. In the midst of the city's rebuilding of burned-out government buildings, retail buildings, and private homes, I discovered my professional path and soul.

John G. Williams, Superintendent of Baltimore's Bureau of Recreation, and a refreshingly different voice among the White establishment, believed that park and recreation services could make a difference in people's lives. As part of my orientation, he mentored me and encouraged me to attend community meetings to determine what direction the city was going to take following the urban riots of 1966 and 1967. Baltimore was one of those large southern cities near the Mason-Dixon Line, whose municipal services had only recently been desegregated due to civil rights legislation. While at these meetings, I met many city officials, community activists, and U.S. government "Great Society" staff, including Clarence Pendleton, who would later become Director of NRPA's Urban Affairs Bureau and then Chair of the U.S. Civil Rights Commission.

It was apparent to me that the field of parks and recreation was not contributing to the solution of urban problems (later discussed in the Kerner Commission Report) or improving the quality of urban life. There were extensive programs and services in Baltimore, but they were unorganized. The wealthier, outlying sections of the city and older established White ethnic neighborhoods often had better equipment and facilities and received more resources to serve their constituencies. The poorer inner city, and mostly African American, sections of Baltimore not only had inadequate facilities but their residents participated much less frequently than Whites in city-sponsored events.

A Fair Share

Following these meetings I came to believe that a community or government-sponsored recreation agency would not be effective in providing meaningful services unless it viewed the entire context of a participant's personal, social, and physical milieu. By targeting neighborhood residents as potential service providers, working with housing authorities, convening various agencies who impacted people on a regular basis (e.g., school officials, health service workers, police, fire, social workers), organizations could better serve people because they would understand not only recreation preferences but also factors which constrained people from being able to engage more fully in leisure. These constraining factors, such as poor health, inadequate housing, insufficient transportation, limited economic resources, and broken social networks, deterred poorer community members from participating in their fair share of recreation experiences.

During my internship with the Baltimore Bureau of Recreation I conducted a survey of many large municipal leisure service agencies and respected leisure service professionals throughout the country. I wanted to know what their organizations were doing to meet the recreation needs of underserved community members. I received an interesting response from Richard Kraus, then teaching in New York City. He had just conducted a study of the five boroughs of New York and several suburbs in New Jersey. He reported that for the organized provision of recreation to be viable, professionals had to first assist residents in reaching a threshold of basic needs (food, housing, transportation, etc.). This perspective changed my thinking about the recreation and park profession's ability to serve as a vehicle for enabling people to experience the joy and benefits of leisure.

In my first coauthored book, *Recreation and Leisure Service for the Disadvantaged*, George Butler, longtime Director of Research for the National Recreation Association, wrote one of two forewords. He said, "Black people, the majority group in many urban ghettos, have rarely enjoyed a fair share of public recreation opportunities. They have been commonly denied access to parks and other public recreation areas although some cities provided separate properties for their use."[1]

The early leaders of the recreation and park movement—Jacob Riis, Jane Addams, and Joseph Lee—recognized that recreation could help alleviate despair and uplift people from poor living conditions and overall social malaise. Recreation agencies were initially viewed as a mechanism for integration and community building.

Clearly, our task as service providers meant we had to acknowledge the totality of the living conditions of people in our service domain, the physical and social environments of a locale, and the capacity and skill sets of organized recreation and park departments to meet the recreation needs of everyone in the community. The threshold concept helped us understand what was needed so that all people—especially at-risk, underserved groups—could realize recreation benefits.

New Service Delivery Paradigm

Soon thereafter, as a doctoral student at Oregon State University, I had the opportunity to study under David Gray. Later, while teaching at San Jose State University, I spent many wonderful hours engaged in conversation with him as my mentor on a textbook. We talked every other Thursday evening for two years. He would fly up to northern California to teach a management course at the University of Southern California's satellite campus in Burlingame. It was during this time that he had been formulating a definition of recreation derived from years of professional practice, teaching, and research into the human condition. His definition of recreation stopped me cold. He said:

> Recreation is an emotional condition within an individual human being that flows from a feeling of well-being, and self-satisfaction. It is characterized by feelings of mastery, achievement, exhilaration, acceptance, success, personal worth, and pleasure. It reinforces a positive self-image. Recreation is a response to aesthetic experience, achieve-

ment of personal goals, or positive feedback from others. It is independent of activity, leisure, or social acceptance.[2]

That definition demanded a comprehensive view of the human condition and a vision of recreation experience that outstripped the conventional thinking of the day. Dr. Gray's insights, combined with Richard Kraus's findings about leisure service delivery to disadvantaged groups, helped me formulate, in collaboration with Bill Niepoth, Dennis Howard, and John Williams, a service delivery model I could embrace and teach with passion and commitment. I came to realize that service delivery could be restructured to enable front-line leaders to interact more freely with community members, seek their input, and engage them in the delivery of services. In this manner, recreation professionals could operate within a collaborative network of agencies and individuals to meet a myriad of needs along a continuum from direct service provision to removing barriers to participation. These changes began to occur in the 1970s as more articles and textbooks began to demonstrate how holistic delivery of recreation services could benefit the entire community. Changes came slowly, but come they did, and it was rewarding for me to play a part in that unfolding of events.

Pedagogy for the Dispossessed

The source of my professional mantra, my daily teaching "vitamins," and my inspiration for encouraging students to discover their soul and pursue a path of professional integrity, was thus borne out of civil unrest and an incomplete understanding of the nature of recreation experience and how it could benefit the human condition. That recreation could be part of a larger service delivery paradigm, while recognizing its unique contribution to an individual's personal growth and development, was a startling discovery for me. It has fueled my academic work and my professional life for almost 40 years.

There was, however, a disconnect for me as an academic. On the one hand, I was free to espouse concepts on how the park and recreation profession might revise its approach to service delivery. On the other hand, the profession appeared uncomfortable assuming a significant community role beyond the narrow definitions and rubrics of mid-20th century, white middle-class America. It became a day-to-day challenge for me to make a compelling case for elevating park and recreation services to a more central role in the lives of all community members.

I needed to convince city officials, and park and recreation professionals alike, of our field's potential to make much more significant contributions to enhancing the quality of community life. Similarly, I believed that university programs needed to develop curricula that fostered a more comprehensive understanding of human behavior, an understanding that would lead to a more equitable distribution of services to minorities and other low-income citizens.

It was hard for students to grasp the idea that park and recreation professionals should help people obtain assistance meeting basic needs by working with other human service organizations. This all seemed overwhelming and outside the customary realm of what park and recreation professionals and academic departments in universities had understood to be the purview of organized park and recreation services. Like many of my colleagues, I found myself searching for a pedagogy that would acknowledge and articulate a holistic leisure service paradigm. My challenge became one of encouraging other scholars to understand and then advocate for a more profound mission. I thought our literature should reflect a heightened awareness of new concepts and insights that could improve professional practice and enable students to better prepare themselves for a new leisure paradigm.

In the past 40 years, research on the human condition and on a more egalitarian approach to the provision of leisure services has spawned greater insight and deeper understanding of how parks and recreation can significantly change a person's life in a positive way. Not only is there increased understanding of how leisure can contribute to the improvement of individual well-being, but there is increasing evidence of the role parks and recreation can play in enhancing a community's social capital. And while our services have clearly made a difference in the quality of public life, our greatest challenge remains one of ensuring that every community member, regardless of age, gender, sexual orientation, race and physical or mental capacity, has equal access to park and recreation opportunities.

Looking Back, Moving Forward

As I reflect on my years of engagement in the field of parks and recreation, working both in academe and in the private sector, I am convinced that we must be advocates and catalysts for change. We have gained sufficient insight to know that people can be uplifted by the helping hands of park and recreation professionals. We must profess that recreation is a civil right for all community members, and we must seek to promote opportunities that will ensure everyone is granted their "fair share."

In my four years back from my second "retirement," I have come to believe that we now have an even better sense of how the recreation experience is a tonic that provides people with a greater sense of self-worth and self-fulfillment. Fueling my professional passion is an emerging "civic care" philosophy, the role of servant leaders, and the capacity for parks and recreation to improve the lives of the disadvantaged, disenfranchised, and dispossessed members of our society. While embracing the core values of respect, dignity, fairness, integrity, and inclusion as the foundation of my educational mission, I continue to fight for a fair share for all.

28

The Accidental Administrator

Bob Wolff

An old friend recently sent me Bob Dylan's new "Not Yet Dark" CD for my 60th birthday. We then began a series of long distance conversations about our roots, career paths, and what the future might still hold for us. While most of the talk focused on friends, family, and jobs we've had over the years, what stood out for me was how many educators had influenced my life's direction. And while I cannot say with certainty that my own teaching, scholarship, service, and administrative contributions have had an impact on anyone, I can say that several other educators, whether they knew it or not, had a significant impact on me.

The first of these was my high school counselor whose words still resonate in my mind. "Son," he said, "you better choose a trade, because you will never make it in college." Soon thereafter, in Vocational Machine Shop, I met a caring, motivated teacher who was willing to adopt the entire group of "never going to make it" kids. Mr. Wasilof spent five hours a day teaching and motivating us to excel. His teaching extended far beyond machine shop skills. His lessons included money management, ethics, choosing the right spouse, and avoiding bad choices. It was in Mr. Wasilof's machine shop that many of us tasted success for the first time. He invested in individuals that the "system" was willing to give up on.

My first job out of high school was in a unionized machine shop. The income allowed me to buy a brand new red convertible. Life was good, or so I thought. The high school training had paid off. I could easily double the shop's established production rates, but I soon learned Mr. Wasilof had not taught us everything. At the end of the first week of doubling the rates, my coworkers waited for me in the parking lot. They explained how they had worked hard to set the rates, and how they didn't like a newcomer "raising the bar." I quickly understood the meaning of their "explanation" and my production rates dropped accordingly. I left shortly thereafter to work at a piecework-oriented machine shop, a shop that rewarded extra effort.

A Tool and Die apprenticeship followed a year later at U.S. Steel's Lorain, Ohio Works. My main role was to analyze, draw, and then replace broken parts brought to us from around the sprawling steel mill. It was both challenging and rewarding to reproduce those intricate parts. At the time, I thought the job would last a lifetime, but a draft notice soon interrupted my "lifetime" work at the mill. This was the first of many times my plans were changed for me. As some wise person once observed, "Life is what happens while you're making other plans."

I was inducted into the Army on October 20, 1965. What struck me on that cold October day was the large number of "trade school" inductees. We were all 19 and 20-year olds and we had no idea what was ahead of us. It turned out that Vietnam was ahead of us.

After a tour in Vietnam, I returned to the Tool and Die shop, but my enthusiasm for that kind of work faded. One night after work, and after several beers, four of us who had recently returned home from the Army decided it was time for a change. We enrolled full-time at Lorain County Community College for the 1968 winter term. On the first day of registration, the clerk insisted I pick a major. Having had no college prep courses in high school, I chose what the person in front of me chose—marketing. I traded in my blue collar for some blue examination booklets.

In the fall of 1969, I transferred to Ohio University, leaving behind the security of old friends and study partners to seek a university experience. It was there, during a sophomore class in "Organizational Theory and Behavioral Management" that I met Dr. Paul Hersey and Dr. Kenneth Blanchard. They team-taught the class, using their new book, *Management of Organizational Behavior*. Everything clicked in that course. Their teaching style was something special. Dr. Blanchard has since gone on to international fame, his career launched by *The One Minute Manager*. I have read most of his books, used "situational leadership" as the basis for my administrative style, and tried hard to "catch people doing things right."

The joy at Ohio University was short-lived. During the spring of 1970, following the National Guard debacle at Kent State University, many Ohio University students acted out. The university administration, fearing for the safety of the students, sent us home early with a "pass" for all the spring quarter courses.

I decided to transfer to the University of Akron, an urban university with more nontraditional students. While there, my interactions with professors laid the groundwork for my long-term goal—to return to a university with Ph.D. in hand to become a marketing professor.

Upon graduation, I secured a sales job at a national corporation in my hometown of Lorain. I was going to spend one year in a training program learning the equipment and sales techniques necessary for success. I would be selling a specialized welding product to construction companies. Two weeks into the training, one of the company's sales representatives suddenly resigned his position in Los Angeles. When asked if I would consider replacing him, I jumped at the chance. I threw a couple of suitcases and my SCUBA gear into the trunk of my car, loaded my bicycle and enduro motorcycle onto a trailer behind it, and headed west.

In Los Angeles I became a serious recreationist. I lived for weekends. I rode my motorcycle across the high desert, across the sand dunes north of Blythe along the Colorado River, and on special occasions I spirited off to Baja, Mexico to ride on the sand dunes along the Pacific Ocean. Camping also became a way of life, and on other occasions I boarded boats in Long Beach Harbor late Friday or Saturday night for four- to six-hour journeys to the outer Channel Islands for lobster and abalone dives. When I didn't have the money or the boats were booked, I dove off the coast at Palos Verde Point.

Even though California life was good, I decided to return to Ohio to start a MBA program at The Ohio State University in the fall of 1973. Everything progressed as planned until the spring of 1974 when my fiancée convinced me to join her on a spring break trip to Bridger Bowl, Montana. It was on that ski trip that I met two assistant professors who had just received their doctoral degrees in Outdoor Education/Recreation from The Ohio State University. I still remember my astonishment. "You mean to tell me you can make a living as a professor doing these things!"

I completed the MBA, and later that summer I walked into the School of Physical Education and Recreation to inquire about a change of direction. Dr. Charles Mann explained that with no academic background in physical education or outdoor education/recreation there was little he could offer me. I thanked him and was heading out the door when I turned and said, "Oh, by the way, I'll be a licensed SCUBA instructor by the end of next summer." He invited me back in and we began to chat. My avocational and vocational interests were welded together that afternoon.

Soon thereafter, I met Alex Urfer, a fellow Ph.D. student. He was one of several teachers in the Program of Outdoor Pursuits (POP), and a great role model. An exercise physiology and outdoor education major, he was intense and driven. We formed a fast friendship and devoted countless hours to expanding and refining the POP. Soon, just like California, the weekends and interim breaks were filled with adventure. During the winter and summer breaks I taught SCUBA in the Florida Keys, off Andros Island in the Bahamas, and at Glover's Reef off the coast of Belize. Spring Break was reserved for bicycling from Central Florida to Georgia, averaging 50 to 60 miles a day. The POP courses provided me with a wealth of experience and abundant stories for my newly discovered career.

I felt like a kid in a candy store. While Kenneth Blanchard had become my administrative guru, I now discovered new mentors—Aldo Leopold, Mike Csikszentmihalyi, David Johnson, Terry Orlick, Paul Petzoldt, and Karl Rohnke. At an Association for Experiential Education conference at Asilomar, California, I was inspired by Willi Unsoeld's stories of adventure. I also met Dr. Betty van der Smissen. Her well-prepared legal guidelines and writings on risk recreation programs sparked my interest in the law, and a respect for the proper planning that should go into any adventure course. By the time I left The Ohio State University with my Ph.D. in the summer of 1978, I felt I was well-prepared for my first academic position.

I was one of three professors hired to start a new undergraduate parks and recreation management program at the University of North Carolina at Wilmington. There were few courses and fewer students. I would lead the outdoor recreation track. Our goal was to build a program worthy of accreditation.

The first five years were a blur. My teaching assignment was four courses per semester. Along with my outdoor recreation-related courses, I added separate law and liability, conflict resolution, travel and tourism, and commercial recreation courses. I was the faculty advisor for, and an active participant in, three student clubs. My door was always open and I wasn't able to say no to any student or administrative requests. I arrived at the office every morning early and left late, five days a week. I traveled to and held offices in state and national associations. I regularly presented papers at conferences. I took students on interim summer break adventures; bicycling the Blue Ridge Parkway, sailing in the Bahamas, and windsurfing in Florida.

To stay current and keep the classes relevant, I worked at the Wilmington Parks and Recreation Department several summers. In 1980, my wife and I also started a windsurfing business, teaching at three park and recreation sites in a two-county area during the summers. At first we just taught windsurfing, but soon we opened a storefront location, selling windsurfing boards and other equipment. We had to hire more employees to cover the expanding operation. In my fourth year at the university, I became the curriculum coordinator—and my two sons were born.

We secured professional accreditation in its fifth year. I also applied for tenure and promotion. Confident I would breeze through the process, I prepared the documents and went back to what I had been doing. A mixed tenure and promotion decision (tenured but not promoted) rocked my world. The committee said I just didn't write enough. I was stunned, but in retrospect, I had become exactly what I set out to be. Before that day, there was never a concern about motivation, focus, questions about life or career choices. I was living my dream. I was teaching exciting courses to excited students, quoting regularly from a growing literature, and meeting and interacting with the leaders in my field at conferences. Now, however, I stood at the proverbial fork in the road. I could write more and be promoted or stay on the same course. Not wanting to give up what I loved doing, I opted for simply trying to do more. After all, I still thought I had the best job in the world, and memories of a high school naysayer were still fresh in my mind. Proving someone wrong can be a powerful motivator.

About this time, Dr. Charles Pezoldt, Operations Director of Miami-Dade County Parks and Recreation Department, acting on behalf of Florida International University (FIU), recruited me away from Wilmington. The university needed someone to revive an undergraduate and graduate park and recreation management curriculum. Dr. Ron Perry, the lone professor and curriculum coordinator, had died two years earlier. Dr. Pezoldt convinced me FIU was a university on the move. Believing Miami would be a great place to build a program and a career, I resigned my tenured position to start fresh as an untenured Associate Professor at FIU in the summer of 1986.

Just before arriving in Miami, FIU's president and provost resigned, with my dean resigning shortly thereafter. At the end of the first year, with no administrator in office who had anything to do with my hire, the College of Education's Acting Dean called me into her office. "I'm not sure we should have hired you," she began. "Nothing against you personally, but we may not have the resources to hire additional faculty, and accreditation is out of the question. Please stop any program development until we hire a permanent dean." Then, to my surprise, she added, "However, you do have a business background and I need an Acting Assistant Dean of Administration and Budget. Since you can't proceed with program development, would you consider that job?"

After conferring with Dr. Pezoldt, I accepted the job. I viewed it as yet another challenge and only a small bump in the road. Eventually, I would be asked to assume the leadership of not just the park and recreation management curriculum, but of a Department of Health, Physical

Education and Recreation. Hiring new faculty, securing scarce resources, advocating on behalf of programs and faculty, being the spokesperson for the department, fighting for faculty and student rights, balancing the budget, being the person between administration and faculty, and "looking for people doing things right" were all responsibilities that came naturally to me. I carried out that Sisyphean-like challenge for nine and one-half years before accepting yet another challenge as my college's Associate Dean for Administration, Enrollment Management, Budget and Alumni Affairs, a challenge that continues to this day.

As I listen to Bob Dylan's "It's not dark yet, but it's getting there" it is clear to me that he isn't singing about my life. My future is bright. It always has been. My willingness to adapt and adjust to changing circumstances, and to play the role required of me, has enabled me to make a good life in higher education. The smiling students, the inquisitive minds, the successful graduates, the long friendships, the freedom to choose battles, the flexible schedules (even in administration), the belief that I'm making a difference, are all part of that life. Where else can these things be found? I've lived on the other side of the fence. I've experienced the "real" world.

Regrets? I have a few, but none more haunting than never thanking my high school shop teacher, Mr. Thomas Wasilof, for the extraordinary difference he made in my life.

When You Come to a Fork in the Road...

29

Frank Guadagnolo

In 1958, prior to my high school graduation from Amos Alonzo Stagg High School, an English teacher required us to turn in a paper based on an interview with someone of note. My interview was with the "Grand Old Man of Football" himself, Amos Alonzo Stagg. At that time, Mr. Stagg was 95 years old. After spending nearly an hour with him at his home, it was evident that he had not lost any of his passion for teaching and working with students; in fact, he was still coaching football at the local junior college and would frequently visit with our high school foot-ball team. Along with his passion for teaching he displayed a rare humil-ity. This was evident not only from my interview with him, but also from the fact that literally hundreds of awards and photographs, both national and international, were simply stacked around the room or placed in card-board boxes. My interview, coupled with Mr. Stagg's speech to the first graduating class of Stagg High School, convinced me that teaching stu-dents was a worthy career. But teaching would have to wait, for as Yogi Berra so confidently said, "When you come to a fork in the road, take it," and my first fork would take me in another direction.

Upon completing my undergraduate degree in Recreation/Physical Education I accepted a full-time position in industrial recreation, now referred to as employee recreation. During my nearly ten years as a prac-titioner it was these four years that proved most exciting. The company, and its 20,000 employees, was in the business of developing rocket en-gines for both space exploration and military purposes. Our charge was to deliver the very best recreation experiences possible to the employees and their families in order to maintain not only employee morale but also to attract top scientists from around the world. Since the United States was in the middle of a space/arms race with the Soviet Union, budget constraints were never an issue. Whatever funds we needed were simply provided through government "cost plus" contracts.

Imagine how creative you can be with unlimited funding. I recall the staff meeting at which we decided we needed to improve the quality of our promotional pieces. A few days later we "bought" an animator from Disney Studios to address the problem. It was also during this period that I was introduced to the "real" world of politics and shadow organizations. During my first year, I was asked to be one of the many chairs of the United Way campaign. I was responsible for collecting pledge cards from several hundred employees. In our initial meeting with management I made the mistake of asking what percentage of employees usually gave. After a minute or so of deafening silence one of the Vice Presidents said, "One hundred percent of course."

Within a week I had received contributions from all but one employee. It was now the day of reckoning. As I passed through the mahogany lined hallways of central administration with its plush carpeting I wasn't sure what to expect. "They" already knew that there was one holdout. Within a matter of minutes "they" were on the phone to the holdout's father who also worked for the company. The conversation with the father went something like this: "Sonny boy makes a token contribution or there may be two unemployed family members." Clearly, political correctness had not yet found its way into corporate America.

My second experience involved the close relationship I had established with top management. Because of my particular interest in fitness I was asked to start a rehabilitation program for company leaders who had experienced one or more heart attacks. Working with cardiologists and staff at the University of California Medical School in Davis, we developed individualized programs for a dozen Vice Presidents and Division Managers. Over time I became good friends with most of them. These close relationships with top management created an environment where I could do no wrong in the eyes of my boss, his boss, and his boss's boss.

In the second year of the rehab program the company lost most of its government contracts. It was then announced that the workforce would be reduced from 20,000 to 4,000 in the next 18 months. It was apparent to me that our recreation program was also expendable. While thinking about where I would head next, a company Vice President approached me. He acknowledged that the recreation facilities and their 500 acres were about to be sold off, but he also wanted to know whose position in our division I would like to take over. I decided it was time to pack my bags.

After completing a master's degree in Recreation Administration in the spring of 1965, I accepted a supervisory position in municipal recreation in a moderately-sized bedroom community just north of Berkeley, California. I soon became Director of the Department and spent a few years furthering my education in politics. With a City Council comprised of two Democrats, two conservative Republicans and one moderate Republican, life became almost schizophrenic. We never knew how the Council would vote on a given matter.

The Machiavellian tendencies I eventually embraced resulted from being caught between relatively conservative City Council members and a Recreation and Park Commission composed primarily of residents who were faculty at the University of California at Berkeley. (Remember this was the 1960s.) The Commission wanted the Department to waive facility fees for residents who were on welfare. Their thinking was that "kids inside the swimming pool can't be getting into trouble." The Commission rallied residents in the community who were not only welfare recipients but who also had various physical disabilities to put pressure on the City Council. On a Monday evening, without any advanced warning, City Council chambers overflowed with residents in wheelchairs, individuals with visual impairments, and others demanding a waiver of fees.

Whenever the Commission employed these strategies the Council would adjourn for a personnel session. They would then return and announce that the City Manager and yours truly retained our jobs on a 3-2 vote. There were a number of 3-2 votes during my tenure. These weekly adventures coupled with various dealings with the local chapter of the Hell's Angels and the Oakland chapter of the Black Panther Party certainly contributed to a number of restless evenings. In fact, on one occasion I received a death threat when I secured federal funding to establish one of the nation's first community recycling programs. It was, to say the least, an exciting time.

Upon completion of my doctorate at Oregon State, I accepted an offer from Penn State in the fall of 1974. While Penn State had a great reputation as a research university, the expectations in the mid 1970s were far from what they are today. As noted in the Kerstetter essay, at that time tenure could be obtained if you were a decent teacher and published a couple of articles annually. This was due in part to the fact that enrollments in the major had reached an almost unmanageable 700 students. Teaching, grading, and advising consumed most of our time.

As with most new faculty, I inherited courses that I wasn't prepared to teach. Fortunately, with almost a decade of experience behind me, I was able to bring much to the classroom. I handled the introductory course, and I was given an administration course that suited me. A third course involved taking new majors on a one-week trip to the east coast to visit various recreational settings that might translate into career opportunities. This class gave me a week to get to know the undergraduates. After a day or two in the van, students opened up, and I learned much about their trials and tribulations. More often than not students gave high ratings to this one-credit experiential class. I took note of that and decided where appropriate "hands-on experiences" should be incorporated into my subsequent courses.

As noted in the title of my essay, each of us is faced with various choices as we pursue our careers. This was certainly true in my case. For example, for the past 20 years, after being tenured and promoted to Associate Professor, I was faced with decisions that boiled down to whether I took the path that advanced my career or the path that best served the Department's needs. While they weren't necessarily mutually exclusive paths, it was apparent that the investment in time and energy it would take to do justice to departmental needs would likely minimize my chances of acquiring the rank of full professor.

Prior to taking the departmental fork, the Dean of the College asked that I prepare my papers for consideration for promotion to full professor. I put the request on the "back burner" since I was already submerged in the minutia required to develop a commercial recreation option to counter a dramatic reduction in student enrollments in the public sector option. It then became even more obvious that I should have heeded the Dean's request since new duties and assignments pulled me still farther away from what was required for promotion. Not only was my life becoming filled with administrative responsibilities, committee assignments, and service, but the promotion bar to full professor was being raised at the same time. To paraphrase Bob Dylan, "The times, they were a changin'." I raise this issue not because of any regrets, but rather as a cautionary note for those facing similar forks in the road. For untenured faculty, there really are no such options.

For various periods of time over the past two decades I served as the Department Chair, Associate Director of the Program, Professor-in-Charge of the undergraduate program, and Professor-in-Charge of the Professional Golf Management option. Reflecting back on my decisions to serve in these positions, I can say with considerable certainty that I took the correct fork. Of course, at various times there were a number of lateral trails taken off the main forks that should have been ignored. However, feedback from colleagues, practitioners, students, and parents confirmed that I had indeed made a difference. And just like Amos Alonzo Stagg, my plaques, certificates, photographs, miniature Nittany Lion statues, and other forms of recognition are now boxed, recycled, or otherwise put away. The fond memories, however, are, and will always remain, on display.

Connecting with Others

30

Gene Lamke

I have been at one university my entire career. I transferred to San Diego State University (SDSU) from the University of Nebraska-Lincoln after my sophomore year and, after receiving my bachelor's degree from SDSU in 1968, I became a graduate assistant in recreational sports while working on my master's. In 1969, I was hired full-time to teach three sections of the same course and administer the recreational sports program. Now, 37 years later, having made it through the tenure and promotion process to full professor, I serve as the chair of a department dedicated to teaching undergraduate students in recreation, parks, and tourism.

How might I have made a difference? Was it through teaching? Was it through other professorial activities such as writing, securing grants, or speaking? Or was it through my service activities to the profession and the community?

Many years ago I had an opportunity to hear Dr. Donald Bartlett speak about how one person can make a difference in this world. His words ring true to me to this day. He described his life and how one person made a difference in it, and how he was trying to do the same for others with whom he came into contact. There is some bond, some connection that allows one person to reach another: finding it is the key.

For me, connecting with others is the only tangible way to make a difference. Whether it is through teaching, research, writing, leadership, or service, the medium is immaterial. Developing that connection is what matters. Some in higher education do not make a difference because they lose sight of that connection. They are excited about their field or academic specialty, but they get lost in themselves. Reaching others is the litmus test. Standing in front of a classroom enables me to do just that. Teaching is what I truly love to do. It makes me come alive.

When I left my position as recreational sports director and moved, full-time, into classroom teaching, I met a writer and motivational speaker named Patricia Fripp. She was guest lecturing in a special one-unit course at SDSU, and I had an opportunity to visit with her. During our conversation, we were sharing our speaking and lecturing experiences when she concluded, "You're an adrenaline freak, a deadline person who lives off that adrenaline rush one gets when you must meet a deadline or are in front of others." I had never really thought about it before, but after mulling over what she said, I knew she was right.

I have been selected a dozen times by outstanding graduating seniors in our department as the "most influential faculty member" in their undergraduate career. I am well-aware that these were not "outstanding teacher" awards. Many of my colleagues did a better job of teaching and promoting learning than I did. Some were more demanding, more organized, more creative, and better presenters than I. I was chosen, I'm sure, because of my ability to relate to students, to relate the subject matter to them, and to help them understand the significance of the material. That was not due to mastery of subject matter; rather it was how I approached the subject matter and how I motivated students to learn it.

In *Coach: Lessons on the Game of Life*, Michael Lewis describes a coach he once had who made a huge impact on his players' lives. One quote in the book really hit home. "There are teachers with a rare ability to enter a child's mind; it's as if their ability to get there at all gives them the right to stay forever."[1] That statement resonates with my experience. It is what I have tried to do throughout my career. I have tried to get into people's minds and remain there forever.

Why didn't I choose research and writing to accomplish the same goal? The answer lies in how I got my start. I was a graduate assistant pursuing a master's degree. I was then hired to run a program and teach. I didn't become a college professor by completing a doctoral degree; therefore, my preparation to engage in scholarship was limited.

I did, however, have a strong foundation in teaching, and I wanted to do it well. I was constantly on the lookout for ways to improve. I was a library rat, always seeking out topics, activities, and new ideas to bring into the classroom. I looked for innovative ways to communicate. I explored different ways to connect. Since I was only 23 when I began teaching, relating to students was not a problem. Teaching fit my personality and my skills. It is what I was prepared to do best.

I thoroughly enjoy making presentations at professional conferences and meetings. For me, it is a natural extension of the classroom. It forces me to make connections, draw learners in, illustrate how certain educational lessons apply to their jobs, and then motivate the audience to employ what they learn from me. I receive no greater satisfaction than to have someone tell me, after they have been in a class or an educational session of mine, that they have been able to use what I taught.

I believe there are three things that make great teachers. First and foremost, they are passionate and enthusiastic about what they teach. Second, they strive for quality in what they present and how they present it. Third, they constantly renew themselves and their material. They are always on their game. The best teachers I have had were completely absorbed in what they were doing. They truly believed that what they were communicating was important and that mastering what they were teaching was essential to future success. Dr. John Zoeger, my high school zoology teacher, was one of those teachers. He drew us into the material. I still think about him often and wonder how many students he reached through his teaching. Dan Dustin and Janna Rankin were colleagues who had that same attribute. They were inspirational because of their enthusiasm for their work. Their enthusiasm rubbed off on me.

Great teachers never stop learning. They understand that the more they know, the better they can teach. Those who think they know it all or aren't interested in discovering anything new are doing a disservice to themselves and their students. How can they do justice to their work if they are not life-long learners themselves?

A current colleague of mine, Lori Sipe, is always finding new material and new ways to teach it. She is one of the most innovative professors I have ever known. Her classes are dynamic, and her students are engaged. That is what I have always aspired to be—an innovative, dynamic teacher who knows what he is doing and knows how best to teach the material to students.

Generally, people in this profession are committed to being great teachers, great writers, great thinkers, or great servants, and most direct their energies accordingly. Often professors are known for a special area of expertise. That does not describe my career. I am a generalist. Everything appeals to me. I don't want to miss anything or neglect anything. I have wanted to be a great teacher, a great writer, and a great servant. I have wanted to be great in everything at the same time. But my interests have been too varied and my efforts in any one area too thin, resulting in work that has never been good enough to make a significant difference by itself. My hope is that the sum of my work—the connections I have made, my investment in teaching, my genuine commitment to students, and my university and community service—do add up to something special.

Recently, I was asked by our local Chi Kappa Rho Chapter of Professional Women in Leisure Services to give the luncheon address at their Boss's Day celebration. "Trends for the Future" seemed a simple enough topic, and 30 minutes was reasonable. When I arrived, I found a room full of former students now practicing in the field of recreation, parks, and tourism. Collectively, they spanned the five decades I had been at SDSU. I knew just about everyone in the room. After giving my talk and enjoying some casual conversation, I was particularly pleased to see and speak with one of my former students who had also taught in our department. We chatted for about five minutes. Then, before departing, he said, "You have had a big influence on many of the people in this room during your career at SDSU. Many of us are here because of you. I hope you know that. I hope you know you have had a big impact on us and this profession." As I looked the room over one last time, I began to entertain the possibility that maybe, just maybe, I had made a difference after all.

Accentuate the Positive
Marilyn Jensen

A tugging at my sleeve and a gentle nip on the ear roused me from a deep sleep. Morning had come—at least as far as Tucker, the dog of the house, was concerned. He was much more interested in a morning walk and breakfast than he was in the fact that I'm supposed to be retired now and enjoying creature comforts like sleeping in. Nonetheless, his persistence provided all the motivation I needed to leave the warm bed and greet yet another fall day.

With leash and dog in hand, I found myself reflecting in the morning stillness about my career path and the academic life I had so recently departed. What impact did I have? What changes did I make? Who motivated me along the way? What were the turning points? Immersed in my thoughts, a cat crossed our path, and Tucker jerked me hard back to reality. Reflection would have to wait.

Back in the kitchen with Tucker fed and the coffee brewing, I continued to think of my career and how it had evolved. Certainly it had not been a straight line from Minot, North Dakota to California State University, Long Beach. My family was continually on the move when I was growing up. Our residence in any one place seldom lasted more than a few years. We traveled from the plains of North Dakota east to Minnesota, west to the Pacific Coast, from California northeast to Idaho, and then back to California again.

Each stop was an adventure. There were barnstormer airplane rides above Washington's wheat fields. In Oregon we ice-skated to grammar school on frozen canals. In Idaho there were horses to ride and deserts to explore, and in California an ocean and mountains to enjoy. I was so fortunate to have parents who placed limits but not chains on my teenage activities. Taking risks within reason became part of my philosophy of life.

Thinking about those formative years made me realize that as a faculty member I had always tried to afford my students the same kinds of opportunities. Yes, I wanted to provide a structure for their learning, but I didn't want to do it in a way that would diminish their creativity or sense of adventure. My mother had a pet phrase that has stayed with me throughout my entire personal and professional life. "Don't let other people plant weeds in your garden." I have always interpreted that to mean we can become whatever we want to in life, and that we shouldn't let others set limits for us. I have passed this adage on to thousands of college students over the years who otherwise might have allowed the negative thoughts of other people to thwart their ambitions.

As I drained the last drop of morning coffee, it was time to make an administrative decision. What should I do with the rest of the day? Should I think about planning an upcoming committee meeting on campus? Should I take Tucker to his agility training class? What about that new book I wanted to read? But I was hooked. Thoughts of the "who, why, and when" of my academic life were not to be ignored. It was as if my mentors, Mary Wiley and David Gray, were sitting by my side, urging me on. I began to think about the rich experiences that filled my university years.

Dr. Wiley, the Founding Chair of the Department of Recreation at San Jose State University, had an uncanny knack for infusing her passion for the field of parks and recreation into the hearts and minds of her students. Her quick wit and disarming smile were captivating. Her commitment to providing a strong professional foundation for her students was bolstered by input from practitioners, politicians, academicians, and recreationists alike. She was tireless in projecting a vision of what the profession she served could become. This was during the glory years of parks and recreation in California when new cities and organizations were springing up overnight and the demand for highly educated park and recreation professionals was insatiable. Dr. Wiley wasn't interested in turning out great numbers of graduates; she was interested in turning out young professionals who had a strong academic foundation that would sustain them and ensure their success as they elevated the field's level of professionalism.

Dr. Wiley's classes featured a constant stream of park and recreation stalwarts, including George Hjelte, Josephine Randall, Pauline des Granges, George Crawford, and Alta Sims Bunker, who shared the spotlight with State Recreation Director Sterling (Skip) Winans. Authors George Butler, Charles Brightbill, Harold Meyer, Gertrude Wilson, and Gladys Ryland shared their thinking as well and encouraged us to debate their ideas. Educators like Ardith Frost and Bill Niepoth sharpened our perspectives, too. We knew these people were important, but we didn't truly understand until much later in our lives just how significant a role these pioneers played in the evolution of the park and recreation profession.

Thinking back on my own tenure as a faculty member and administrator, it is easy for me to now see why I also felt it important to expose my students to the leading thinkers and experts in the field. I was following the example set by Dr. Wiley. I encouraged my students, as she had hers, to participate actively in professional conferences, committees, workshops, and meetings conducted by the field's leading specialists. I wanted my students to be exposed to cutting edge thinking in the same way I had been during my undergraduate years.

Although I began my career in municipal recreation, it didn't take long for a quiet man by the name of David Gray to recruit me onto the faculty of California State University, Long Beach. He was a wonderful mentor and I benefited greatly from his compassionate demeanor. An excellent listener who displayed a sharp wit and sense of humor, he had the ability to make you want to exceed your own expectations. Despite the naysayers and skeptics who disparaged my newfound interest in using computers to solve many of the problems facing the park and recreation profession, Dr. Gray gently reassured me by saying, "Stay the course. People just aren't ready yet."

Feeling somewhat like Johnny Appleseed, but buoyed by Dr. Gray's support and wise counsel, I continued to buttonhole anyone willing to listen as I grappled with the effects that computers could have on traditional organizational practices. This was a time when computer program boards weighed many pounds and computers themselves filled large rooms. It was the very beginning of the computer revolution. Along the way, I subjected hundreds of students and practitioners to my ideas and research results related to computer applications in park and recreation settings and information systems for local governments.

Eventually, my interest in organizational culture led me to take on increasingly larger administrative responsibilities, the first of which was Department Chair, and the last of which was Vice President of California State University, Long Beach. From the latter "perch," I was able to better observe the political context within which park and recreation departments labored to make their way. Battles between the hard and soft sciences were commonplace, and I observed the many difficulties encountered by park and recreation departments when fighting for their fair share of the fiscal pie.

As Department Chair I followed my mother's advice. I admonished the park and recreation faculty not to allow others to plant weeds in their gardens. Dr. Gray's "Stay the course," became my personal mantra as program needs increased. I sometimes felt that we in parks and recreation were being punished for doing well with inequitably fewer resources. We were always being asked to do more with less. I encouraged students to be patient and remain positive if change was taking longer than they thought necessary, all the while grappling with my own impatience with administrative foot-dragging and institutional bureaucracy. Still, I had the advantage of having learned from some excellent role models over the years. I was also smart enough to surround our students with dedicated faculty who had come to the university with real-life field experience, and who, without question, understood that accentuating the positive was the name of the game.

Long Beach State's present park and recreation faculty agrees with my perception of what academic life should stand for. They are professional, diligent in their attention to student needs, collegial with one another, and focused on promoting positive relationships between the university and the community. Their classrooms are full of a rich tapestry of experiences that challenge and encourage risk-taking without the fear of failure. Through it all, they guide, nurture, and expect their students to be successful. How could I hope for more?

Perhaps the reason I sleep comfortably now and remain optimistic is because I can see in my mind the faces of countless graduates of our program. They come together often for reunions. They network. They represent their cities, their nonprofit agencies, their therapeutic programs, and their commercial endeavors with pride. There are doctors, lawyers, and even professors among them. They are as happy to see their faculty mentors as we were to see ours. Some shuffle their feet in embarrassment and admit they aren't working in the field of parks and recreation, but they quickly add that most everything they learned has been put to good use in their current line of work. Three very different examples include an undertaker who says he is better at working with grieving families than anyone else in his company because he learned requisite skills as well as management know-how in our program; a newly retired woman who spent her professional career training staff and negotiating multimillion dollar mergers in the international business world, who has made a point of coming back to Long Beach to talk with us and thank us for her formal education and her ability to care for the human side of an otherwise harsh business world; and a graduate who has just returned from his third tour of duty in Iraq as a National Guardsman, giving full credit for his leadership ability to the time spent as a student in our department.

I could go on and on, but I won't. Knowing that our Recreation and Leisure Studies Department at California State University, Long Beach continues to develop students in a positive and challenging way allows me to conclude that the lessons learned from my own experiences were influential in pushing the current faculty and students to new heights. For me, that contribution, and taking Tucker for his daily walk, is satisfaction enough.

32

Doing What Needs to Be Done

Patricia Delaney

I am officially retired from the California State University system. How do I feel about this? I was 15 years old when I got my first paying job. Since then I have always worked—until now.

My decision to retire was the result of many months of pondering and checking resources. I still miss the students. I do not miss the endless meetings, the annual rewriting of the previous year's committee reports, and the superciliousness of some faculty members. Initially, though, I had the most trouble receiving a retirement check each month when I had not actually worked for it. It took time, but I adjusted.

As I was thinking about how I reached this point, my brother asked me, "How did you get into Recreation?" I was not a product of the playground. The nearest playground was over a mile away and we hardly ever went there. I did not go to camp. I never learned to swim. In fact, until I was in 7th grade, we had no organized Physical Education at my school. So I grew up feeling awkward and having very few physical skills.

When my brother asked that question, my mind instantly presented me with the image of a small one-story building on the public high school campus. Built in 1939, it was a social hall which was used for club meetings and parties. In the fall of my sophomore year, I transferred from parochial school to this high school. I knew very few students, but one of them invited me to the "Back to School" party of a club called "Ice-Breakers." It was held in that social hall. We played mixer games, danced, and enjoyed light refreshments under the unobtrusive but watchful eyes of an older woman.

As I participated in this and other school events, I became acquainted with the older woman. She was the Recreation Director for the school. She was not a credentialed teacher but the adviser and chaperone for most of the extracurricular clubs, committees and all social events. I followed her around and decided that she had a neat job.

After high school graduation, I went to UCLA looking for a major that would get me a job like hers. The freshman counselor was unaware of any such course of study and told me to major in Sociology. However, in the spring, in the office of the Women's Physical Education Department, I discovered a paper listing the courses for a major in Recreation. The faculty adviser was Dr. Norman Miller. I went to see him. The next fall I came back as a Recreation major.

My parents, my sorority sisters, the men I dated, friends on and off campus—nobody had heard of or understood what I was majoring in or why. Additionally, I came from several generations of Midwestern Americans who believed that fun and playtime were earned by work. Leisure and recreation were not a basic human need. So choosing a major in Recreation was a divergence from certain traditional values. Nevertheless, I felt I was on the right track and the classes had meaning for me. I managed to graduate with a B.S. degree in four years. I took the two required field work courses but I did not feel ready to work in the field. So I applied for, and was accepted in, graduate school. My dad could not believe I was going to get a master's degree in Recreation.

Two life-changing events occurred during the year I was in graduate school. In the spring semester, my adviser, Dr. Miller, asked me to serve as his recorder for a research session he was chairing at a state-wide conference of the California Recreation Society to be held in Long Beach. I went and dutifully recorded the session. Also, I studied the conference program and walked through the Exhibit Hall. Since it was Easter vacation, I went back the next day and the next. It was an eye-opening experience as I learned about the number and variety of recreation and park agencies in California.

The second event was, by pure chance, sitting next to a man by the name of David Gray during one of the seminars of the aforementioned conference. He worked as the director of a nature museum in Griffith Park for the Los Angeles City Department of Recreation and Parks. In the summers, he and his family moved to the Eastern Sierra where he managed a family camp for the Department. It had cabins for 120 guests and 20 staff, a dining hall, and a lodge. He offered me the job of directing the camp's recreation program. I felt I needed camping experience, so I accepted.

After graduation, I went to Camp High Sierra with much insecurity and very few skills. Thank goodness David was patient or I never would have survived. His style of management was very laid-back. He seldom intervened, but he knew *everything* that was going on. He wanted people, including me, to reach out, to try, to learn by doing. If I started failing, he was right behind me with just enough help. Although I did not recognize it at the time, I was learning through observation and experience, a new style of teaching and leadership.

In the fall, after returning to Los Angeles, I began a full-time year-round civil service job with the Department of Recreation and Parks. Why that agency? I knew I needed much more experience and skill improvement. David spoke well of the department as a training agency. Also, I could not find a job like the one held by the woman at my high school.

For five years, along with two male recreation directors, I provided classes and programs at a large park-playground-recreation-center-swimming pool complex with baseball and football fields, a wooded picnic area used for day camp, and tennis courts. You learned to do most everything because you had to. As my motivation for the job waned, I wanted to move into supervision. The majority of the personnel in the department were men. I was relatively young. There was an undeniable, though never admitted "glass ceiling."

A position for a citywide supervisor became available in a nearby smaller municipality. I was hired. The position involved being responsible for all the playgrounds and day camps (including all the school playgrounds during the summer), as well as all citywide special events and programs. Most of the employees I supervised were part-time, except in the summer. On the school playgrounds, male teachers took over. They were close friends with the Director of Recreation and they held these summer jobs for some time. They ran sports programs for boys. They ignored or even joked about my requests for a greater variety of programs and more "inclusion." I learned some do's and more do-not's in regard to supervising employees, conducting staff meetings, and providing in-service training.

While I was there, and because I needed an alternative environment, I began taking evening graduate courses in the doctoral program at the University of Southern California. The students in the seminars were from Health, Physical Education, and Recreation backgrounds. Our reports were varied and the discussions were lively. This experience provided good cross-disciplinary information and friendships. These in turn helped me stay in the supervisory position even though my motivation for the job had diminished considerably.

As an assignment for one of the classes, I chose to survey the three undergraduate Recreation Education curricula in the state universities in my geographical area. I Interviewed the Department Chairs at San Fernando Valley State, Long Beach State and Los Angeles State. The next fall, I received a call from the Chair at Los Angeles State asking me to teach a 400-level course one evening a week covering dance programs in

Community Recreation. I was still in the supervisory position but I accepted the offer. I felt qualified to teach the course.

My work experiences had required teaching different kinds of dance to children, teens, and adults. From my supervisory position, I knew how to work with commercial dance instructors as well as musicians' union officials. I could guide the students through the organization, production, and problems of dances with hundreds of teen, adult, or senior participants. Although I was unsure about teaching college students, I was highly motivated to share information with them that I thought they would need in future jobs.

Several months later, the Chair offered me a half-time position for the spring semester. I was more than ready to leave the supervisory position, so I accepted. In those days, my master's degree made me eligible for a teaching position (even tenure-track) in the CSU system. The next year I was hired full-time. Little did I know I would be on that campus for 38 years.

CSULA was built to be a liberal arts college for 5,000 students. It has grown to more than 20,000 with possibly the most diversified student body of any CSU campus. It is a commuter university with almost all students working part- or full-time. Many of the students also look after their own immigrant parents or other older relatives and/or their own children. English typically is not spoken in the home. They are the first family members to finish high school, let alone go on to college. Yet the "face," the pride of the whole extended family, is dependent upon their success. Feelings of inadequate time, pressure, and stress are evident.

When I began teaching, I do not recall being given any ideas, directions, or expectations on how to be a professor. I did not know how to reach college students or how to put a course together. The course outlines were sparse. Furthermore, collegiality among faculty was difficult to achieve. I found that course materials meticulously gathered were not shared. To my eyes, it seemed as though experienced faculty picked up a book, walked down the hall to the classroom, closed the door and began to talk.

I may have had a lot of motivation to share information, but I was dismayed by the process. It quickly became apparent that I would need to use most everything I had learned in my own education and in my years in the field to develop the courses I was assigned to teach. Self-assurance about what and who I did know and what I had done in the field, along with a genuine desire to prepare students for success in the field, provided my motivation for teaching. Additionally, I was determined *not* to repeat what I had observed in my own course work; I was not going to put students to sleep in my classroom.

About five years after I began teaching, I happened to meet the Deputy Mayor of the City of Los Angeles at a Christmas social event. We chatted and I answered her questions about where I worked and what I did. In the spring, she called asking if she could recommend to the mayor my appointment to the Board of Recreation and Park Commissioners. By City Charter this was a five-member citizen board. They were the head of the Los Angeles City Department of Recreation and Parks. They met every Thursday morning. I obtained permission from the Chair to be away from campus on Thursday mornings.

Because it was an administrative board, the meeting room was usually overflowing with people, most of whom wanted to speak. Our meetings were taped but there were also newspaper reporters with microphones. If it was a controversial issue or vote, there would be two to three television cameras. It was exciting, but scary. I learned a whole new side of my chosen field. I had an insider's view of administering a very large metropolitan recreation and park agency. We dealt with federal and state grants and budget issues. There were personnel problems. The public was frequently unhappy about the purchase or the nonpurchase of land or certain uses of public land. I learned first-hand about the importance of protecting the Department and at the same time placating the politicians.

To me, this was an incredible opportunity and spine-tingling motivation to share current events and real-life problems with my upper division and graduate classes. I could, and did, bring in yesterday's copy of the *Los Angeles Times*, which carried a front-page story and picture of a problem or decision regarding Los Angeles parks. Where appropriate, I gave students the necessary background information. We discussed the pros and cons relative to the kinds of decisions administrators must make. After the fact, and after "fogging" names and dates, I used copies of some of my actual agenda reports. We had mock Commission meetings in class. Five students became commissioners; I served as the administrator; and the rest of the class were irate citizens or worried politicians. It was real. It was now. And nobody went to sleep!

I served on that Board for five years: the last year as Chair. Then a new Mayor was elected. A year later, I was contacted by a staff member from the Los Angeles County Board of Supervisors. The Board wanted to appoint me to the Los Angeles County Park and Recreation Commission. The Commission was advisory and met monthly. It was a very different experience. The meeting room was usually empty and seldom was Commission business deemed newsworthy. Once in a while my appointing Supervisor would call me in to discuss an issue, but compared to the City Board, it was quiet. Nonetheless, it was valuable to me, because it provided me with current information for my classes. Eventually, my appointing Supervisor was not reelected. I was glad to relinquish Commission status.

My approach to teaching was governed by my understanding of the Master Plan for Higher Education in California, which specified that the CSU system was to be the work force engine, especially at the undergraduate level. Students were expected to graduate and be ready for full-time jobs. Jobs in parks and recreation were mostly "doing" jobs, whether someone managed a major sports complex, became the Executive Director of a Region of Girl Scouts, worked in Therapeutic Recreation, or rose to become the Director of a city, county, or district department.

With few exceptions, faculty taught 12 semester or quarter units each term and had 3 units each term for student advisement, committee work, etc. On my campus, research and publishing were not encouraged in the Recreation Department, nor was release time available. Campus committee work was expected and community involvements received mild acquiescence. Therefore, I viewed my faculty position as one of preparing students for professional positions. Perhaps because of UCLA's undergraduate and graduate emphasis on theory, I felt a strong need to combine theory with current practices in the field. During the first five to seven years of teaching, my experience in the field was still relevant and my "war stories" still cogent. During the next 12 years, my service as a Commissioner provided me with numerous real-world examples and problems to help make my classroom come alive. To stay motivated and be an effective teacher, I needed a steady stream of current information about developments in the field from a variety of sources.

Like other CSU faculty, I remained close to people in the field. When I began my first full-time job with the Los Angeles Department of Parks and Recreation, I joined the California Park and Recreation Society and went to conferences most years. The public recreation, therapeutic recreation, and even some of the voluntary agency people I met became my role models and colleagues. When I was at the university, they became my guest speakers, fieldwork supervisors, and field trip resources.

Many of the early faculty members at the CSU campuses came from the field. In some cases, we had known each other for years outside of academe. Every fall, I went to Asilomar to the California Society of Park and Recreation Educators (SPRE) conference, and there I found answers to questions, access to resources, and sharing of ideas and solutions to problems. There was camaraderie and caring that was extremely motivating and helpful to me.

In time, I also joined the National Recreation and Park Association (NRPA) and went to its conferences. I worked with groups and committees and met more wonderful educators and practitioners. Through attending meetings, I visited city, county and university departments in other states and learned new ways of accomplishing goals on very limited budgets. Best of all, my professional "family" grew and became more diverse. Wherever possible, information I obtained was woven into my courses.

Knowing educators and practitioners in California and across the country gave me a boost when I was lonely on my own campus. Local, regional, and national conferences were my annual morale boosters. They reminded me that I did belong and was a contributing member of the field I had chosen for my life's work. In fact, the older I get, the more I realize that even when discouraged, the reason I never wanted to leave the field of parks and recreation is because of the quality of the people I have come to know.

Why was this "belonging" of such import to me? From my perspective, chairing committees, holding offices, and writing short journal articles for professional organizations gave me, and hence my academic department and campus, some sort of stature. I felt the same about the two commission appointments. All of these were in parks and recreation, not some other discipline. Additionally, all of them provided source data which went into the courses I taught.

Other faculty in my Department did not do these things and rather openly resented the fact that I did. There were long-standing and difficult personnel problems. Even with several retirements, cohesion was poor. At one point, the Department was dissolved and the curriculum placed within the Physical Education Department. The situation did not improve. The courses needed updating. However, students were still interested in the major. Within the university's service area, there were positions available for which a bachelor's degree in Recreation was preferred. Nonetheless, word came from the Chancellor's Office that the B.S. and M.S. degree programs would be discontinued and that the program was no longer open to new majors. I was appalled that the career path as well as the whole discipline of parks, recreation, and leisure was not recognized as a valuable and important component of CSULA's curricular offerings and degree programs.

Shortly thereafter, the new Dean called me to her office. She told me she was giving me "release time" the next term so that I could be retrained to teach other courses. It was almost like starting over. I chose two courses in Physical Education, "shadowed" the instructors, read the text, and walked in to teach. My initial motivation was fear. "What if, what if, what if...?"

I continued to teach those two courses until I retired. These were not "my" majors. Their career goals were different from "my" students'. Yet, as I got to know them, their concerns for earning a desired grade, their worries about a future job, and pressures placed on them by their families and finances were the same. I found myself wanting to help them be successful in their studies.

Reflecting on these and other experiences, I have come to two conclusions. The first is that while I was working in the field, serving on the two Commissions and being involved with professional organizations, my main motivation was for *me* to succeed; that is, to learn, teach, and contribute. The second is that when I began teaching at CSULA and working with students, my main motivation was to help *them* succeed. Although they did not know it, in my mind they were like my own children; I worried about them and longed for them to succeed.

Did I make a difference? Occasionally, former students will find me at a meeting or conference. When they tell me about their advancement in the field, when they remind me about classes we shared, when they want me to meet their families, then I think perhaps I did.

Working with university students was a source of joy for me. It kept me going all those years until I retired. Although I wanted to be a Recreation Director at a high school and never planned on being a professor, it turned out to be the right job for me. It was where I was supposed to be.

33

Embracing Serendipity
Linda Caldwell & Ed Smith

Individually and jointly, we try to make a difference. So for this essay we decided to address the topic of making a difference by employing both of our voices. Our comments are based on our 27-year life partnership and 17-year research partnership.

Linda's Perspective

I think I first became aware that I wanted to, and could, make a difference when, at a young age (my parents talk about me being seven), I picked up a piece of litter my beloved grandfather "GoGo" threw on the ground and scolded him because it was the wrong thing to do. For some reason that had an effect on my family, and although I wasn't aware of it at the time, I had just learned that I could make a difference.

When I was in middle school in 1969 I could either be found participating in a leadership program at the YWCA or "grooving" with my hippie friends at coffee houses. During that time, I also volunteered in a swimming program for developmentally challenged youth. I remember one such boy my age, who wrote rock and roll songs and felt sad because he couldn't go to the coffee house. I made sure he got there and hung out with us.

I believe I've always had an instinct to want to make things better, and, in retrospect, I gravitated to the field of parks and recreation to do just that. I have always cared, but I learned that caring isn't enough. Respect is also an essential ingredient. You can care, but if you don't have respect for all creatures and the natural world, your caring can only take you so far. I learned that both from working with customers in a craft store (I still have nightmares about the "old ladies" and their crocheted pearls) and from working with individuals with disabilities and in psychiatric facilities. To truly make a difference, genuine respect for others' abilities, wishes, and interests is essential, as is a genuine respect for humanity in general. I have found this to be a critical component in working with students, youth, and colleagues from all cultures and with different types of backgrounds. I have also found that it is important to acknowledge what you don't know and to continually be open to learning in all formal and informal situations.

As important as caring and respect are, I also recognized that to make a difference I had to develop more skills to be better prepared to take action from a learned position. My education at Penn State helped me develop professional skills in therapeutic recreation and outdoor education. Those skills served me well in my five years as a practitioner. I ran a therapeutic recreation department at a large nursing home, managed seven community living facilities in two counties for adults with developmental disabilities, worked on a psychiatric unit, and ran environmental education programs in a large urban area for two summers. I felt like I was making a difference, but I also felt limited by what I didn't know. I needed more knowledge and skills.

It finally dawned on me that what I was missing was science. I clearly had a social work orientation but realized during my master's degree work at North Carolina State University that not only did I need to know more about administration, I needed to understand the research process and how research results could be applied in professional practice.

My understanding of what this really meant was limited at the time, but I knew that I had to pursue more learning. The journey began in earnest at the University of Maryland during my doctoral studies, but that learning has come to fruition only in the last ten years at Penn State. As with many other things in my life, I've been a very slow learner.

I've come to appreciate that meaningful research is a long-term endeavor that includes careful planning. It also involves a lot of serendipity: being in the right place at the right time and taking advantage of emergent opportunities. It also means putting yourself in places where opportunities might occur. I've worked on building a coherent and systematic research agenda that addresses core questions involving leisure as an essential element; but leisure doesn't necessarily frame the questions I examine. I believe my research needs to address important social problems that can be addressed by the inclusion of leisure. This has led me to adopt a prevention orientation to my work.

I also value "inter-, multi-, trans-" disciplinary work, and I've come to understand that no one owns knowledge or a base of knowledge. I have also learned to step out of the recreation and leisure "box" to communicate the importance of leisure to other fields. That might be the biggest contribution I have made, and I now make it my personal goal to help other professional and scientific fields "get" what we are about. This frequently challenges my comfort level, and I rely heavily on science and theory to explain why "we" are important players on the allied health team. We should be proud that we can use science to help us speak to others, but there is much work yet to be done in this regard.

I believe a successful research agenda involves teamwork. Thankfully I have learned that I don't have to know how to do everything. I used to think I had to, and it was paralyzing. I am not good at many things, and realizing that this limitation is "okay" makes for a better research team. This orientation also gives me the freedom to try bigger things, such as NIH grants. These "big stakes" or "high profile" grants are possible if we ask the right questions, frame our research more broadly, and work as interdisciplinary teams to focus on important, socially relevant issues. I think the more we can get these kinds of grants, the more we will make a difference overall as longitudinal research is allowed that helps us untangle important causal, mediator, and moderator relations.

One of my joys is helping others make decisions and think through their choices. Working with students at all levels on appreciating or conducting research that makes a difference is highly satisfying to me. Current models of academic excellence stress the integration of scholarship across research, teaching, and service. To me, this means working with practitioners, and being involved in state, national, and international organizations. Making a difference means being a good citizen and contributing to my academic units and various professional organizations.

I have also learned that progress is not linear. At the 2005 Penn State graduate school commencement ceremony, Dr. Arden Bement, Director of the National Science Foundation, made a statement that really resonated with me. He said, "I believe that the human imagination thrives best on a 'spiral model.' The spiral proceeds gradually upwards in an ascending, circular motion. At its worst, this process can feel an awful lot like going around in circles. But when it is working correctly, the circles are leading us ever higher and traversing much more interesting territory." Countless are the times I have felt like I was going around in circles. In retrospect, these have often been ascending circles or spirals, and they did indeed take me into very interesting territory.

Throughout this journey many people have made tremendous differences in my life. Perhaps the most important of them has been Ed, who I met during my practitioner years, and who cared about similar things. We became life partners and eventually research partners on numerous projects.

In 1988 we wrote "Leisure: An Overlooked Component of Health Promotion"[1] together. It was our first coauthored article, and little did I know that it would not only foreshadow my own research agenda, but it would also foretell an exciting joint research agenda that would take Ed and me to destinations throughout the world, destinations that would be both professionally and personally rewarding. In the process, Ed, the "leisureaholic," taught me, the "workaholic," that to make a difference, you also need to slow down and enjoy life.

Ed's Perspective

In my repeated attempts to encourage Linda to practice the benefits of leisure that she preaches, I have noticed that this tendency to work long hours, nights, and weekends, is not unique to her. Many professors do this, convinced that one more paper, one more grant, one more presentation, one more (fill in the blank) will make a difference. But a difference in what? Tenure? Full professor? Life fulfillment? As the prophet Yogi Berra once stated, "If you don't know where you're going, you'll end up someplace else." Maybe the trick is to figure out where you want to go.

So much of professional development is serendipitous. Recognize this and foster it, but maintain a balance. Chance meetings with colleagues, bright students, administrative opportunities, new grant announcements, and shifts in societal interests, are constantly teasing us into new directions. Tenure committees don't want to hear this, but many professors wander for a while, searching for an agenda to pursue. Along the way, if they're lucky, some of it comes together and the tenure portfolio looks as if everything was planned. The truly smart and honest folks recognize some of this serendipity, and, while they continue to formulate and gather a concerted professional persona, they remain open to ending up in Yogi's "someplace else." Five years ago I could not have predicted doing what Linda and I are doing today in our research. Stuff happens.

In 1972, while hippie Linda was frequenting coffee houses, making things with beads, and evolving into a life-long do-gooder, I had my first interview as a college instructor. A fresh master's degree in Sociology qualified me for a position in a small rural college where no one else wanted to be. Beard trimmed, hair shortened, and paisley tied, I met with the ex-military Dean. "What will you do," he inquired, "when controversial issues such as civil rights, Vietnam, or women's lib are raised in class?" Five minutes later, after explaining how I would attempt to present all sides of the issues and elicit diverse input from students, I concluded what I thought was a slam-dunk response. "You can go one step further," he added. "Tell the truth."

Should we, as college professors, tell the truth or question the truth? One of the differences we can make is to train people how to do both. Many years ago, a United States president (I think it was Harry Truman), was quoted as saying, "What I really want is a one-handed academic." Our education trains us to be objective, critical, and constantly weighing the "other hand's" opinion. This objectivity and neutrality serves us well within the confines of the ivory tower, allowing for educated debate and liberal discourse. Outside the ivory tower, the tools of battle change.

Aging hippies, however, shouldn't use battle analogies. Instead, the outside world uses terms like "promising approaches," "informed policies," and "science-based practices." A career shift to Public Health provoked me to step into this world and afforded me the opportunity and obligation to see if I could make a small contribution to improving lives. Fortunately I had a partner who shared this vision. As Linda and I have merged our research interests we have gone outside the ivory tower and entered the worlds of recreation and public health providers, school teachers and administrators, and other community service providers. Here, making a difference requires us to tell the truth as we know it. We do this knowing full well that the truth needs to be spelled with a small "t."

College professors have at least three choices in deciding how to make a difference, all of which have their relative merits. They can fulfill the holy trinity (teaching, research, service) by staying within the confines of the university. These professors are usually very good at teaching others to question the truth. An alternative way to fulfill the trinity is to venture outside the walls and collect data in the "real world," analyze it, and make statements regarding relationships among variables and the policy implications that follow from these relationships. These professors are very good at teaching how to question the truth, and how to develop theories about the truth. The third group, what Monty Python might refer to as the "grail seekers," attempts to work within the "real world," armed with their versions of the truth. This process requires the ability to take a stand, sit on "the other hand," and work through the messiness of the "real world." Randomized research trials become school board meetings, variables become questions that offend some parents, policies become people, and obstacles become broken buses.

It is this latter group that Linda and I have joined. Over the last few years we have been doing this internationally, and, while it sounds like a cliché, our lives have been greatly enriched through these experiences. A very cool thing is that we can do this together. It's one thing to disagree with a colleague and then not have to deal with her for a week; it's quite another if you go to bed with her that night.

The other person I go to bed with every night is myself. Most of the time I really like that person and where he's going. However, in 1997, after 25 years of teaching undergraduates, I realized I was rapidly becoming disillusioned with that part of the job. In those years I had taught 18 different courses to over 8,000 students in seven different departments. It was boring, I was becoming cranky, and I was tired of looking for the few bright eyes in the sea of apathy staring at me waiting to be entertained. Teaching undergraduates is the bread and butter of most departments and I had run out of enthusiasm.

Fortunately, universities like Penn State allow you to reinvent yourself. A combination of grants, teaching graduate students, and some new administrative responsibilities made it possible for me to fashion a new position for myself which totally changed my outlook. I had been one of those professors counting the ticks on the retirement clock, but now I am reengaged, reenergized, and really enjoying myself. Being a professor is fun again.

In order to make a difference you have to be comfortable in your own shoes. While Linda and I have taken different paths to our current collaborative relationship, her convictions remain at the core of our efforts to make a difference: caring and respecting others, making it last, continuing to develop personal skills, adopting a transdisciplinary approach to our work, and, most importantly, recognizing that change, both personal and professional, is not linear. Our ongoing quest for truth, that serendipitous "spiraling upward," is a journey we continue to enjoy taking together.

Pardon My Reservations

Tom Goodale

34

The title "professor" conveys the notions of scholar and authority and thus an elevated status. Certainly the privileges and perks of life in academe make us, in some senses, special. Of course we think we've made a difference, but don't most people in most walks of life make a difference? John Gardner (in *Excellence*) convinced me they do:

> We must learn to honor excellence (indeed to demand it) in every socially accepted human activity, however humble the activity, and to scorn shoddiness, however exalted the activity…. An excellent plumber is infinitely more admirable than an incompetent philosopher. The society that scorns excellence in plumbing because plumbing is a humble activity and tolerates shoddiness in philosophy because it is an exalted activity will have neither good plumbing nor good philosophy. Neither its pipes nor its theories will hold water.[1]

W. L. Goodale's pipes held water though mostly they carried milk. He was, quite literally, chief cook and bottle washer of a small milk processing plant, Goodale Dairy Inc., an extended family business. He worked six days a week—sometimes a half or full seventh day, too— starting at 4:00 a.m. and seldom returning home until 3:00 or 4:00 p.m. He held the plant and the business together, again almost literally, for nearly 40 years. Profit was not even a prospect; a few family members and loyal employees had steady work and the bills were paid. Supermarkets and agribusiness put thousands of small dairies out of business, during the 1960s mainly. Goodale Dairy went out of business in 1970, sold what tangible assets it could, paid the bills and closed the doors. W. L. Goodale retired.

He took his retirement benefits "lump sum" as there was no choice. After 40 years of 70-hour weeks, his total retirement package was a used pick-up truck. It was a '65 Ford. Yellow.

In 1954, W. L. Goodale was chosen "Cortland County Dairyman of the Year" by the Cortland County Dairymen's Association. He received a certificate, 5 x 8 inches, mounted and laminated on wood. That's it.

That he made a difference there can be no doubt, although he thought only about meeting his responsibilities and worried, for much of his life, about not being an adequate provider. All my thinking is colored by his story, to a large extent the story of a generation. His favorite book was *The Grapes of Wrath.* I have his copy; his "Dairyman of the Year" certificate, too. They remind me of my responsibilities. My thinking is also colored by his expectations of me. In the event of some malfunction or accident requiring his and other dairy employees' attention, I was often assigned new tasks with no time for instruction or preparation. Small businesses lack that kind of organizational slack. Still, there was never any doubt—on his part, at least—that the job would be done at least adequately.

While a grad assistant at Illinois, my mentors, especially Ted Storey, had a similar influence for a similar reason, assigning me tasks and expecting them to be done well enough. But I would never have made it to graduate school had it not been for Harlan "Gold" Metcalf, long-time chairman of what was then known as Cortland (NY) State's Recreation Education Department. He convinced the Admissions Department, which had rejected my application, that I deserved a second chance. My record certainly did not merit his faith, but he gave everyone a second chance, and believed in all his students. That alone, made them better.

Elsewhere in this volume John Crompton noted that we are often driven by the need to validate the faith of those who believed in us along the way. That is certainly my case. Add to that the unspoken corollaries; the serendipitous nature of encounters and accomplishments, and the obligation to share credit with those who are due. All this should remind us that a large dose of humility should accompany "our" accomplishments.

More Caveats

A second caveat arises from a utilitarian streak. Utility refers to the consequences by which decisions and actions should be judged. To what extent do they contribute to "the greatest good of the greatest number in the long run?" That is derived from the quite natural hedonistic impulse to seek pleasure and avoid pain, while simultaneously guided by what is referred to as "common sense ethics" or "moral intuitions." The result is that, at least with Bentham, utility leads in the direction of equality, because the first duty imposed by utilitarianism is the duty to alleviate misery: hunger, illness, exposure to the elements or to abuse, and so on.

The point, hopefully obvious, is that there is a moral hierarchy to utility, and the caveat, or at least my own misgiving, is that a greater or better difference might have been made had I made different decisions or had events unfolded differently. So I have the greatest respect for those who do the difficult things: teach "special education" classes and work with those with special needs, feed the hungry and shelter the homeless, provide palliative care for the terminally ill or potable water for those dying of dysentery and dehydration. Thus, there is a world of difference, although the tax advantages are the same, between a donation to Harvard, whose endowment *earned* four billion dollars from investments last year, and a donation to a shelter for Boston's homeless. Could we be using our time and energy and other resources more usefully?

A third caveat, or just my misgiving if you prefer, arises in an institution that is very successful in some respects but failing in others. The failures can be seen, for example, in the fact that education has increasingly become a private good rather than a public one, or in the fact that, system-wide, universities have exacerbated disparities in wealth and opportunity rather than ameliorated them. Such macro-level concerns suggest we may be winning a few laps but losing the ongoing race between education and catastrophe. It can leave you feeling like an apologist and wondering if there is something better to do.

A fourth caveat, or misgiving, arises from the ambiguity about the purpose of education and the marks of an educated person. In *The University: An Owner's Manual,* Henry Rosovsky, then Dean of Harvard's Faculty of Arts and Sciences, wrote, "It may well be that the most significant quality in educated persons is the informed judgment that enables them to make discriminating moral choices."[2] By that standard we are graduating many uneducated people, which is not an endorsement of "character education" but rather an illustration of the ambiguity about purpose. We all hope the purpose is more than simply preparing for work, but there seems little agreement about what it is.

Unsolicited Advice

Clearly, talk of making a difference leaves me uneasy. If my misgivings are shared by others, they become caveats: that is to say, cautions for us all. In any case we all seek to make a difference and sometimes we do. Again, some of that is luck and some credited to others as much as to one's self. To the extent that conscious decisions have helped make a difference, here are a few suggestions, based on observations about activities that worked out well for me and for my colleagues. My colleagues will recognize in this unsolicited advice some measure of "do as I say and not as I do."

The first bit of advice is of the "do as I say..." variety; try to focus your energies. That is not easy, especially for junior faculty, the very ones who most need to do it. Godbey advises junior faculty to go for tenure (if tenure is still around) as soon as possible. To some that may sound selfish, but unselfish ends can be served as well, as noted later. For now, suffice it to say that being pulled in so many directions, spending so much time on this rather than that, experiencing many intrusions or distractions, even if all true and all worthy, appear to others as, at best, lack of discipline and, at worst, excuses. In addition, your greatest contribution likely flows from a melding of what you can contribute uniquely, your own centrality to department and university mission, and your ideals. Simply put, focus on what makes the greatest difference.

One simple strategy to help maintain focus is to volunteer to serve on committees. This is not counterintuitive; you'll serve on some committees anyway. So volunteer to serve on those you believe are important, and don't volunteer for more than your fair share. Individuals' understandings and priorities differ of course, but I always volunteered to be the department's library liaison, one beauty of which is that it is usually a one-person task, and I was always ready to serve on the committee that handled reappointment, promotion, and tenure decisions. Shaping your program's library and personnel resources, without the headaches of administration, seems a good way to make a good difference. For the same reason, in those rare instances when the department can limit enrollment, volunteer to work on admissions if you can actually decide who is or is not admitted. Alas, for undergraduates at least, this is only a dream in most departments.

A second simple strategy is to maintain a healthy skepticism about intellectual fashions that come our way now and again, such as leisure counseling or values clarification or, more recently, self-esteem. Monitor to see if evidence emerges regarding the value of the fashion. Be respectfully patient; some fashions have real staying power while others simply don't pan out. But patience has its limits. If there are tortoises and hares in academia, be a tortoise plodding along on paths already rich in ideas and some promising evidence, however distant from the current fashion.

Since my entire career was spent in universities with no graduate program or fledgling ones, my experience was almost entirely with undergraduates. That has probably colored my view that the biggest difference can be made at the undergraduate level. In fact, I believe the best teachers should teach the introductory courses unless doing so creates significant inequities in workloads or pulls talent from other essential department and university tasks. Many of our colleagues, well-established as researchers, writers, and leaders in research and professional organizations, voluntarily teach introductory undergraduate courses. The department's standard must be set at the outset and must be set high. Doing so really does make a difference.

Students need teachers, and junior faculty need mentors. Being courteous and approachable while remaining a respectful distance is one key. Matters beyond academic and professional guidance may be best left to others, a matter of recognizing your limits, I think. That said, you may be the only one, and perhaps also the best one, a student can turn to. We have, as they say, been around. That is not the same as coddling, a real disservice, as it undermines the objective of producing disciplined men and women. Perhaps students' evaluations of courses and teachers will be higher if they like the teacher, but coddling probably has the opposite effect. If the students are learning they will respect you and that will be reflected in their evaluations.

Most of our colleagues agree that you should be a model of what you want students, and young faculty members, to become. If teachers and mentors can be described as well-versed, conscientious, objective, impartial, and the like, a good difference is being made. Above all, however trite this may sound, in a milieu which purports a commitment to determining what is true and conveying it, denizens must be honest in every way. The gown imposes the obligation to seek and speak the truth based on the most objective evidence available. The practice of science is impossible without that. When the truth is compromised, much real harm is done, and the damage spreads well beyond those implicated directly.

The crux of the matter is integrity, durable and enduring integrity. Pulling your weight is part of that, i.e., taking care of business while minding your own. Complainers and gossips need not apply. But here, too, is another caveat. Universities are not immune from politics. In fact they can be pits in which territorial imperatives can result in unpleasant skirmishes over resources as petty as photocopies, or as significant as cannibalizing faculty positions in blatantly unethical ways.

There are many ramifications of the political dimension of universities. The first is that minding and taking care of business necessarily includes being politically astute. Otherwise you may be minding and taking care of business elsewhere. So while avoiding rumor and gossip, you must nonetheless keep your eyes and ears open. There are times when a network is needed in order to avoid being blindsided. There are times when allies are needed. Besides, lone rangers may be alone for good reason. Even if right and courageous enough to go up the hill alone, the odds of returning with all your faculties and resources intact are improved if other rangers make the climb with you.

To repeat what was said in the opening paragraph, that most of us in academia make a difference, is hardly remarkable. Plumbers do, too, if they are any good, and milkmen. But there are two differences worth pointing out.

First, it is easier to evaluate a plumber or a milk plant cook and bottle washer than it is a professor. The criteria are clear: do the pipes hold water, are they up to code, do they pass inspection; is the butter-fat content above or below food and health standards, is the bacteria count acceptable? Perhaps that is why professors, as much as any occupation or worker group, are evaluated almost constantly; course by course for teaching, annually and quite formally for everything else. We are to be accountable even if we are not sure what that means. It is one of the prices of the autonomy and security that go with the job.

Second, because results of a professor's work are intangible, and evaluations thus to some degree subjective, errors occur and injustices result. The most egregious cases generally involve administrators acting not just arbitrarily and capriciously but in deliberate and unethical fashion. Throughout much of my career, I did not believe in tenure. It is irrelevant as a means of protecting academic freedom, and too often it protects shirkers and backsliders and those bypassed by change. But tenure turns out to be useful in this respect; it makes going up the hill to confront un-ethical administrators a little bit less risky. Personal grievances are a poor reason to confront administrators. But if your students or colleagues are threatened or harmed by an unethical administration, climb you must, regardless of tenure or the company of others. That means taking risks, personal ones.

Your vitae will never reflect it but, for example, being a player in the removal of incompetent administrators makes a difference. Sometimes, even to your own financial detriment, it is necessary to make a statement and refuse to passively accommodate unethical behavior, even though your statement may have no effect on the condition and practice at hand. But making a statement still makes a difference in two critical respects. First, you are constructing and preserving the model you want students and colleagues to follow. Second, durable and enduring integrity remains intact. Without it you will not be invited to the table, or have anything to bring to it.

Fortunately, as Woody Allen suggested, making a difference is largely a matter of showing up and being prepared and willing to work. Showing up is merely what we owe those who believed in us, and what we expect from each other. Unless you are in the wrong line of work, earning an equitable income, earning respect, and making a good difference will take care of themselves if you show up. As Lao Tse said, "If you seek a tranquil heart, do your work, then step back."

About the Authors

LARRY BECK, Ph.D., University of Minnesota, Professor, San Diego State University

Dr. Beck's teaching interests include conservation education, environmental interpretation, wilderness management, and the symbolism of park and protected areas in American culture. Currently he teaches "Outdoor Education and Environmental Interpretation," "Outdoor Recreation Planning and Policy," and "Wilderness and the Leisure Experience." Dr. Beck has authored or coauthored three books. *Interpretation of Cultural and Natural Resources* (2003) has been adopted as a textbook at universities throughout the United States and Canada. *Interpretation for the 21st Century* (2002) is used by the interpretive profession internationally and has been translated into Chinese. These two books are among the six core publications used by the National Association for Interpretation for professional certification. Dr. Beck's most recent book is *Moving Beyond Treeline: Meanings of a Wilderness Experience* (2006).

M. DEBORAH BIALESCHKI, Ph.D., University of Wisconsin-Madison, Senior Researcher, American Camp Association

Dr. Bialeschki was formerly a professor in the Department of Recreation and Leisure Studies at the University of North Carolina-Chapel Hill. Her research interests have focused primarily on issues related to women's leisure, outdoor recreation, and human development through the organized camp experience. She has presented her work at state, national, and international conferences as well as published in a variety of research journals. She has coauthored several books, including *Both Gains and Gaps* (with Henderson, Shaw, and Freysinger), *Evaluation of Leisure Services* (with Henderson), and *Introduction to Leisure Services* (with Henderson, Hodges, Hemingway, and Kivel). She has served her profession in a variety of ways, including President of SPRE, President-Elect of the Academy of Leisure Sciences, Co-Chair of the NRPA's Leisure Research Symposium, Secretary of the American Alliance for Health, Physical Education, Recreation and Dance Research Consortium, Chair of the National Standards Board of the American Camp Association (ACA), Editor of *Schole*, and Associate Editor of the *Journal of Leisure Research* and the *Journal of Park and Recreation Administration*. She has received the ACA National Honor Award, ACA Special Recognition Award, and a SPRE President's Recognition Award. She has also been recognized for her teaching at the University of North Carolina-Chapel Hill with a prestigious Tanner Faculty Award for Excellence in Undergraduate Teaching.

HERBERT BRANTLEY, Ph.D., University of North Carolina-Chapel Hill, Professor Emeritus, Clemson University

Dr. Brantley was the first Department Head in Parks, Recreation and Tourism Management at Clemson University. He served in that capacity for 21 years. He focused his scholarly interests on the ethics of resource allocation and environmental management. Dr. Brantley served as President of the NRPA and the Society of Park and Recreation Educators. He also chaired the NRPA-AALR Council on Accreditation, and was elected to the American Academy of Park and Recreation Administration. He served as a member of the Health Education Authority of the South Carolina Commission on Higher Education, as a member of the South Carolina Commission for Parks, Recreation, and Tourism, and as a member and Chairman of the Pendleton District Historical and Recreation Commission. He also serves on the Board of Directors of Textile Hall, Inc., which operates the Palmetto International Exposition Hall in Greenville, South Carolina.

LINDA CALDWELL, Ph.D., University of Maryland, Professor, The Pennsylvania State University

Much of Linda Caldwell's research has centered on adolescents, leisure, and health. She is particularly interested in leisure education and the developmental affordances of leisure. Currently, she is the lead investigator on a National Institute of Drug Abuse-funded substance use prevention program that helps middle school youth learn to use their leisure time wisely. She is also involved with several international projects (Santiago, Chile; Cape Town, South Africa; Lome, Togo) that focus on developing youth competencies, healthy lifestyles and democratic behavior through leisure. Dr. Caldwell has been an associate editor for the *Journal of Leisure Research, Therapeutic Recreation Journal, Schole,* and *Journal of Applied Recreation Research.* She recently served as guest editor for the *Journal of Park and Recreation Administration's* special issue on Youth and Leisure (2000), and is currently the guest editor for a special issue on youth for the *Therapeutic Recreation Journal.* Dr. Caldwell sits on the Board of Directors for the SPRE and the Canadian Association of Leisure Studies, and is a member of the World Leisure Association. In 2001, she received the National Therapeutic Recreation Society Professional Research Award. She loves gardening, photography, scuba diving, and traveling.

MARY FAETH CHENERY, Ph.D., North Carolina State University, retired

Mary Faeth Chenery taught in recreation and leisure studies at North Carolina State University, Indiana University, and the University of Oregon before emigrating to Australia. At La Trobe University, Bendigo, Victoria, she taught outdoor education and nature tourism, and periodically served as department head before retiring in 2002. She now works for peace and the healing of the environment through spiritual education and service.

JOHN CROMPTON, Ph.D., Texas A&M University, Distinguished Professor, Texas A&M University

Dr. Crompton's primary interests are in marketing and financing public leisure services and tourism. He has authored or coauthored five books and a substantial number of articles in the leisure, tourism, and marketing fields and directed scores of studies for recreation resource and service providing agencies. Dr. Crompton has conducted numerous two- and three-day workshops on marketing leisure services and has lectured in a number of foreign countries. On seven occasions he has delivered the keynote address at the respective nations' annual national conferences. Dr. Crompton is a past president of the Society of Park and Recreation Educators, the Texas Recreation and Park Society, and the American

Academy of Park and Recreation Administration. He is also a recipient of the NRPA's Literary Award, the Roosevelt Research Award, and the Travel and Tourism Research Association Travel Research Award, among many others.

PATRICIA DELANEY, M.S., University of California at Los Angeles, Professor Emeritus, California State University, Los Angeles

Ms. Delaney received her B.S. and M.S. degrees from the University of California at Los Angeles. She taught 14 different undergraduate and six different graduate courses, all requiring different readings, preparations, forms, materials, and examinations. Her articles have been published in the *California Park and Recreation Magazine, Parks and Recreation, Spirit*, and *The Anchora of Delta Gamma*. Ms. Delaney has also given 47 presentations at conferences, meetings, workshops, and training sessions in 15 states. Honors and awards include the Fellow Award from the California Park and Recreation Society (1975), and the Special Award from the California Association of Park and Recreation Commissioners and Board Members (1978). Her active membership in the NRPA includes positions as Chair of the National Registration Board, Chair of the Pacific Southwest Regional Council, and Research Chair and Awards Chair on the Board of Trustees.

NICK DIGRINO, Ph.D., Texas A&M University, Associate Dean for Health and Human Services, Western Illinois University

Dr. DiGrino, along with his other assigned duties, has oversight responsibilities for the Departments of Community Health and Health Services Management; Dietetics, Fashion Merchandising and Hospitality; Kinesiology; Law Enforcement and Justice Administration; Military Science; Social Work; and Recreation, Park, and Tourism Administration. Dr. DiGrino also served for 18 years as Chair of WIU's Department of Recreation, Park and Tourism Administration. Prior to that, he served for two years as Coordinator of the Leisure Services Curriculum in the Department of Health, Physical Education, and Leisure Services at Iowa State University. Dr. DiGrino received the Illinois Park and Recreation Association Literary Award and the Iowa Park and Recreation Association Gazaway and Associates Research Award. He also received Indiana University's Garrett G. Eppley Distinguished Alumni Award.

DANIEL DUSTIN, Ph.D., University of Minnesota, Professor and Chair, Department of Parks, Recreation & Tourism, University of Utah

Dr. Dustin's academic interests center on environmental stewardship and the moral and ethical basis for leisure and recreation activity preferences and behaviors. A past president of the Society of Park and Recreation Educators and the Academy of Leisure Sciences, he is a recipient of the NRPA's Literary Award. In 1994 he was named an "honorary lifetime member" of the California Park Rangers Association for his contributions to the literature of outdoor recreation resource management and planning. *Wilderness in America: Personal Perspectives; Beyond Promotion and Tenure: On Being a Professor; For the Good of the Order: Administering Academic Programs in Higher Education; The Wilderness Within: Reflections on Leisure and Life; Stewards of Access/Custodians of Choice: A Philosophical Foundation for the Park and Recreation Profession*; and *Nature and the Human Spirit: Toward an Expanded Land Management Ethic* are among his works as a contributing author and editor.

PHYLLIS M. FORD, Re.D., Indiana University, deceased

A foremost national expert on outdoor recreation and camping, Dr. Ford was a graduate of the University of Massachusetts, Arizona State University, and Indiana University. She spent much of her career in higher education administration, holding administrative posts at the University of Oregon, University of Iowa, Washington State University, and Michigan State University. Her academic interests varied, but her passion was outdoor education and camping. Dr. Ford received 15 distinguished service awards during her career, and she was an officer of the American Alliance for Health, Physical Education, Recreation and Dance. Among her many works were *Leadership and Administration of Outdoor Pursuits* and *Principles and Practices of Outdoor/Environmental Education*, and among her many honors was the Hedley S. Dimock Award from the ACA.

GEOF GODBEY, Ph.D., The Pennsylvania State University, Professor Emeritus, The Pennsylvania State University

Dr. Godbey has authored or coauthored eight books and approximately 100 articles dealing with leisure behavior, history and philosophies of leisure, leisure service organizations, and the future of leisure and leisure services. He has been President of the Society of Park and Recreation Educators and the Academy of Leisure Sciences. He has testified before committees of the United States Senate and Presidential commissions. Godbey has won the National Literary Award from the NRPA and the Distinguished Alumnus Award from SUNY-Cortland. Dr. Godbey has written for and been featured in a wide variety of mass-circulation magazines and newspapers and has been featured extensively on network television. He is a founder of Venture Publishing, a publisher of scholarly books and textbooks in leisure studies. Godbey has given invited presentations in 18 countries and several of his books and articles have been translated into Chinese, Korean, and Spanish.

THOMAS GOODALE, Ph.D., University of Illinois, Professor Emeritus, George Mason University

A past president of the Academy of Leisure Sciences, Dr. Goodale previously taught at SUNY-Cortland, Wisconsin-Green Bay, and Ottawa (Canada) where he also served a term as Chair of its bilingual program in Leisure Studies. He has served as an editor of *Leisure Sciences*, and an associate editor of *Leisure Sciences, Journal of Leisure Research*, and other journals, and is coauthor (with G. Godbey) of *The Evolution of Leisure: Historical and Philosophical Perspectives* and coeditor (with P. Witt) of *Recreation and Leisure: Issues in an Era of Change*. Dr. Goodale is a Distinguished Alumnus of SUNY-Cortland, Distinguished Colleague of the Society of Park and Recreation Educators, recipient of the National Literary Award from the NRPA, and recipient of an honorary doctorate of letters from the University of Waterloo, Ontario, Canada. His principal professional interest is a liberal studies approach to teaching undergraduates about leisure.

FRANK GUADAGNOLO, Ph.D., Oregon State University, Associate Professor Emeritus, The Pennsylvania State University

Dr. Guadagnolo assumed various roles during his 31 years at Penn State. Most recently (1995-2005), he served as Professor-in-Charge of the Professional Golf Management program within the Department of Recreation, Park and Tourism Management. In addition to carrying out his administrative responsibilities, Dr. Guadagnolo taught undergraduate and graduate classes in law, marketing and administration; chaired and served on more than 100 masters and doctoral committees; conducted feasibility studies involving economic impact, consumer preferences, and buying behavior; and presented the results of his research in the United States and abroad. Dr. Guadagnolo served on various national and state committees, including the Board of Directors of the Society of Park and Recreation Educators, and was as an associate editor of the *Journal of Park and Recreation Administration*.

KARLA HENDERSON, Ph.D., University of Minnesota, Professor, North Carolina State University

Dr. Henderson is a Professor in the Department of Parks, Recreation, and Tourism Management at North Carolina State University. She has been on the faculty at the University of North Carolina-Chapel Hill, the University of Wisconsin-Madison, and Texas Woman's University. She has given numerous presentations throughout North America, Europe, Asia, and Australia. She publishes regularly in a variety of journals and has authored or coauthored several books: *Both Gains and Gaps* (with Bialeschki, Shaw, and Freysinger), *Dimensions of Choice, Volunteers in Leisure* (with Tedrick), *Introduction to Leisure Services* (with Sessoms), and *Evaluation of Leisure Services* (with Bialeschki). She is currently Co-Editor of Leisure Sciences. Dr. Henderson has contributed to the profession in a number of ways by serving as President of the Society of Park and Recreation Educators, President of the American Alliance for Health, Physical Education, Recreation and Dance Research Consortium, President of the Academy of Leisure Sciences, and on numerous state, national, and international boards and committees. She received the Jay B. Nash Scholar Award, the Julian Smith Award, the NCRPS Special Citation, the ACA Honor Award, the SPRE Distinguished Colleague Award, the North Carolina Recreation and Park Society Honor Award, and the NRPA Roosevelt Excellence in Research Award. When not working, Karla enjoys hiking in the Rocky Mountains, running, playing her trumpet, and reading and writing wherever she goes.

DENNIS HOWARD, Ph.D., Oregon State University, Phillip Knight Professor of Business, University of Oregon

Dr. Howard's principal research interests focus on the application of consumer behavior theory to sport and recreation issues. His research in recent years has concentrated on the development of a scale for measuring the dimensions which motivate and sustain sport spectatorship. His latest book with John Crompton is *Financing Sport*. He has served as a co-chair of the NRPA's Leisure Research Symposium, as a member of the Society of Park and Recreation Educators Board of Directors, as President of the Oregon Park and Recreation Society, as an associate editor of *Leisure Sciences*, and as a member of the Editorial Board of the *Journal of Sport Management*.

MARILYN JENSEN, Ph.D., University of Southern California, Associate Vice President, Academic Affairs/Dean of University Academic Programs, and Professor Emeritus, California State University, Long Beach

Dr. Jensen enjoyed a long and distinguished academic career in teaching and administration. She served as Chair of the Department of Recreation and Leisure Studies at California State University, Long Beach from 1974 to 1975 and again from 1976 to 1989. She then moved into university level administration from 1989 until 2000. Among her many honors are the Citation and Fellowship Awards from the California Park and Recreation Society, the Distinguished Service Award from the Southern California section of the ACA, and the Distinguished Alumni Award from San Jose State University's Department of Recreation and Leisure Studies. Dr. Jensen was a pioneer in applying the advancement of computer technology to higher education.

DEB KERSTETTER, Ph.D., The Pennsylvania State University, Associate Professor, The Pennsylvania State University

Dr. Kerstetter teaches and conducts research in the areas of marketing, consumer decision making, and tourism. She has authored or coauthored approximately 50 journal articles, a number of book chapters, and conducted research for federal, state, local and private/nonprofit recreation/tourism agencies. Dr. Kerstetter has conducted marketing workshops for the Professional Golf Association, the ACA, and several tourism groups.

She has also coordinated research symposia at national and regional conferences and been a member of various national and regional boards associated with recreation and tourism. Her contributions to the field have been recognized by external organizations such as the Society of Park and Recreation Educators, the Resort and Commercial Recreation Association, and the Travel and Tourism Research Association, as well as internal governing bodies such as Penn State's Schreyer Institute for Teaching Excellence.

GENE LAMKE, M.S., San Diego State University, Professor, San Diego State University

Mr. Lamke's primary areas of expertise are in recreational sports management, leisure service delivery and programming, and organization and program administration. He has written several articles in a variety of refereed and nonrefereed journals, and he has given more than 200 conference presentations. He has keynoted conferences in Canada and the United States and has lectured at universities in several countries. Mr. Lamke has been a member of the Society of Park and Recreation Educators Board of Directors, President of the National Intramural-Recreational Sports Association, President of the California Society of Park and Recreation Educators, and President of District XII, California Parks and Recreation Society. He has garnered over $2,000,000 in grants and contracts for recreation services and currently serves as Project Director for Camp Able at Coronado, an aquatic-based camp for children and youth with disabilities.

ROGER MANNELL, Ph.D., University of Windsor, Professor and Dean, College of Applied Health Sciences, University of Waterloo, Canada

Dr. Mannell is a psychologist and professor of recreation and leisure studies. He was Director of the Centre of Leisure Studies at Acadia University in Nova Scotia before joining the University of Waterloo. Roger's work is focused on the psychological study of leisure and time use, and he has employed a variety of research methodologies, including laboratory studies and the experiential sampling method. In particular, he has been interested in social and personality factors that influence the ways in which people choose to use their leisure and how these choices affect the quality of their lives. Currently, his research includes examining the impact of time pressure and stress on family leisure and lifestyles, and the relationship between the use of leisure and mental health. He is the coauthor (with Douglas Kleiber) of the book *A Social Psychology of Leisure*. Dr. Mannell was the 1989 recipient of the Allen V. Sapora Research Award and the 1991 NRPA's Theodore and Franklin Roosevelt Research Excellence Award.

LEO MCAVOY, JR., Ph.D., University of Minnesota, Professor Emeritus, University of Minnesota

Dr. McAvoy's primary line of research is in outdoor recreation and education, specifically studying the personal and social benefits of participation in environmentally related activities and the management of human behavior in outdoor recreation settings. This applied research has been supported by federal, state, and local agencies and has been published in a variety of scholarly and professional journals. He is coauthor of *Stewards of Access/Custodians of Choice: a Philosophical Foundation for the Park and Recreation Profession* (with Dan Dustin and John Schultz). Professional service has included serving as an associate editor for *Leisure Sciences*, as a co-chair of the NRPA's Leisure Research Symposium, and as a research and training consultant on a number of projects for public and private outdoor recreation and outdoor education agencies.

JAMES MURPHY, Ph.D., Oregon State University, Professor and Chair, Department of Recreation and Leisure Studies, San Francisco State University

Dr. Murphy's scholarly interests include concepts of leisure, delivery of services, holistic management perspectives, and services for the economically and culturally disadvantaged. Author or coauthor of seven books, six book chapters, and many articles on these themes, he has also given many presentations and workshops. Dr. Murphy has been an associate editor of the *Journal of Leisure Research*; an editorial advisor for *Leisure Today*; and an editor and coeditor of *Schole: a Journal of Leisure Studies and Recreation Education*. Dr. Murphy served on the Society of Park and Recreation Educators Board of Directors for two terms and is a past president of that society. He has been Director of the California Park and Recreation Society, and chair or member of committees of several professional organizations. He has received eight awards for his contributions to teaching or to the literature in the recreation field, including being the recipient of the NRPA's Literary Award. A scholarship in his name has been established at San Jose State University.

J. ROBERT ROSSMAN, Ph.D., University of Illinois, Professor Emeritus and Dean Emeritus, Illinois State University

Dr. Rossman is an author, speaker, and consultant on recreation program design and management. He has held a variety of roles in park and recreation administration for more than 38 years. Most recently, he was Professor and Dean of the College of Applied Science and Technology at Illinois State University, Normal, Illinois where he still holds the titles of Professor Emeritus and Dean Emeritus. The Department of Leisure Studies at the University of Illinois selected him as a recipient of the Charles K. Brightbill award for demonstrated outstanding ability. The Department of Recreation and Park Administration at Indiana University also presented him with the Garrett G. Eppley Distinguished Alumni Award. He received the NRPA's Literary Award, and he is a member of the Honor Society of Phi Kappa Phi and the American Leisure Academy. In 2006, Dr. Rossman was selected to present the Jay B. Nash Scholar Lecture by the American Association for Physical Activity and Recreation.

RUTH RUSSELL, Re.D., Indiana University, Professor, Indiana University

Dr. Russell's research portfolio includes studies in retirement satisfaction, leisure satisfaction, higher education pedagogy, and tourism's impact on developing countries. Most recently she has ventured into work on leisure and the humanities. Bringing research into the world of professional implementation, she is the founder of the NRPA's Leisure Research Roundtable held annually in conjunction with the Leisure Research Symposium, and cofounder and coeditor of "Research into Action," a regular column in *Parks and Recreation* magazine. An author of five textbooks and cofounder of *Schole: A Journal of Leisure Studies and Recreation Education* and the SPRE Teaching Institute, Dr. Russell has received six distinguished teaching awards, served as President of SPRE, and is currently responsible for undergraduate academic affairs for the Indiana University Bloomington campus. Dr. Russell has also served as a Trustee to the NRPA.

MARK SEARLE, Ph.D., University of Maryland, Vice President of academic personnel, Arizona State University West

Dr. Searle's research interests have been focused on the social psychological aspects of leisure behavior with particular attention on the issues of aging and constraints on leisure. Most recently, he has expanded his focus to include the linkage between health and leisure behavior. He is the coauthor of *Leisure Services in Canada: An Introduction*, the first Canadian text of its kind, and is past coeditor of the *Therapeutic Recreation Journal*. In addition, Dr. Searle has served as an associate editor of the *Journal of Leisure Research, Schole, Therapeutic Recreation Journal*, and *Recreation Canada*, and he has served on the Boards of Directors of the Canadian Association for Leisure Studies, Canadian Fitness and Lifestyle Research Institute, and the Manitoba Parks and Recreation Association. He is the recipient of the American Academy of Park and Recreation Administration's Outstanding Dissertation Award and the Province of Manitoba's Prix Award for Research.

H. DOUGLAS SESSOMS, Ph.D., New York University, Professor Emeritus, University of North Carolina-Chapel Hill

Dr. Sessoms' scholarly interests include acts of professionalism such as certification, accreditation, and professional preparation; sociology of leisure; and the nature and role of the leisure service delivery systems. He has contributed significantly to the literature and authored, coauthored or edited several textbooks. He is a past president of the Academy of Leisure Sciences, and past chair of the NRPA/AALR Council on Accreditation, SPRE, the National Examination Certification Committee, and the North Carolina Recreation and Park Society. He has received the NRPA's Literary Award and Distinguished Professional Award, the University of Illinois's Brightbill Award, New York University's Distinguished Alumnus in Recreation Award, Distinguished Fellow Awards from SPRE and the North Carolina Recreation and Park Society, and the Southern Region Harold D. Meyer Award.

ED SMITH, Ph.D., University of North Carolina-Chapel Hill, Professor, The Pennsylvania State University

Dr. Smith's research focuses on the design, implementation, and evaluation of school-based programs to improve the lives of adolescents. The prevention of substance abuse, risky sexual behavior, and other problem behaviors are the key foci of these initiatives. As part of this research, he works with program providers, developers, teachers, and administrators to improve programs by incorporating pragmatic evaluation findings. The settings for these programs, both domestically and internationally, have included schools, health clinics, camps, community centers, and recreation centers. This research has been supported with over $12,000,000 from a number of sources including the National Institutes of Health (NIDA, NIMH, NCI, NICHD), The United States Navy, The United States Department of Justice, State Health Departments (PA, NJ, NC, WV), Provincial Ministries (Ontario, Quebec), and private foundations. Since 2001 Ed has been increasingly involved with international research efforts and has had the opportunity to work with collaborators in a number of countries including South Africa, Togo, Slovenia, the United Kingdom, Germany, Australia, Malaysia, Chile, Guatemala, and Colombia.

STEPHEN SMITH, Ph.D., Texas A&M University, Professor, University of Waterloo

Dr. Smith is a Professor in the Department of Recreation and Leisure Studies, University of Waterloo (Canada). He worked at Michigan State University before emigrating to Canada in 1976. His research and teaching focuses on tourism, especially statistics and economics. Steve is an elected Fellow of the International Academy for the Study of Tourism, and of the International Statistical Institute (ISI). He chairs the ISI's Marco Polo Committee on Tourism Statistics. In addition to his academic research, Steve works with the Canadian Tourism Commission (he chairs their Research Committee) and consults with a variety of tourism agencies.

LOUIS TWARDZIK, Re.D., Indiana University, Professor Emeritus, Michigan State University, deceased

Dr. Twardzik earned his B.S. degree from the University of Notre Dame in 1948, his M.S. and doctorate degrees in Park and Recreation Resources from Indiana University in 1950, and completed additional graduate work in Political Science at Wayne State and Michigan State Universities. He served in the U.S. Marine Corps in World War II and the Korean Conflict. His career began in the State of Tennessee as Director of State Parks. He came to Michigan State University (MSU) in 1960 as an assistant professor and extension specialist in the Department of Resource Development. He served as Professor and Chairman of the Department of Park and Recreation Resources until 1982. He served as teacher and advisor to students majoring in Park and Recreation Resources and as a Park and Recreation specialist for the Cooperative Extension Service. Retiring in 1991, he continued to work full-time as a volunteer for MSU as Professor Emeritus and the director of several international, national, and statewide projects and invited lecturer for undergraduate and graduate level classes. He received many awards throughout his career, authored numerous publications, and held more than 150 appointive and elected offices in state, national, and international professional societies and associations. Following his retirement, MSU's Department of Park and Recreation Resources created the Louis F. Twardzik Distinguished Alumni Award, which is now given annually. Throughout his life, he focused on family, faith, and a commitment to education.

PETER WITT, Ph.D., University of Illinois, Professor and Elda K. Bradberry Chair of Recreation and Youth Development, Texas A&M University

Dr. Witt's major research interests are in youth development, youth recreation services, and program evaluation. He is codeveloper of the Leisure Diagnostic Battery (with Gary Ellis), coeditor of *Recreation and Leisure: Issues in an Era of Change* (with Tom Goodale), coauthor of *Recreation Programs that Work with At-Risk Youth* (with John Crompton), and coauthor of *Recreation and Youth Development* (with Linda Caldwell). Dr. Witt is the editor of the *Journal of Park and Recreation Administration*, and former editor of the *Journal of Leisure Research, Therapeutic Recreation Journal*, and the *Journal of Leisurability* (founding editor). He is the 2004 recipient of the Robert W. Crawford Achievement Prize from the National Recreation Foundation for his work in the area of youth development, and he has received the NRPA's Distinguished Professional Award and Roosevelt Research Award; the SPRE and TRAPS Distinguished Colleague Awards; the AALR's Outstanding Achievement Award; and the Sapora and Brightbill Awards from the University of Illinois. He is an elected member of the American Academy of Park and Recreation Administration (President 2004) and has served on the Board of the Texas Recreation and Parks Society and SPRE. Dr. Witt was previously at the University of North Texas and at the University of Ottawa in Canada.

ROBERT WOLFF, Ph.D., The Ohio State University, Professor and Associate Dean for Administration, Enrollment Management, Budget and Alumni Affairs, Florida International University

Dr. Wolff focuses his teaching and research on the marketing and legal aspects of parks, recreation and sports management. Known as an excellent teacher, Dr. Wolff has authored or coauthored three book chapters and numerous articles in a variety of professional venues. He has managed seven grants totaling $1,000,000. He frequently serves on department, college, and university committees as well as on state and national committees. His service responsibilities have ranged from committee chair assignments to being elected president of a state society, to receiving multiple "Certificate of Appreciation" awards over the years.

ANDERSON YOUNG, Ph.D., The Ohio State University, Professor, State University of New York at Cortland

Dr. Young is Distinguished Teaching Professor and Graduate Coordinator in the Department of Recreation and Leisure Studies at the State University of New York at Cortland. He chaired the department for 13 years and now teaches courses on resource management, camp administration, and environmental history. Dr. Young is a founder of the Coalition for Education in the Outdoors and editor of its serial publication, *Research in Outdoor Education.*

NOTES

Chapter 1: The Gift

1. Nelson, W. (1981). *Renewal of the teacher-scholar: Faculty development in the liberal arts college,* p. 21. Washington, DC: Association of American Colleges.

2. Cahn, S. (1986). *Saints and Scamps: Ethics in academia,* p. 78. Totowa, NJ: Rowman and Littlefield.

3. Ibid, p. 46.

4. Goheen, R. (1969). *The human nature of a university,* pp. 78–79. NJ: Princeton University Press.

5. Nelson, p. 7.

6. Boyer, E. (1987). *College: The undergraduate experience in America,* p. 131. New York: Harper and Row.

7. Giamatti, A. (1981). *The university and the public interest,* p. 30. New York: Atheneum.

Chapter 2: Does This Path Have a Heart?

1. The way I did this was to create a little learning community, a writing group. Four of us—a minister, a therapist, a sociology graduate student, and I—got together every two weeks and brought some writing we were working on to share and to receive feedback on.

The article I wrote took an entire semester to complete and was revised in major ways four or five times. I think it helped that the group was diverse and outside my own field.

2.   Peck, M. S. (1987). *The different drum: Community making and peace*, p. 65. New York: Simon and Schuster.

3.   Piveteau, D., & Dillon, J. (1977). Two scholarly views on religious education: Lee and Westerhoff. *Lumen Vitae, 1*, 7–44, p. 19.

4.   Rilke, R. M. (1992). *Letters to a young Poet, #4.* San Rafael, CA: New World Library.

Chapter 6: On Reading and Professing: Recounting a World of Privilege

1.   Pieper, J. (1952). *Leisure–The basis of culture.* New York: New American Library.

2.   Bishop, D., & Jeanrenaud, C. (1980). Creative growth through play, and its implications for recreation practice. In T. L. Goodale & P. Witt (Eds.), *Recreation and leisure: Issues in an era of change*, pp. 81–99. State College, PA: Venture Publishing.

3.   Bloom, B. (1956). *Taxonomy of educational objectives, handbook 1: Cognitive domain.* New York: David McKay Company.

4.   Frazer, J. (1987). *Time—The familiar stranger*, pp. 327. Redmond, WA: Tempus Books.

5.   Ibid, p. 337.

6.   Goffman, E. (1959). *The presentation of self in everyday life*, pp. 144–145. Garden City, NY: Doubleday.

Chapter 19: A Very Privileged Form of Service

1.   Stewart, I. (1989). *Does God play dice? The mathematics of chaos*, p. 141. Oxford, UK: B. Blackwell.

Chapter 20: "Faith-Based" Teaching

1. Dustin, D. [Ed.] (1990). *Beyond promotion and tenure: On being a professor*. CA: San Diego State University's Institute for Leisure Behavior.

2. Dustin, D. (1992). The dance of the dispossessed: On patriarchy, feminism, and the practice of leisure science. *Journal of Leisure Research, 24*(4), pp. 324–332.

Chapter 22: A Gleam in the Eye

1. Louv, R. (2006). *Last child in the woods: Saving our children from nature-deficit disorder*. NC: Algonquin Books of Chapel Hill.

Chapter 25: On Undergraduate "Benevolent Coercion" and Graduate Collegiality

1. McDermott, J. (Ed.). (1977). *The writings of Williams James*, p. 8. IL: University of Chicago Press.

2. Huxley, T. (1971). *T. H. Huxley on education; A selection from his writings*. UK: Cambridge University Press.

3. Mill, J. (1957). *Autobiography*, p. 26. New York: Liberal Arts Press.

4. The comments in this section expand upon those which appeared in Crompton, J. (1998). University teaching—A very personal perspective. *Schole, 13*, pp. 81–90; and reflect those which were made in Crompton, J. (2005). Issues related to sustaining a long-term research interest in tourism. *The Journal of Tourism Studies, 16*(2), pp. 34–43.

5. Kelly, J. (1989). To be a scholar. *Leisure Sciences 11*, p. 249.

Chapter 26: Beyond the Social Science Citation Index

1.   Howard, D., & Crompton, J. (co-senior authors). (1980). *Financing, managing, and marketing recreation and park resources.* Dubuque, IA: W. C. Brown Co. Publishers.

2.   Howard, D., & Crompton, J. (2004). *Financing sport.* Morgantown, WV: Fitness International Technology.

Chapter 27: A Fair Share for All

1.   Nesbitt, J., Brown, P., & Murphy, J. (Eds.) (1980). *Recreation and leisure service for the disadvantaged: Guidelines to program development and related readings.* Philadelphia: Lea & Febiger.

2.   Gray, D., & Greben, S. (1974). Future perspectives. *Parks and Recreation, 61*, p. 49.

Chapter 30: Connecting with Others

1.   Lewis, M. (2005). *Coach: Lessons on the game of life*, p. 12. New York: W. W. Norton & Company.

Chapter 33: Embracing Serendipity

1.   Caldwell, L., & Smith, E. (1988). Leisure: An overlooked component of health promotion. *Canadian Journal of Public Health, 79*(2), pp. 44–48.

Chapter 34: Pardon My Reservations

1.   Gardner, J. (1961). *Excellence*, p. 86. New York: Harper & Rowe.

2.   Rosovsky, H. (1990) *The university: An owner's manual*, p. 107. New York: W. W. Norton & Co.

Other Books by Venture Publishing, Inc.

21st Century Leisure: Current Issues, 2nd ed.
by Valeria J. Freysinger and John R. Kelly

*The A•B•Cs of Behavior Change: Skills for Working
With Behavior Problems in Nursing Homes*
by Margaret D. Cohn, Michael A. Smyer, and
Ann L. Horgas

*Activity Experiences and Programming within
Long-Term Care*
by Ted Tedrick and Elaine R. Green

The Activity Gourmet
by Peggy Powers

Adventure Programming
edited by John C. Miles and Simon Priest

Assessment: The Cornerstone of Activity Programs
by Ruth Perschbacher

*Behavior Modification in Therapeutic Recreation:
An Introductory Manual*
by John Datillo and William D. Murphy

Benefits of Leisure
edited by B.L. Driver, Perry J. Brown, and
George L. Peterson

Benefits of Recreation Research Update
by Judy M. Sefton and W. Kerry Mummery

*Beyond Baskets and Beads: Activities for Older
Adults with Functional Impairments*
by Mary Hart, Karen Primm, and Kathy
Cranisky

*Beyond Bingo: Innovative Programs for the New
Senior*
by Sal Arrigo, Jr., Ann Lewis, and Hank
Mattimore

*Beyond Bingo 2: More Innovative Programs for the
New Senior*
by Sal Arrigo, Jr.

*Boredom Busters: Themed Special Events to Dazzle
and Delight Your Group*
by Annette C. Moore

*Both Gains and Gaps: Feminist Perspectives on
Women's Leisure*
by Karla Henderson, M. Deborah Bialeschki,
Susan M. Shaw, and Valeria J. Freysinger

*Client Assessment in Therapeutic Recreation
Services*
by Norma J. Stumbo

*Client Outcomes in Therapeutic Recreation
Services*
by Norma J. Stumbo

*Conceptual Foundations for Therapeutic
Recreation*
edited by David R. Austin, John Dattilo, and
Bryan P. McCormick

Constraints to Leisure
edited by Edgar L. Jackson

*Dementia Care Programming: An Identity-Focused
Approach*
by Rosemary Dunne

*Dimensions of Choice: Qualitative Approaches to
Parks, Recreation, Tourism, Sport, and Leisure
Research, 2nd ed.*
by Karla A. Henderson

*Diversity and the Recreation Profession:
Organizational Perspectives*
edited by Maria T. Allison and Ingrid E.
Schneider

*Effective Management in Therapeutic Recreation
Service, 2nd ed.*
by Marcia Jean Carter and Gerald S. O'Morrow

*Evaluating Leisure Services: Making Enlightened
Decisions, 2nd ed.*
by Karla A. Henderson and M. Deborah
Bialeschki

*Everything from A to Y: The Zest Is up to You!
Older Adult Activities for Every Day of the Year*
by Nancy R. Cheshire and Martha L. Kenney

*The Evolution of Leisure: Historical and
Philosophical Perspectives*
by Thomas Goodale and Geoffrey Godbey

*Experience Marketing: Strategies for the New
Millennium*
by Ellen L. O'Sullivan and Kathy J. Spangler

Facilitation Techniques in Therapeutic Recreation
by John Dattilo

*File o' Fun: A Recreation Planner for Games &
Activities, 3rd ed.*
by Jane Harris Ericson and Diane Ruth Albright

*The Game and Play Leader's Handbook:
Facilitating Fun and Positive Interaction,
Revised Edition*
by Bill Michaelis and John M. O'Connell

*The Game Finder—A Leader's Guide to Great
Activities*
by Annette C. Moore

*Getting People Involved in Life and Activities:
Effective Motivating Techniques*
by Jeanne Adams

Glossary of Recreation Therapy and Occupational Therapy
by David R. Austin

Great Special Events and Activities
by Annie Morton, Angie Prosser, and Sue Spangler

Group Games & Activity Leadership
by Kenneth J. Bulik

Growing With Care: Using Greenery, Gardens, and Nature With Aging and Special Populations
by Betsy Kreidler

Hands On! Children's Activities for Fairs, Festivals, and Special Events
by Karen L. Ramey

Health Promotion for Mind, Body and Spirit
by Suzanne Fitzsimmons and Linda L. Buettner

In Search of the Starfish: Creating a Caring Environment
by Mary Hart, Karen Primm, and Kathy Cranisky

Inclusion: Including People With Disabilities in Parks and Recreation Opportunities
by Lynn Anderson and Carla Brown Kress

Inclusive Leisure Services: Responding to the Rights of People with Disabilities, 2nd ed.
by John Dattilo

Innovations: A Recreation Therapy Approach to Restorative Programs
by Dawn R. De Vries and Julie M. Lake

Internships in Recreation and Leisure Services: A Practical Guide for Students, 3rd ed.
by Edward E. Seagle, Jr. and Ralph W. Smith

Interpretation of Cultural and Natural Resources, 2nd ed.
by Douglas M. Knudson, Ted T. Cable, and Larry Beck

Intervention Activities for At-Risk Youth
by Norma J. Stumbo

Introduction to Outdoor Recreation: Providing and Managing Resource Based Opportunities
by Roger L. Moore and B.L. Driver

Introduction to Recreation and Leisure Services, 8th ed.
by Karla A. Henderson, M. Deborah Bialeschki, John L. Hemingway, Jan S. Hodges, Beth D. Kivel, and H. Douglas Sessoms

Introduction to Therapeutic Recreation: U.S. and Canadian Perspectives
by Kenneth Mobily and Lisa Ostiguy

Introduction to Writing Goals and Objectives: A Manual for Recreation Therapy Students and Entry-Level Professionals
by Suzanne Melcher

Leadership and Administration of Outdoor Pursuits, 3rd ed.
by Jim Blanchard, Michael Strong, and Phyllis Ford

Leadership in Leisure Services: Making a Difference, 3rd ed.
by Debra Jordan

Leisure for Canadians
edited by Ron McCarville and Kelly MacKay

Leisure in Your Life: New Perspectives
by Geoffrey Godbey

Leisure and Leisure Services in the 21st Century: Toward Mid Century
by Geoffrey Godbey

The Leisure Diagnostic Battery: Users Manual and Sample Forms
by Peter A. Witt and Gary Ellis

Leisure Education I: A Manual of Activities and Resources, 2nd ed.
by Norma J. Stumbo

Leisure Education II: More Activities and Resources, 2nd ed.
by Norma J. Stumbo

Leisure Education III: More Goal-Oriented Activities
by Norma J. Stumbo

Leisure Education IV: Activities for Individuals with Substance Addictions
by Norma J. Stumbo

Leisure Education Program Planning: A Systematic Approach, 2nd ed.
by John Dattilo

Leisure Education Specific Programs
by John Dattilo

Leisure Studies: Prospects for the Twenty-First Century
edited by Edgar L. Jackson and Thomas L. Burton

The Lifestory Re-Play Circle: A Manual of Activities and Techniques
by Rosilyn Wilder

Marketing in Leisure and Tourism: Reaching New Heights
by Patricia Click Janes

The Melody Lingers On: A Complete Music Activities Program for Older Adults
by Bill Messenger

More Than a Game: A New Focus on Senior Activity Services
by Brenda Corbett

The Multiple Values of Wilderness
by H. Ken Cordell, John C. Bergstrom, and J.M. Bowker

Nature and the Human Spirit: Toward an Expanded Land Management Ethic
edited by B.L. Driver, Daniel Dustin, Tony Baltic, Gary Elsner, and George Peterson

The Organizational Basis of Leisure Participation: A Motivational Exploration
by Robert A. Stebbins

Outdoor Recreation for 21st Century America
by H. Ken Cordell

Outdoor Recreation Management: Theory and Application, 3rd ed.
by Alan Jubenville and Ben Twight

Parks for Life: Moving the Goal Posts, Changing the Rules, and Expanding the Field
by Will LaPage

The Pivotal Role of Leisure Education: Finding Personal Fulfillment in this Century
edited by Elie Cohen-Gewerc and Robert A. Stebbins

Planning and Organizing Group Activities in Social Recreation
by John V. Valentine

Planning Parks for People, 2nd ed.
by John Hultsman, Richard L. Cottrell, and Wendy Z. Hultsman

The Process of Recreation Programming Theory and Technique, 3rd ed.
by Patricia Farrell and Herberta M. Lundegren

Programming for Parks, Recreation, and Leisure Services: A Servant Leadership Approach, 2nd ed.
by Debra J. Jordan, Donald G. DeGraaf, and Kathy H. DeGraaf

Protocols for Recreation Therapy Programs
edited by Jill Kelland, along with the Recreation Therapy Staff at Alberta Hospital Edmonton

Puttin' on the Skits: Plays for Adults in Managed Care
by Jean Vetter

Quality Management: Applications for Therapeutic Recreation
edited by Bob Riley

A Recovery Workbook: The Road Back from Substance Abuse
by April K. Neal and Michael J. Taleff

Recreation and Leisure: Issues in an Era of Change, 3rd ed.
edited by Thomas Goodale and Peter A. Witt

Recreation and Youth Development
by Peter A. Witt and Linda L. Caldwell

Recreation Economic Decisions: Comparing Benefits and Costs, 2nd ed.
by John B. Loomis and Richard G. Walsh

Recreation for Older Adults: Individual and Group Activities
by Judith A. Elliott and Jerold E. Elliott

Recreation Program Planning Manual for Older Adults
by Karen Kindrachuk

Recreation Programming and Activities for Older Adults
by Jerold E. Elliott and Judith A. Sorg-Elliott

Reference Manual for Writing Rehabilitation Therapy Treatment Plans
by Penny Hogberg and Mary Johnson

Research in Therapeutic Recreation: Concepts and Methods
edited by Marjorie J. Malkin and Christine Z. Howe

Simple Expressions: Creative and Therapeutic Arts for the Elderly in Long-Term Care Facilities
by Vicki Parsons

A Social History of Leisure Since 1600
by Gary Cross

A Social Psychology of Leisure
by Roger C. Mannell and Douglas A. Kleiber

Special Events and Festivals: How to Organize, Plan, and Implement
by Angie Prosser and Ashli Rutledge

Stretch Your Mind and Body: Tai Chi as an Adaptive Activity
by Duane A. Crider and William R. Klinger

Therapeutic Activity Intervention with the Elderly: Foundations and Practices
by Barbara A. Hawkins, Marti E. May, and Nancy Brattain Rogers

Therapeutic Recreation and the Nature of Disabilities
by Kenneth E. Mobily and Richard D. MacNeil

Therapeutic Recreation: Cases and Exercises, 2nd ed.
by Barbara C. Wilhite and M. Jean Keller

Therapeutic Recreation in Health Promotion and Rehabilitation
by John Shank and Catherine Coyle

Therapeutic Recreation in the Nursing Home
by Linda Buettner and Shelley L. Martin

Therapeutic Recreation Programming: Theory and Practice
by Charles Sylvester, Judith E. Voelkl, and Gary D. Ellis

*Therapeutic Recreation Protocol for Treatment of
Substance Addictions*
   by Rozanne W. Faulkner

The Therapeutic Recreation Stress Management Primer
   by Cynthia Mascott

The Therapeutic Value of Creative Writing
   by Paul M. Spicer

Tourism and Society: A Guide to Problems and Issues
   by Robert W. Wyllie

Traditions: Improving Quality of Life in Caregiving
   by Janelle Sellick

*Trivia by the Dozen: Encouraging Interaction and
Reminiscence in Managed Care*
   by Jean Vetter